D1806643

# THE PATHWAY OF FAITH

Rosie Hindmarsh

PRESS

www.xulonpress.com

# CONTENTS

# PREFACE

*R*osie's book is written just as she speaks, without any airs or graces.

*"Just as I am, without one plea, but that Thy blood was shed for me, and that Thou bidst me come to Thee, O Lamb of God, I come."*

As these few lines from Charlotte Elliott's hymn (found in many hymn collections) illustrate, the reader will soon discover that Rosie is totally committed to her Lord and Redeemer the Lord Jesus the Messiah. [Yeshua is His Hebrew Name.] So committed indeed that often she lapses into talking directly to her heavenly Father. For example, she addresses the reader as normal (Chapter 11):

'I was praying all the time, for Father had said, "Every place you put your foot I have given to you." ' The next sentence however is addressed to her Lord, before she resumes her usual narrative style:

' "I received it, Lord".
'We arrived at the village and I was introduced to the chief.'

Rosie tells her story best in her own words, with passion and sincerity. This fact makes her testimony and message all the more glorifying to the God Whom she loves with every fibre of her being.

In order to digitise the text, Rosie read the manuscript aloud, recorded by a video camera, from which it was keyed in to a computer. Heartfelt thanks are due to him who undertook this labour of love at God's prompting (he gets an "honourable mention" in the book, as does the editor). The book has since been edited to correct (most) typographical errors, spelling and punctuation, and clarify meanings. Where the spelling of some names was unclear, the world wide web was consulted; it found many but did not seem able to decipher some of them. Such details, however, do not detract from the overall aim of the book which God gave to Rosie, as she describes, to show how He uses her to His glory.

Finding the right publisher for the book took a few years. However, the right time to publish is always our Lord's time; He used the editor to alight on Xulon Press as our Lord's choice of publisher.

Glossary, for non-Geordies:

| | |
|---|---|
| Bairn | child |
| Clarts | mud |
| Geordie | native of Newcastle, or the North East more generally. |
| Kiddled | poked the embers (of a fire) into life again (an old Northumbrian word). |

In Chapter 17, Waggai is pronounced like "Wag-eye".

# CHAPTER 1

# How I found The Lord Jesus Christ and how it helped with my bereavement

*M*y story begins in 1975, on February 28th, the day I accepted Jesus Christ as my Saviour. It was about seven thirty to eight o'clock in the evening, my children out to play and my husband Jimmy working in the garage. I was all washed up and ready for tomorrow, bait up for my husband and things ready for the bairns for school. I was in the living room, but I was so upset in my mind. My friend was telling me some gossip, during the day, and I was saying, "Never mind! Don't listen; some people have nothing better to do but gossip. They are jealous about how happy you are, and what you have."

To my horror, she then said, "What about you then?" to which I said, "What do you mean?"

Her answer devastated me, implying I fancied her brother because we danced together. I was so shocked and speechless. Fear gripped me, first for my Jimmy, we loved each other so much, and then for the man's wife, for they too were very happily married. I came home and worried myself all day after, never saying anything to Jimmy when he came home; but now, still very much in fear, with the house quiet, I got down on my knees in front of the fire and began to pray, asking Jesus Christ, pleading to protect both my dancing partner and his wife, and my Jimmy. I poured my heart out, weeping that to fancy him was the last thing on my mind.

I just loved to dance, and he was very good; and so when he asked me to dance I just loved it. We would be dancing together and Jimmy, who could not dance, would sit with my partner's wife and watch us. We always, or very often, went out together, when there was a good band at the club. We were such friends, but nothing else. I poured all these things out to Jesus and then did what Will Curry at work talked about. He said it was not enough to go to church, you had to make the commitment, and pray, and ask Jesus into your heart, repent of your sins and receive the salvation. I was not quite sure what all that meant, but I knew I had to do it that night, to save our love for each other and protect any further gossip about our friends. I wept and wept.

I do not know how long I was on the floor, but when I got up I felt so clean, as though I had been washed from head to toe, inside and out. I knew all we had talked about was true: I was saved.

The next day I was back in to work. I could not wait to tell Will what I had done. He was thrilled. He said I would have to go with him, the next Sunday, and tell the people in the service. Will was a lay preacher in the Methodist Church. He said he would give me a verse or two to read and then I would share what Jesus had done for me. It was all arranged, I would go with him and tell my testimony. He gave me a Bible and showed me what I would read, then tell the people what Jesus had done.

I was excited and came home and shared it all with Jimmy. I had to share everything; why I had asked Jesus into my heart, in the first place; because of the gossip and my fear for us and our friends. Jimmy loved me so much and I loved Jimmy so much. He was quite happy if I was happy, but we never went back to the club again. Jimmy said it was as though I was guilty, as though I really had something to hide, but I said, if people could talk about you to that degree when it could have damaged two marriages, we were best not going at all. As for myself, I had no desire to go again.

When the next good band came and our friends phoned to meet up to go, I wanted to meet up, but then to share what I had done. I had accepted Jesus Christ, my Lord, into my heart and I did not want to go back, not only to the club but anywhere - I did not want to dance any more.

They asked Jimmy to go but Jimmy said "If Rosie is not going, it would be no fun for me to go without her".

I did not mention the gossip, because my Jesus had really come into my heart, and where, before, I had showed off with my dancing, I found I no longer wanted to dance at all. It was sad, really, that I lost my friends because I accepted Jesus; they no longer wanted to know me.

As the time was drawing near for me to go with Will, I had to read and read my verses. I was so afraid I would make a mistake; my reading was very bad. I was a dunce at school, I could not read or spell, my writing was very bad; in anything that would do me any good, I was bottom of the class, but in music or physical training (P.T. in my day) I was very good. So Sunday came and I went with Will, read my piece, then put my Bible down and began to share what Jesus had done for me. It was like I was on fire to tell my testimony.

So it continued: Will would give me a scripture reading at the beginning of the week and I would practise and practise until Sunday and then share about my Jesus. I could not wait to get home to tell Jimmy what had happened.

The next thing happened at work; I was in the fringing room and we fringed all the baby rugs and travel rugs and picked the blankets clean, before they went down to the wash. Well, after a little while, Will got me transferred to the showroom, where I then worked alongside Will. It was wonderful, talking to all the people, it was like being back at home delivering the milk and talking to all the people; I loved it. One day a lady went downstairs to the toilet and turned on the little heater for hot water; well, she scalded her hands and arm. She came back upstairs to the showroom and I went forward to listen to her, as she told me what she had done. I asked her if I could pray for her and as I did she was so surprised and shocked, both at the same time, but left ok.

After a week or so Will and Margaret, his daughter, took me to a meeting. Some wonderful preacher was coming to speak, so I took my tape recorder to record it. For some reason I was quite excited, and, while we were sitting chatting, the strangest thing happened. My mouth was moving, but strange words were coming out. I did not understand what was happening. Just then the meeting began and, lo and behold, the man was speaking about the Holy Spirit, baptism of the Holy Spirit and the gift of tongues. I was amazed, for, as before he spoke, I believe that is what happened. I did not need to ask to receive, my Lord had already given it to me, and then brought the man to tell me what Jesus, my Lord, had done. O, the thrill of receiving the gift of tongues. So wonderful, I used it and used it in my prayer times.

Everything seemed so wonderful and my new life with Jesus was moving on. I was hungry for His Word. I was in the Bible as much as I could, reading it and trying to understand the Scriptures. I carried my little green Bible with me and I had asked Jimmy if I could have a big black Bible, which had been Jimmy's Aunt Lizzie's. She had places marked, so I would read to see what Aunt Lizzie was reading and wondering what our Lord had been saying to her.

After quite a long time, a year or more, I was in the showroom, Will had gone out and it was coffee time. As I always did, I got out my little green Bible and as I opened it at 1 Corinthians 7:13-16, I was so thrilled, in a way, as my Lord was speaking to me about Jimmy and my bairns. How wonderful, Lord, not that I would leave, we were so happy, but to see what my Lord was saying was such a comfort, for our children also. But somehow, I felt it was a warning and He was showing me, to prepare me.

Summer was well through and Jimmy was poorly, nothing terrible, just not himself, and so I would help. He was very anxious about jobs to be done, so I would paint the eaves. Jimmy had built our home himself; it was a bungalow, and so the eaves were not very high. On a beautiful day, Jimmy still not too good yet, he was off work. I asked for the time off, making light of the things to do. I got the ladders out and up I went, moving along quite well, when my foot slipped and down I went. To save the paint, I hooked my arm in the ladder, which broke my fall and, yes, I saved the paint: but o, I pulled the muscles out of my arm. My shoulder had taken the full weight; I was hanging by one arm. I unhooked myself, found the rung of the ladder again, managed to get down and walk round the house to where Jimmy was and told him what I had done. By this time, the pain was so bad, I was not sure if I had broken my arm, I could not move it at all. We phoned the doctor, who said go straight to the hospital, as I would need an x-ray. So, off we went and no, it was not broken, but very badly bruised, so I was off work too. I knew our Lord was giving us this time together. Jimmy had to wash me and dress me. I could still work with one hand so we laughed together, he had to peel the potatoes for the dinner, cut things, which took both hands, and I could do the things in between. This went on for about a fortnight to three weeks. The hospital had said it would take time to heal; bruises were just as bad as a break, so we were really having fun, like being on holiday, the bairns at school all day so we were having such a great time; plus the jobs were being stroked off the list. By the time I was able to use the arm, and

13

hand, and put pressure on it, gripping things again, Jimmy was back to work and doing fine.

The weekend was coming up, and this was my children's first youth club dance. Josephine was having a friend to stay, so it was pressing trousers and shirts for the boys and getting things ready for the girls. Jimmy also was going out, he was on duty to take the colonel out to a meeting, so it was flasks of coffee and a sandwich for Jimmy, a good book and a rug, as he stayed in the Land Rover, out of sight really, waiting for the colonel, so off everyone went and I continued to iron.

At ten o'clock, Jimmy came in. He was laughing; we hugged and kissed, which we did every time either one of us left the other one. Our love was so strong; I could see the love shining in Jimmy's eyes, so I packed in ironing and we had coffee and went through into the room. There was a good film on, Friday night, so we cuddled up together and watched the film. When it was finished, we hurried ourselves and got into bed, for this was Edward's first job of responsibility: to see everyone in safely and to lock up; so we laid waiting, cuddled in.

They came; he locked the door and, supposed to be quietly, went to bed amid giggles from the girls. We loved each other so much; we kissed again and just loved each other - and Jimmy died. I felt the breath go out of his body. I knew he was gone.

Immediately the words came, in a twinkling of an eye, "You will be changed".

I first of all froze with shock; then, what to do? My senses were reeling thinking of the bairns, what to say, what to do, how to handle everything? I first went to Edward to go and fetch uncle Lister, Jimmy's brother, who lived up the road from us. I don't think the bairns were asleep, with the excitement of the night, where they had been and all they had done. I got dressed.

Lister came with Edward. He phoned the doctor and they got Aunt Ada to come round; she just lived round the corner from us, her garden backed on to ours. She also was a widow; Uncle Tom died not long after Edward was born and, on clinic days, Lister would run me down in the post van to Ada's to chat and for company, once a month. So, after the doctor came, Ada and the doctor laid Jimmy out. While all this was going on, I went in to tell Josephine. I was so thankful her little friend, Marian, was with her. I don't know what I said, how I put it, anything; for Josephine was her Daddy's girl. How she loved Jimmy. I knew, in lots of cases, that the girls are Daddy's and the boys are Mammy's - it certainly was this way with us. Everyone finished what had to be done and left.

The bairns settled down again and I went into the room, kiddled up the fire, sat on the floor in front of it, and broke. I wept and wept - how would I manage? Fear gripped me, like a chain; I had never signed a cheque book, the boys were at the age they needed their Dad, the scars that would come because of losing their Dad, Josephine would break her heart, fear of all manner of things, how would we manage? In all this turmoil I must have fallen asleep. Next day, it was all over the village.

I phoned to tell my Mam and my family. Margaret, Will's daughter, came around. All I could say was "I'm alright".

I knew my Lord was with me. There were no scenes or breakdowns in front of people; I seemed to be calm. My brother and his wife came and my sister and Mam. Mam loved Jimmy, He had been so good to her and ever since we married, Mam came every weekend with Mary, the lady I worked with on the milk round. I'm not sure who stayed with me first, Noel's Joan (that's my brother's wife) or Joan, my sister; but they both came and stayed for the night and went home the next day. Then the other one stayed the next night.

15

I prepared for the funeral, baking, making the plans, so much to do. I was all right during the day and people were calling in to see me and see if I was all right. A couple called, friends of Margaret and Will. They talked about my Lord and the funeral and in the conversation they asked if Jimmy was "saved". To which I answered, that I did not think so, I never heard him make the commitment. To which they then replied, "O well! That's that, then, isn't it?"

I said, "What do you mean?"

The answer was, "Well! He will not go to heaven, if he was not saved".

I was so shocked, I could not believe the Jesus I knew, and loved, would cast my Jimmy, whom I had loved, out of heaven. I prayed and prayed that Jesus would save my Jimmy.

The day of the funeral arrived. What was said and done, I remember very little. I was numb; I went through the motions for Mam and my bairns.

Life had to go on: I must live for them now.

# CHAPTER 2

# The coming to terms with bereavement and moving on.

*I* did my best to be light hearted, to carry on. I never went back to work at the mill or go with Will to preach. Father Peter was at the Church of England, my church, and so we had prayer meetings and Sunday school, and I started to work with Peter, but I mainly stayed at home to look after my bairns.

Edward, at fourteen, went from a boy to a man. He left school the following year and all he wanted to do, or be, was on a farm. All his school pals were on farms and Edward was always at one or the other friend's farm. I was down the road, one day, and got on talking to Mr. Thompson from Metcalfe's. They were merchants for the local farmers. He went round all the local farms getting orders and such like. So I asked him if he knew of anyone needing a lad to take on, to work. He suggested I try Mr. Walton at Flatterton. Edward and I must have talked about it, so I phoned Mr. Walton to make an appointment to see him. With having no one to talk to, I really depended on my Lord. Well, I prayed about everything and more and more trusted what I was hearing. He was leading me and guiding me. I went to see

Mr. Walton, praying all the way there, not to be afraid, not to say the wrong things, not to weep. My thoughts were going round and round. What would he say? What would I say? How would it go?

I turned in at the gate, quaking in my shoes, rang the bell and I was invited in and ushered into a small living room on the back side of the house, and waited. Mr. Walton came in and took the lead, asked me some questions about Edward. Edward had not done well at school, but Jimmy and I were extremely pleased with his housemaster at Ponteland. He had suggested sending Edward to Kirkley Hall, which was a college for farm workers to learn their trade, or ways of agriculture in farming. His written work had been his let down. He always had difficulty expressing himself and, because he was left handed, his writing was not good, but for the practical work, he received full marks. We were pleased with his housemaster, so this was all that I had, really, in Edward's favour. But this man was wonderful, he said for Edward to start right away. I came out and walked back to my car, got in and broke down and wept with thanksgiving and drove home.

I would like to say that for six months my Lord carried me. There is a picture called 'Footprints' with one set of footprints walking away in the sand. The story goes, that the man asked our Lord, "Why only one set of footprints during the difficult times, whereas there had been two sets previously? Why did You leave me then?" And our Lord said that He carried the man through the difficulty, the difficult times. Well, I knew this was true, I knew I was being carried.

Will too had died, and Margaret now wanted to be a missionary and go on the mission field, as she said there was nothing to hold her here now. Both her mam and dad had gone home to Jesus, so she was making plans to find out where to go, how to go. Margaret was very good at what she did, and very right in how she did things, so it was not long before she had prayed and doors were opening for her to go to Japan.

We used to go to a prayer meeting, once a week or so. At one time at this prayer meeting it came twice that I would write a book. The title would be "The pathway of faith". The Lord put into my mind "through two or three witnesses" and this was said twice in the same night (Bible confirmation Matthew 18:16 and 20). For Margaret, we were talking and sharing and praying, in preparation for Margaret's going away. It was also very hard because all of my props were being taken away, so my dependence was even more on my Jesus. We helped each other; there was quite a lot to do and a special service, where Margaret gave her testimony and shared how she was going to be a missionary in Japan. Kay and I went with Margaret to set her on the train to London before flying off to Japan. There were tears and goodbyes, and Margaret got on the train and Kay and I left to come home.

I remember holding Kay all the way home. She sobbed and sobbed, she and Margaret were such great friends and she really was so upset that Margaret was going away. Margaret used to write quite regularly, but o my, homesick - not saying she was homesick, but reading between the lines, so I hardly talked about what was happening at home. I kept off the subject and kept talking about the Lord and what He was doing: what He was teaching me, asking questions to know more about where she was and what she was doing; in my letters to cheer her on, sort of thing, answering things she was saying. I don't know how long it was, but next thing, Kay was going out to join her.

This was wonderful, really, to have her best friend with her. "O Jesus! How great You are, answered prayer really, a break for Margaret." Two, the Bible says (Deuteronomy 32:30), can put ten thousand to flight. She would have someone to talk to, to pray with, to work with, and for that person to be her best friend. "O Father! You are so great."

As for me, my beloved Jesus was teaching me, wonderful in His grace. He gave me 1 John 2 verse 27. What encouragement for me. Then it was 2nd Timothy 2 verses 19 to 26. Then chapter 3 verses 1 to 6. I would pray through the Scriptures.

By now I was learning to read fast, still not good at spelling, going into prayer meetings and sharing and listening to others. You had your quiet time in the morning before you started the day but, back then, I couldn't - too much to do in the morning: getting the bairns off to school and Edward off to work.

He always wanted to know what he would have next. He would eat his breakfast, then want to know what was in his bait; come home from work and want to know what was for dinner; loved his food. They all loved their grub. After dinner, they would all do what they wanted to do and this was my time to be with my Lord. I would talk to Him and read the Word.

I was given a tape of Kathryn Kuhlman, which I listened to and wept, asking my Lord for the gift of healing, for this was her gift. Then I was given a book to read, "Rees Howells: Intercessor" by Norman Grubb. This book really spoke to me. The more I prayed and talked to my Jesus, the more this person's book came alive. I identified with this book, the things our Lord was showing me. We have to get rid of the flesh: if you are angry, confess it to Jesus, ask to be freed of it and it will go - but then it would come back. "So, what happened, Lord?" I was rid of the spirit of anger, but you see, we open the door again and let it back in. We want to do it - things - our way, and Jesus said, "No, do it this way".

The Bible says (Matthew 16:24-25) always to die to self, live to Jesus Christ, our Lord, for all things in our character that we have to deal with: anger, bitterness, jealousy, greed, gluttony, criticism, bad language, bad habits, pride. "The fruit of the Holy Spirit is love, joy, peace, patience, kindness, goodness, faithfulness, gentleness, self-control" (Galatians 5:22-23). Believe you me, this is not easy, but all these things are possible to him who believes (Mark 9:23). When the bad things come rushing in to my mind, I use my gift of tongues and disperse them. I was learning new things every day. My faith was so strong, and when I learnt anything, then my Lord took me on to the next step.

Roly (my friend's son) had grown. Time was moving on. David was two years behind Edward, so it was coming up for David to leave school, and with David leaving school, my pension would drop drastically.

Jimmy was forty-nine when he died, but I was eleven years younger. Because of my age, my widow's pension dropped to twenty-five pounds a week and the pension I had for the bairns dropped from sixty pounds odd, to nil, with David leaving school. The money I received after Jimmy died was very much less than when he was alive, so I would have to go back to work to have sufficient to live; so from learning and reading, and learning to pray, I now must pray for a job.

I only wanted to serve my Lord. "Take me Father, where can I serve You?" I was praying this on a daily basis.

Jimmy and I had sixteen years of such love. Some people don't know what love is. My prayer, Father, was, "If I could give back the love my Lord had given me, that I had with a man like Jimmy", because my Lord was touching me so much.

At every turn of discussions we had in the house, I was passing this on. Discussions about everything, I would teach the bairns my Lord's way and doing things the world's way. I used to begin with making them come to church with me, and they would always come, until one day, Jesus showed

21

me that He wanted them to come because they wanted to come, not because I wanted them to come. It was such a release, no more pushing to get them to come. It was a laugh too, because when anyone came to the house, the bairns would say, "Don't ask Mam anything, or you'll get a lecture, Acts 2".

I was going to Peter's to the prayer meeting and one week Elsie and I met outside, both arriving at the same time. She was very serious and began to tell about her mother's friend, who had been in a bad accident, so we agreed that we would ask Peter if we could pray for her. We rang the bell and went in. The meeting was good, prayers coming and hearts being soothed and comforted by our Lord, as things were shared and prayed about. Confession is good for the soul, Jesus said: Luke chapter 12 verse 8, "And I say to you, everyone who confesses Me before men, the Son of Man will confess him also before the angels of God".

The meeting ended and while we were getting our things together, I remembered Elsie. O, we had not prayed. I went to Elsie and said, "I forgot all about your neighbour, Elsie, I'm so sorry, but don't worry, I'll bring him up before the Lord tonight, in my prayer time".

This was accepted and we hugged each other and went our separate ways. That night I went to bed, but this was my time with Jesus. My bed was covered with my Bible, concordances, my daily readings, and I did one with "Streams in the Desert" where the lady was brought out with our Lord in gentleness. It was given to me by one of my sisters in Christ Jesus, when I was still going to Bob and Alan's prayer meeting, just after Jimmy died, and I still read this book every day. So, as always in my prayer time alone with my Lord, wherever I had been, or whatever I had been doing, when I felt in my spirit something was wrong or troubling someone, or something just did not sit right, I would pray it all back to my Lord as soon as I had space.

Sometimes I would go to the toilet, just to be able to get alone with my Lord and pray back for whomever, or whatever. Jesus said, "Take every thought captive." In 2 Corinthians 10 verse 5 - listen to this - "We are destroying speculations and every lofty thing raised up against the knowledge of God and we are taking every thought captive to the obedience of Christ." Isn't that just something wonderful? My Lord taught me that one, because the moment after I pray, I may forget and it might be important for the other person or people, so I did it straight away.

So tonight, I was going through all the prayers again, for all who had been at the prayer meeting. When I had finished, I then went to Elsie's mother. Well, it was wonderful; I was so in the Holy Spirit that I left my body. This is true. I found myself travelling along the hospital corridor; the smell of the ether was so strong. I stopped at the base of this man's bed, in the ward, and I began to pray, in my heavenly language, the gift of tongues. I seemed to be there quite a long time and then I was finished. I travelled back along the tiled walls of the corridor and out, and then I was back in bed. I did not look at the clock, but I felt I was away a long time. I put everything away and lay down and slept. Next morning I went round to church. I knew Father Peter would be there and I shared what had happened. Peter seemed to pass it off and looked at me as if I had taken leave of my senses, so I told nobody.

Time was creeping on for David leaving school, no word from our Lord about a job, or work. I was still lifting him every day, when David himself came in from school and said, "Mam, the café at the end of the village is up for sale."

My thoughts went wild. "My, what we could do in there, Lord."

I went back to when I was small. My Mam had to work all day, every day, to bring us up, and so in the summer holidays she would put me on the bus out of Rothbury and tell the local driver to put me into the Felton bus at Morpeth, and tell him to put me off at Felton, and I would stay at my Auntie Jane's where she had a guest house and a café.

Uncle Jim had a massive sandpit; the wagons used to come in and out all day. I had to behave myself, but I loved going. On Saturday, I would go with Uncle Jim, to Alnwick, to the market. They would be buying all that was needed for the following week. They would buy me a bag of cherries off the marketplace and at the lunchtime they would take me into the café for lunch. They always sat at the same table. O, it was very posh. Uncle Jim would order: soup to start, then main course, then sweet, mine was always beautiful home-made ice cream - Ah! He then would finish what business he had to do and we would travel home - what a day.

At night, the guests had come for so long, they had become Auntie Jane and Uncle Jim's friends and would come through from the dining room into the kitchen, and so I was always asked to sing. I was so small and very shy, so shy I could never sing in front of other people, but Uncle Jim would open the dining room door, and then stand me on a chair, behind the door or just inside the room. Because no one could see me, I could sing my heart out. I was told by Auntie Jane that my Mam used to sing. So memories were flooding back about Auntie Jane's café. Because it was tea-time, when there were no heavy plates to carry, I was allowed to help set the tables and I would carry the cake stand, full of wonderful home-made cakes. And, when I cleared the tables, there would be pennies left for me. Auntie Jane said I could keep them and spend them on market day.

"O Father! Here I was again, tottering on the edge of something wonderful, and could I do it?"

# CHAPTER 3

# The preliminaries
# of buying the café.

*T*he little shop was a paper shop, and some of everything really: groceries, off-licence, there was an ice cream machine in the shop, a drapery in the middle and a chip shop, which had been closed for years, a big flat upstairs and a back-shop for store.

There was no way I could do this. "Lord help me!" I needed my Jesus to confirm it.

I prayed and prayed my heart out. Then one morning I got up and I had a calendar, on my dressing table, with a text on for the day and then a write-up of what God was saying. Just on passing, I tore it off, and there it was, "I am with you."

My mind reeled again. I don't think I took in where it was from in the Scriptures (later I found it, Matthew 28:20). I don't think I read the write-up. It was just so right, it hit me between the eyes. How I got through my day, I don't know, but at night I went home to my Jesus with fear and trepidation and prayed with my heart in my mouth. The witness in my spirit was "Yes" - but "O Lord! How would I do it?"

Three businesses in one and I could hardly add up. I waited and waited, afraid to go along and ask about it. A week went by, then the second week and I still was in such fear of how I would do it. At last I plucked up the courage to go along to the café and see, praying again, "Lord, stop it! Or bless me to know it is You."

I rang the bell, or knocked on the door and Betty let me in. I said why I was there and we began to talk. She showed me round the place and told me all about it, but I really was not listening. I was away with the eyes of the Lord. How wonderful! I did not want the drapery: this would be the café and re-opened chip shop. After we finished going round, we said our goodbyes and I said I would be in touch. I came out and sang all the way home, praising and thanking our Lord.

I went in to my Jesus with such joy, thinking of how I could witness to all the customers. My mind was going fifty to the dozen. The ideas I would use and what would the work be like? Then I came down with a big bang and started to think and pray my next move.

The next move: I phoned my brother Noel, first to say what I had done, then to ask for the number of his accountant. Noel was thrilled for me. He gave me his accountant's number and so I phoned him.

I then made an appointment, which was the next day. As always, because he was an important man, fears started to creep in and so I was keeping myself busy to occupy my mind. By night, I was nearly frantic. "O Father, help me!" I prayed through again and slept.

Next day, I got myself ready and away I went. The appointment was in the morning. I arrived in good time, still praying for wisdom. Here I was again out of my depth. Afraid of man, afraid we would talk about me. Would I understand? These men have such jargon of their own. I felt a bit like Julie Andrews, when she got off the bus to go to her job with the Von Trapp family, with six or seven children singing, "I have confidence in me."

The door opened and I was ushered in to the office. A gentleman came in; we introduced ourselves, then I began my story about the shop. He listened very quietly, very studiously, till I finished. Then he began: did I own my own house? Yes. Was there mortgage to pay on it? No. He was a quick spoken man, no nonsense, the kind of man straight to the point, no shilly-shallying.

"Good!" he said, "We sell your house, as quickly as possible, get a good price, for we don't want to be paying a mortgage on the shop and pay too much interest. Go straight up and see Mr. Bolam now and get him to value the house. Let me know how you get on, and when we have some answers, then I will come up and see what the business is worth."

He stopped speaking, silence, I was dismissed, shook hands, "Bye bye."

I was back out on the landing, shaking from head to foot. I could not sell Jimmy's house. Dear Lord, I could not do it. The bairns had lost their Dad, now I was going to sell our home? I came down the stairs in a stupor, my heart thumping so hard and opened the door on to the street. The car I had parked at 'The Queen's', but I turned up the street to go to Peter Bolam's. I got there, opened the door and went in.

Now Peter and I were at school together, in the same class. I was not quite so afraid of Peter. We shook hands. I must have been a little pale. He offered me brandy, jokingly, and asked what he could do. In my state of shock, I related my story to Peter; what the accountant had said, expecting sympathy, or something. But, to my surprise, he said, "Great! I'll come up tonight, after work, after five, or thereabouts."

O my, o my, it gets worse. I thanked him, came out of his office, walked back down to the car. "O Lord, what could I do now?" I decided to go and tell Noel and Joan. It was now lunchtime, so they would probably be stopped for their lunch.

You see, Noel was in business himself and his schedule was always tight from one job to the next. I arrived, right enough they were both in. They welcomed me in, then I shared what had happened, what had been said, frantically telling everything. They listened in complete silence. By the time I had gone through everything, we sat staring at each other. Then I said I would have to go, the bairns would be coming off the school bus, and I hadn't told them anything yet and I must be there before Peter came.

I went back to the car and began to drive home. "Here I was again, Father," tears beginning to flow so fast I don't know how I could see to drive. "I don't know it Lord; I can't do it."

Then our Lord spoke to me, almost in an audible voice, "You said, your all or nothing."

"But, Lord?"

"No buts."

And indeed, I had taken and said this to my Lord, "I give in."

Suddenly, calm came over me. I had my peace back. "Trust in the Lord with all your heart and do not lean on your own understanding" (Proverbs 3:5).

How or what I did not know, but my Lord had it all in hand. I calmed down, my tears stopped and I then began to pray again, "Please, Father, be with me. Go before me; make a way for me to be able to tell the bairns. I don't want them hurt. I don't want to give them any more shocks. They've had enough with their Dad. Please, heavenly Father, help me."

I quietly and calmly prepared our meal. Josephine came in first, then David. Just chitchat, "How was school?" etc.

We sat down for tea and I told them what I had done. There was no scene, not a flicker, really, of anxiety, very down to earth, quite matter of fact. Josephine said, "You can't sell Dad's house," finished tea, changed and went off to play, or out.

David, with a little bit more emphasis and expression, said, "I'll serve the fish and chips," and off he went.

I'm not sure who came next, Peter or Edward, but Peter was quite impressed. He looked through the downstairs, and then asked if he could look in the loft. We got the steps and up he went. After a little while, he came down again, walked the boundary line up to the back fence, out to the front gate, came back in and said, "I can see why you didn't want to sell. Very compact, no wasted space inside, built on steel, very well built, good bit land."

He then said, "House worth fifty thousand," something like that, "You could possibly get planning permission to build another house on the land, so you're looking at twenty five thousand for the land, with planning permission."

I then said, "My Jimmy built it."

Every part of it was built with love. It took him two years and nine months, every evening and every weekend. The steel was from a building they took down off the camp. He got it down to the site and cleaned every girder, treated it, then painted it. Noel, Jim and Lister came up one Sunday to erect it the old fashioned way, with block and tackle. Sweat and strength, pulling on the ropes, to get the gable end in position and then bolted together. The shape and the size were all there when they completed this shell of steel. The lads all came back to us to eat, at night. When it was finished, Jimmy was so happy; couldn't wait to start the brick and the blocks. What a man! What a job to tackle, holding down full time work and building his own home, his castle.

When he was finished on the bungalow, I walked four mile down the road, pushing three bairns in the pram; painted out a room, scrubbed the floor, cleaned the window, pushed the bairns home and had the dinner ready for Jimmy when he came home at night. The excitement, which we felt with both of us finishing it, was just so wonderful.

It was time to move. Edward was coming up five years old, David was three and Josephine was two. Edward went down on the back of Jimmy's scooter. I walked with the two bairns, the little ones. Charlie, good old Charlie, he was the milkman of our village and it was the farm's wagon. If you wanted help, Charlie was always ready to give you a hand. Our neighbours helped collect furniture when we were leaving, and I'm not sure if George came with us, to help unload.

We called the house 'The Sheiling,' O my! After our meal at night, the bairns had beautiful baths. Josephine had her own little room and the boys shared a room. We went into the sitting room. Jimmy sat down with his feet in front of the fire. "O Father, he was so happy, so proud."

Peter left and Edward came home. Like the little ones, I told Edward, and like Josephine and David, he just listened while he ate. Then said, "You can't sell Dad's house, Mam."

I cleared away. Must have been a weekend, as Mam came every weekend to stay. I would go for her on a Friday and take her home on the Monday, so I brought Mam up and told her all about the café. But with Mam, I could really share that it was going into full time work with my Jesus.

On the Saturday, Noel and Joan arrived. "Could we go along and see the café?" So off we went.

Mr Elliott was there on the Saturday. This was the owner of the café. He showed us right through downstairs then we went home. I made coffee and we all just chatted. Noel said that he and Joan had been discussing the situation and decided they would like to come into the business with me. That way, I wouldn't need to sell the house. Well, my heart leapt within me. "Dear Lord! What a mighty God You are." I just about leapt up into the air. "Wow! O joy, such joy!" I was speechless.

Noel continued, we could do this, and that, how this would work and so on, and so on. I came back down to earth with a bump. He was excited now, ideas racing through his mind and the prospects of owning the café. When he'd finished, I then said, "But Noel, my reason for going into the café is to serve my Lord."

I told them my testimony, how I had received my salvation through Jesus Christ my Lord, and the work was to proclaim this; how I did not want the drapery - that would be the café. So I would proclaim through the café and the chip shop, to all who passed through and also through the papers and the groceries to the local people. He put his hands on my shoulders and said, "I don't know anything about that, but if that was what you want to do," he said, "I admire your faith. You go ahead."

We then said our goodbyes and Noel and Joan left. From nearly having the answer to my heart's ache, I was so flat and empty. The following week I took Mam home. I was so heavy in my heart and at night while talking to my Lord, I would say, "I'm so afraid Father. It's so big, three businesses in one really, I'll never do it."

Then I was kneeling, half sitting, on the floor beside the bed with my books spread out in front of me and Father said, "If you put in what you have, I'll do the rest."

I did have money in the bank, that an uncle had left Jimmy. "O my Lord!" I opened my first reading and it was the story of Uzzah when he put out his hands to save the ark and died instantly. King David was furious, but he really was the one in the wrong, because he was not told to bring the ark back into Jerusalem on the cart with the oxen. The Levites were to carry it back in. (2 Samuel chapter 6). Father was really speaking to me again, this time through the Word. We always need the Word to verify what the Holy Spirit is saying. It is a spiritual principle that the Spirit and the Word work together.

Next morning I got on to the phone to the accountant and said, "Go ahead! Buy it! We're on our way."

After a week of men being men, I was told I would have to go along and sign the papers. I made the arrangements with Betty, for the best time to come to meet Mr. Elliott. Well, in a day or so, news came, Mr. Elliott had been in an explosion, in another business he had, a bakery I think, somewhere down the country and was now in the burns unit, with very bad burns to his hands, so we did not know how long this would take before he was well enough, or how long before he could hold a pen. "So, what now Lord?"

I think it was about this time: the decision was taken that I should go along to work, and learn the ropes. So I duly went in, on regular days, to work. I was very nervous; my maths at school was nil. Putting up the papers in the morning was no bother. Getting off to the stocktaking, no bother. Making ice cream, no bother. Going to cash and carry, no bother. What a joy meeting the people, having a laugh, o, you got all the gossip of the village. That was tremendous because I could pray about it and take it all to the Lord. I was learning new things every week; when we suddenly heard it was back on the market, to sell. I could not believe my ears. What was going on? A little bit hanky-panky, methinks? I was cross.

On telling Noel, he said the ball was in my court, "Knock 'em down in price." The books were not terribly startling.

"Knock him down," the accountant said.

"But, I have an agreement; I cannot knock him down. You go yourself and talk to him, but I'm not going. I have an agreement."

From this, I went back to Noel. He said, "Well, do as he says; go yourself. Take the bull by the horns and tackle him yourself."

"O Father! I don't like this; I go!"

I thought that was the solicitor and the accountant's job. What could I achieve?

When the evening came, I went back to my Lord with a heavy heart. "What's wrong Lord? Where have I gone wrong?"

I checked it all out with Jesus. No, everything seemed to be ok. "So, why the delay? And what a trick to play to try and take the rug out from under my feet."

Confirming it: "Father! If it's I who have to go, now I know I'm not going alone. It is almost a year now. How can I be a good Christian, being cross with a man who has suffered with such burns, and such incapacity to himself? He needs love and understanding." I talked it all through with my Lord.

I had my peace back and I was in a better frame of mind; still a little afraid of the man, but decided I would go and see him. Who knows what our Lord had in mind?

I was asked to go to a Lydia prayer meeting in Whitley Bay, so I went with Barbara (who had hosted my first prayer meeting). I went to Hexham and Barbara and I travelled to Whitley Bay; it was great to meet other women who prayed a lot.

On the way, I had shared with Barbara all that was happening, for with all that was going on we had not seen each other for a while. Barbara said, "If there is a chance, share the tale of the shop with the ladies."

We arrived, introduced ourselves, then down to business. Now I knew I wept a lot in prayer, but was not quite sure if it was my emotions or whether it would be my Lord. But this day, we were praying about the Church, the bride of Christ, and our country. During each item I would sob and sob. Nothing was said, but it was uncomfortable. I was stuffing my hankie in my mouth to make less noise. There were some looks, but nothing was said.

In the break for coffee, Barbara suggested I share, which I did at the end. This lady piped up and said, "How wonderful. I've got the table and the chairs, which have been painted, recovered, and I will get them up to you this week."

"Well, dear, dear Lord!" He again was confirming to me, "Keep going. Everything is in order."

That same week, I went to see Mr Elliott. I said all the things Noel had said: "Books are not good enough. The fact that my accountant did not come is because he had arrangements with you. The agreement must have meant very little to you Mr. Elliott, for you to double-cross me and try to sell it out under me."

To my surprise, he was sorry. "Huh! It was not the way I conducted business." I continued to talk and told him about my stand with Jesus and why I was interested to begin with.

He then said, "Well Rosie! I will deal with you the way it was done with me. You can have the café on the same terms I got it; that is, you rent it from me for five years. At the end of five years, you buy it for the fifty thousand. It won't go up, it will be a signed agreement. That way, you don't need to sell your house, you don't have to knock me down; I will have the papers drawn up tomorrow, and you can come back and we'll sign them together."

You could have knocked me down with a feather. I had not put the house on the market, now I know why.

"O Father! You've done it again. When You do things, Father, how wonderful."

I was in business. I rang Noel to tell him, and the accountant, that we were ready to start. This involved quite a lot with solicitors, on both sides, but 'Praise our Lord,' the wheels were in motion.

# CHAPTER 4

# The café is a success,
# but the call comes to Japan.

*I*t was not long before my solicitor phoned me to go. There
was goodwill to pay, fixture and fittings to pay, first year's
rent to pay; but my Lord said, if I put in what I had He would
do the rest, so I paid, signed the papers at last. While we
waited for the day to move, I went to an auction house and
bought nine tables for thirty-nine pounds. I also bought a
cash register. The drapery was to change into the café and so
all that was to organise. Plans had to be drawn, passed and,
of course, no one was in a hurry but me. Noel came up to see
to that part of it for me.

Mr. Elliott had cleared the drapery and the room was
quite a size. Progress was being made. I also wanted a ramp
up into the building for wheelchairs, so that was approved.
The staff in the shop had been with Mr. Elliott since he
started, so I kept them on. Mr. Elliott suggested to get in
touch with Joyce Lowes who had been the fish and chip shop
cook, when it was open before, so I did. I went round and
asked Mrs. Lowes if she could come and work for me at the
chip shop again. To the joy of my heart, she said, "Yes."

Lesley was one of the girls in the main shop and had already offered to do the serving in the chip shop which would be Thursday night, because it was bingo night at the workingmen's club and the people came in from far and wide. Saturday lunchtime, again people would come, because it's a good handy meal for Saturday lunch. Saturday night was always a good night, because bingo and dance at the club, and Sunday night: the four times a week. Where we live, we are right out in the country and in a very small village, so not enough people to be open every night.

With all this setting in my mind, and talking everything through with my Lord, I then went down to my childhood home, back to Rothbury, for the fish and chip shop man. He was a lovely man. I felt I could talk to him and maybe learn from him, so I knocked on the door. He answered and I shared with what I was doing. I also knew this man, having delivered his milk for eight years, from when I left school till I got married. He invited me in and he was really helpful. He gave me the name of Corbett's, who sell everything to do with fish and chip shops, or any take-away business, so I would get the fat and oil. "Mix half and half, good beef dripping and oil, for the taste," he said, "The dripping for the taste and using the oil makes it go further. It also is better, for the food is not greasy, and cuts down just a little on the calories."

We laughed about that one. Then there were all the food products you could buy. After giving me a list of all these, I asked about the batter. "Was there a secret formula or a knack, or anything special?"

"No," he said, "You buy that ready from Corbett's too. All you add is the liquid and salt, I think. The secret," he said, " is your hot fat and fresh."

I was thrilled with my morning's work. Next to contact was to get the stuff delivered and of course the fish and potatoes. The fish was so beautiful, boxes of frozen, about five or six a week, so it was defrosted, practically, as I used it. Sometimes, an extra box or two, depending on who was in the camp, for the soldiers would phone in for forty suppers at one time. Great! So you had to have spares, if there were a lot. Everything coming along nicely.

Then it was the oil for the tank to be ordered; the pans run on oil. So we were ready for the chip shop. The bairns were quite excited. Jo, in her way. Because they had taken so long, David was now left school, working in a garage.

The next wonderful thing that happened: if you remember, Mam came every weekend to stay. Because of our going into business, I would not have the time to go and get her and take her home, so Mam was wondering how she would cope. She was excited for us, but worried as well and I involved her in everything. Dad had died, a little while back, and Mam loved to come up where she was part of all that was going on. We laughed and cried together. Mam, through all this, gave her heart to Jesus and the times we had were special.

The flat above the shop was really big, we all had our own rooms, big rooms - and there was one for Mam to have, like a bed-sit. It was so big, I suggested this very tentatively, so she would mull it over, no pressure, we would love her to be with us, only if she would like to come. She could come down to be involved or to be private upstairs, whatever suited her. That way, we would be together and she would be part of our new venture. For Mam to give up her independence and leave home was a major step. The family down home would have to come and see us, but that could be done. I'm sure it was left so Mam could take her time.

Next, it was the bungalow: I would have to let it. Well, Robert, my other brother, was in a farm cottage at Longframlington, and the son was getting married, so the farmer wanted the cottage for the son. So Robert and Frances, his girlfriend, would move into the bungalow. Frances was a very clever woman and she worked in the university in

Newcastle, but as we talked and shared about all that was happening, she decided she would like to work in the café too. She would also do all of the books: ledgers, accounts, books, income, outgoings, profits, bills. Everything had to be accounted for, something I was dreading. "Wow, Lord!" What can I say? "My Lord will supply all your needs from His bountiful riches in glory" (Philippians, chapter 4, verse 19). What a mighty God we serve! Even before we ask He has supplied.

"O, my Lord!" The day was coming fast now, so it was packing up at home. The closer it was coming, the more afraid I was getting.

"O, dear Lord, help me!"

Mr. Elliott said he would move out on the Saturday and Sunday morning. I could move in on the Sunday afternoon. Edward brought the tractor and trailer, which really was wonderful; it was not too high to lift things into.

That week the soldiers were having a big do at the camp. We let them borrow our piano. They came about a week before. A lot of them lifted it out of our home into the back of a truck, so when they came to return it, we asked them to bring it back to the café. It weighed a ton and, being so many of them, they handled it well, as we would really have struggled. So we moved.

We could leave some things because it was Robert and Frances moving in. All went well. The big doors into the shop and café also became our front door which was locked and led straight up the stairs, but there was a little back door into the kitchen as well.

Finishing at night, I really did not know whether to laugh or cry. As I went in to my Jesus that night, I poured my heart out, as usual with such desperation. "What have I done?" No turning back now.

I walked through the downstairs, the shop, the café, the chip shop. The bairns were quite happy, I think; they've never complained. It was no good looking back. Move on! I talked and talked till I got my peace back but I had covered everything back into my Lord's hands. Must sleep, early rise in the morning, first day of business.

I rose early and opened up for Lesley to do the papers and I began to prepare for the café. To my joy, I'm not sure whether it was coffee or tea time, but the blessing was: a mini-bus pulled up and they all came into the café and as we shared and talked, they were all believers. "O, what a blessing, Lord!"

We laughed and laughed, what a joy! All the things I had seen about the whole place, being such a witness to my Lord Jesus. Even the name: it had to be "Lydia's Café."

The first reading I read in the pulpit was Lydia, a dealer in purple cloth; so now, this stepping out in faith in business - I had to call it "Lydia's Café."

Another wonderful thing my Jesus showed me to do was to make a card for the tables, like a menu card, only ours was a beautiful white card with a purple "Lydia," on a slant, across the front, and inside was how I came to be there, also the story of Lydia. So my testimony story of Lydia, then the prayer story of Lydia, and a prayer for salvation. Five thousand went off the tables a year.

Thursday came, fish shop night. Edward had to light the pans. We had to turn the oil on and put your arm right through to light it. I was scared stiff to light the gas on the top of the cooker, and put my hand right through to help - "Wow Lord, not me!"

Mr. Elliott said I would never do it, because the bad language of the men was appalling, but within a very short time, all the bad language had stopped and again I could witness. I would be singing and the lads would say, "Come on Rosie, it's not Sunday today."

I would say, "But every day is Sunday when you know Jesus."

It was a wonderful place to talk to the people while you were waiting for their orders. One day a bus stopped; they were on tour, going right up round the highlands of Scotland, and they all came in. There was a couple, Doctor Brown and his wife, who were saved, and the joys were shared. To this day, every Christmas, we write to each other.

Another Saturday lunchtime, the queue was right out of the door and full inside the shop, when the minister came in. Because a good percentage were farmers, he said, "Rosie, I'm trying to get the farmers to come to a lambing service. Don't you think it would be good, laying crooks on the altar, for blessing?"

My Lord gave me the story of the Hebrew people coming out of Egypt, with the blood on the doorposts, and they had to be ready. And I preached my heart out. At some point, the minister had left, and I went forward to the counter and said, "It's not just the crooks He wants to bless, but you, your-selves, because of His love for you." I shared the gospel. It was great: such opportunities to share with the people. If I could share the gospel, even once a day, I was fine, but it was hard work.

Now it was time for Josephine to leave school. There was an open night for parents to go and talk to teachers. Josephine had done well; one of the teachers had wanted her to go into a bank. I was so pleased, but try as I did, I could not persuade Josephine to stay on at school, or go into a bank. So, if she really wanted to leave, then she could work with me in the café. This was her choice, so she served, while I prepared the food in the kitchen.

When we started, I had a local lady who baked buns, scones and cakes, and I tried everything: making dinners, having a salad bar, doing fish and chips. Then I was running out of stuff, so Avril (my son Edward's partner) started to bake for me too. Coffee time, bus-ful in, fifty people coming in, cleaned me out of scones for the day. One day three buses stopped, one after the other, and Mary from along the street came in, rolled up her sleeves and started washing up. O, it was great!

Josephine hated serving in the café, so she suggested I serve and she would work behind the scenes, and work she did.

Bill, from the Hall, wanted to sell one of his big ovens, so I bought it and Josephine and I would start together, but she would carry on; bread buns for the shop, quiches etc., and orders would come in for cakes. She was a tip top little baker. I also got a delivery from our local baker, in Bellingham, for things we didn't bake.

Things were going well. Mam had made the decision to come, so she was coming down, in the afternoon, sitting in the café.

Next thing we heard, the Queen was coming to open Kielder Reservoir and she would have to pass our door. I had huge windows, which I decorated with pictures and flags and streamers. They looked terrific. The day came and we had a fantastic view. The staff were all out on the steps. Mam and I were at the upstairs windows. It was a fabulous day and down she came. She came down a bank, and the corner they had to go round was just opposite us, so the whole entourage had to slow down, right down, so slow it was nearly stop. What a view: our Queen, right at our door. We were waving like mad. She was beautiful and waved back. What a day! Mam talked about these things for days, being so close and because of the corner, how it wasn't just a flash-past.

After a little while, the café was really giving me a lot of business. The Air Force lads were in the camp. To fly, the weather had to be perfect, so they would phone up and ask if I'd cook breakfast at six o'clock in the morning. Because I would do it, I got the business and they would tell me how many. It was great, because what a start to the day: some- times fourteen, sometimes more. I was really blessed. I did not get to talk to the Air Force lads too much. It was just being pleasant and trying to get to know how they liked their bacon cooked and giving a cheery word, maybe a pat on the shoulder if they looked down, or they had had a hard night at the mess, or maybe a new one who was learning and looking worried. I always used to pray for them when they went out that Father would take care of them and keep them safe. Many times I would give the worried one a cuddle, thinking if it were my lads, I would want someone to encourage them. Some of these men were very young.

Time was passing quickly and I needed time to go in to Jesus and spend lots of time with Him. I would fall asleep now while talking to Him, so I had to change tactics and get up an hour earlier in the morning, so I did this and found I would talk to Him all day. I had to: (a) So I would not forget things and (b) Because more and more people had big problems to bring to Him.

My days were getting longer and longer without a moment to spare, but where my Lord had taught me so much, this was now endurance and also strength. I would carry a four stone bag of potatoes under each arm on a chip shop day and at night we closed at twelve; but every thing had to be washed down: the pans, the counters, the tables, all the tops. In the back, everything, the floors, the lot, so there was no smell or traces of fish or anything really, for we used the same tops to bake on in the morning. So it would be one in the morning, and if I'd had a phone call with someone in trouble, I would wash and change and set off for them.

One such night a mother phoned: her little girl had become very ill. The doctor had said it was meningitis and had taken her to hospital. She was only three. So I started to pray the moment I came off the phone. Then, when I finished in the chip shop, I went over. They lived in the Hexham district so this was twenty-five miles or so.

We prayed together and she was so grateful that I had come. We talked and prayed a couple of hours. She was blessed and now felt she was safe. The little girl was sent home in three days, no meningitis. I travelled home, and had an hour's sleep.

I was up again to start the baking. On nights when this happened, I was more awake and had more strength, as if my Lord had given me a whole night's sleep in one hour. It had to be my Lord: I could never have done days and nights like this in my own strength. And I could witness twice as much and sing twice as much the next day. I loved it.

My letters to Mag (Margaret Curry whose father brought me to the Lord) were now more full of my walk with my Lord. The Falklands war was over and we got the lads home: war-scarred maybe, frightened maybe. A truckload would come into the café at once. They just wanted tea or coffee. It was like being in the middle of a war zone. The café would be full of young men, the floor covered with guns. They would sit down and lay the guns on the floor. It was wonderful for me.

I had put on weight; Josephine was always telling me, "Mam, will you sit down and eat." But, no, I just picked at a sandwich here, or a plate there, or something, while I was going. But do you see how God moves, what I was doing? If I had been like my Jo, slim and smart, it would never have worked. I believe my Lord was saying, "It's ok, just love these guys." Because of my size, etc, I could take them in my arms. Grown men would hold me, sobbing, crying for friends shot down, crying because of the shells exploding right next to them, crying with fear. O Father! They would pour their hearts out. Some knew our Lord and we could pray, but the rest, I could only hold tightly and sob with them and bring them to my Lord at night.

The lads would only stay up in the camp for maybe a fortnight, then all change; but I think, in fact I'm sure, that these lads stayed longer. After a while, two ministers came into the café; padres from the camp and thanked me for my work with the lads, saying that I was achieving and had made inroads with the pain and the trauma of these lads, what they had gone through. There wasn't much I could say, that this was the Faith, this was Lord Jesus and I was the hands there. You see, the times that the lads pulled up in the truck and were dropped off and they came in, I would have no-one else in the café and when the time was up and they had to be picked up again, no-one would come in. My time was purely for them.

Another day, the café was fairly busy and a little family were sitting in the centre, when screams went up. The mother had knocked her tea over the baby she was holding in her arms, down her front, down her legs. There was a lady sitting in the window who was a nurse and knew what to do with the baby. She came immediately and asked for certain things to bathe the baby. Then I took the mother away to our back room. After making sure that mam was all right, I left her to wash and dry herself off. She wasn't scalded - "Praise our Lord" - and I came back downstairs to see how dad and the baby were. The nurse had finished what she could do and then handed baby back to daddy. I sat down beside them and took the baby from them. Praying, not out loud, just heart singing to the baby in tongues, nursing her. He finished his tea and by the time mam came back there was no mark on the baby at all. The angry red had gone off the arm and they left all right. "How great You are, Lord."

Lydia's café was getting a reputation and a group of ladies came and, after talking, I was invited up and down the country to give my testimony. This I loved. Then Mag would write in her letters on a regular basis: "I must go to Japan and share my testimony."

There were more and more I could go out to speak and work with. These were women's groups and I was feeling I couldn't go to Japan. Then one morning, in my prayer time, I was sitting on the floor of the office and my Lord said, very clearly, I was going to Japan. This was five in the morning. Japan is nine hours behind us, yet I was so excited, I phoned Japan to tell Mag I was coming.

Margaret said, "Wonderful!" It would be October and I would be the speaker. "Come for a month." Everything was already arranged at Japan.

# CHAPTER 5

# An account of my experiences in Japan

*I* didn't have any money and I did not get a wage, our living and eating was my wage. And this was in the August.

Because I was going out speaking, to the Lydia Fellowship and the Women Aglow Fellowship, I was often told where they were or what they were doing. The Fellowship was coming to Otterburn Hall, so I made arrangements with somebody to take my place in the café; I was going to the meeting. To begin with, when I woke up I felt really ill. Now, it was the first time this had happened to me. I was determined to go, regardless of how bad I felt.

I got washed and got ready and left to walk to the Hall. I walked right through the village; the more I walked, the worse I felt, but I carried on. I turned the corner to head up to the Hall and someone asked if I would like a lift. Boy, did I want a lift? I was dropped, right at the door, still feeling extremely ill.

I went in and the ladies had started, they were singing and worshipping, but I could not worship. Instead, I began to cry, then wail. I knew it was the Holy Spirit, but I did not know what He was doing, but I cried and cried. Then the sickness and the headache left and just about everyone in the room joined in crying and wailing. After a while, the leader came to me, took both my hands and thanked me. She said the conference had started last night, but there was no break-through, and there was no breakthrough this morning, until I had come, and through the weeping and the wailing, the breakthrough came.

Later on, talking to this leader, everything I was feeling that morning was the apathy of the ladies present and the crying was Father God to bring them right in to repentance. This was what Rees Howells talked about with intercession. "O Father!" After the breakthrough came and the people were released, the worship was beautiful, the love and the joy and the praise going up to my Lord.

I got talking to one lady, who said she went to meetings like this every week, in the Great Hall at Hawick. It was a wonderful day and I came home with such joy in my spirit, but also to go to the Great Hall at Hawick. I attended every week and yes, it was wonderful. I shared with the leader that I was going to Japan to work with the missionaries.

He said, "God wouldn't take you out, away from the café to go to Japan."

I said it was my Lord who said I was going.

"No, no," He said, "Never!"

On the way home, I was asking Father for a Word to take to my pastor to verify that I was going. Right enough, in my prayer time, He gave me one. I took it to my pastor the next week. He said, "No way: I had picked that out of the Bible myself."

So on the way home again, I said, "Father! This man is not going to believe me." And that week, a letter arrived with a cheque for eight hundred pounds in. So, when I went back to church on Sunday, I said, "You've got to give me your blessing now, for no-one knew I was going to Japan, but you and Margaret."

When I came home, I phoned Mag and told her about the eight hundred pound cheque. She never admitted sending it but she did tell me to book my flight. She gave me the airport number, the contact and I duly phoned. Now the lady at the airport said, "O, I'm sorry Mrs. Hindmarsh, but flights to Japan are fully booked till next year." I said, "Sweetheart, you've got a flight for me, because I'm going out to work with the missionaries in Japan for a month, so my Lord has got a flight somewhere for me so that I can go."

She said, "Ok. Leave it with me, I'll get back to you later in the afternoon" and she went off the phone. Duly, she phoned me back and told me there was one seat on a flight going the first of October; eight hundred and twenty pounds.

I said, "Book it!"

Now my story changes again. Because in my prayer time I was talking to Father and saying, "Lord, if I can have young people to work with me, their faith would rocket." Because the more you share your testimony, the stronger you become in your faith. The chapel was now never used, so I was asking Father if we could use it alongside the café, with people to stay and they would grow in Jesus. Well, Mr. Wright, the Methodist Minister, arrived, came into the café and asked if I had the keys. I said, "No," but what was he going to do with the chapel?

He said, "Sell it!"

I said, "You can't do that, I've been praying for the chapel for weeks, to work alongside the café."

He went away and, a day or so later, phoned and said, "Mrs. Hindmarsh, put down on paper what you feel our Lord is saying and send it to our superintendent."

So I had a young girl who used to come into the café, not every night, just some nights. She would have tea or coffee and sit and do her homework. This night, I asked her, if I said what to put, could she write me a very official letter, with headings and addresses etc. in the right places.

"O yes." she said, so we set off to write this letter.

When we had finished, I was very impressed and thanked the lassie with great joy. Well, she laughed. I sent it, and in a short time Peter Wright came back on the phone to say the superintendent wanted to see me. It was arranged. "O Heavenly Father, really to have in my mind what You ask for, and Father, show me something I can relate to, as again these men could bamboozle me and I might not know what I was doing, or what I was agreeing to, or what I was not agreeing to, whatever the case may be." Father gave me a Scripture, so when Peter came back, I said, "Go ahead! Make the arrangements." When I put the phone down, I said, "Father, if they don't come to the café to see what You are doing here."

The phone went again and Peter said, "Rosie, the superintendent wants to come to the café."

"Praise The Lord!"

Well, it was Thursday, and he came. We went upstairs to the flat and he asked me a lot of questions, which I answered as well as I could. Then the superintendent laid out two letters. One said I would pay five pounds a week and do whatever God was saying to me, and the other letter said I would stay under the Methodist wing covering, but I could still have the free hand to do God's will. But (exclamation mark) my Scripture was in the middle of the letter. I was so thrilled. I chose to stay under the Methodist wing. Now the superintendent was very pleased. He then said, "Let us pray."

We all knelt down on the living room floor in the flat and we prayed. He handed me the keys. What a privilege.

So I started to have little services on a Sunday evening. Again I really just spoke of my testimony, but as people were coming into the café, I was now sharing about the chapel. The weekend that I confirmed I was going to Japan, we had a service in the chapel, and when it was over, a lady pressed a twenty pound note into my hand. That was my full fare paid.

As I said, there was so much to organise for a month before I could go. Two friends of Margaret and Kay came to stay with us. They thought they could stand in for me, while I was away. Their names were Marty and Rowena. Margaret had said to bring my book with me, but what I had written was not good and did not flow. I was still in so much fear of man, it was not right. Marty worked with, or on books and she read and corrected it, but did not seem very impressed with it. I sent it to a publisher and they sent it back. It was not finished. It was something, I guess, it wasn't a total no.

Round about two to two and a half years had passed, and Mam had become very ill. The last winter she was eighty-three on her birthday in September, so I was sitting up with Mam; she was not eating, but, out of the blue, she would ask for boiled egg and tea, and this would be one o'clock in the morning or some time later. I would go and prepare it and, bless her, she would sit up and eat every bite. We would talk and talk, but all the while she was fighting to live. We were fine, really. Doctor Armstrong, her doctor, said one day that he really did not know why she was still alive. He said her stamina and strength were unbelievable. Then things changed and she began to fail. She said, "Rosie, I'm going."

It had been weeks that she was so strong and we would have such laughs about old times. Mam had had such a hard life. She never complained and I never heard my Mam call anyone. She taught me to sing. She herself was such a good singer. Auntie Jane said that if there had been T.V. in her day, she would have been on it. She also played the violin. When we were little, or when I was little, my eldest sister Joan's boyfriend brought a violin for Mam to tune for him. Jim was full of talent, so Mam did. He then said, "Play something," which she did. But for me, pain in her face tore me to pieces. I had to go out of the room, she was so sad. The music was beautiful. It was the only one time I ever heard her play. Now here we were holding each other and I would read Psalms to her and always soothe her. She knew she was dying. I then asked if the family would help me. One night Noel and Joan would come and another night our Joan would come. She knew them, knew they were there.

Then it was Friday night, it was my turn again. It was also Good Friday because I remember thinking of Jesus and how He died and rose again. Mam was unconscious, but as I sat and read to her she was in such peace and, round about five in the morning, she went home to Jesus, so full of peace.

Going back to Marty and Rowena: one day, very early in the morning, I was baking and I started to weep uncontrollably. Then it stopped and a little while passed and away I would go again. There was such trauma in the sobs. This happened five times. On the last time Marty came to me and said there had been a very bad accident and the weeping was the five people in the accident crying out to God, and Marty said, "You're the bridge between them and our Lord."

I always knew it was intercession, but because Father had shown Marty what it was, I knew I had prayed for the five people. I really felt so humble that Father could use someone like me. Marty and Rowena stayed about a couple of weeks and then decided they couldn't do it. The work was so much, they felt they really could not take it on, so Frances said she would transfer from the shop to the café the time I would be away.

Margaret rang and asked me to bring a plastic container of golden syrup, a gallon from Cash and Carry, as they could not buy it in Japan, and a gallon of black treacle. A gallon? Margaret's Auntie Margaret made her a Christmas cake and some things for Christmas. The time came for me to go, we said our goodbyes and off I went.

The flight was nine hours. There was delay at Heathrow before we left, then we came down at Bangkok to change flights. There were more delays again, they could not get it right; they decided we had to stay the night, so we were taken to a hotel for one night. It was beautiful. We could have a shower and a bed to sleep in. The dinner gong went and I went downstairs to dinner.

Well, I had never seen so much food. Every dish prepared you could imagine and quite a good variety of English dishes too, so I tucked in. I was sitting on my own and a beautiful Filipino girl came and sat next to me. She could speak broken English so she asked me where was I going?

"Japan," I said, "To work with my friends who are missionaries." I told her my testimony.

She listened with no comment till I had finished, then she said when she was very small missionaries came to the Philippines and they told the Christmas story. I asked her if she had made the commitment. "O no," she said.

I asked if she would like to do it now. She said, "Yes."

We bowed our heads in prayer and she repeated what I said. Afterwards we hugged each other and parted. We never saw each other again, but "Praise Jesus," she was saved.

We got back on the bus and travelled back to the airport to continue our flight. I was wondering if Margaret and Kay would be there to meet me, and what it would be like. Everyone on the plane knew I was going to work with my friends who were missionaries, and so many helped me on and off the flights with my gallons of syrup and black treacle and Christmas cake. I took these as hand luggage, in case they burst or something happened in the luggage department, if they were thrown about. So it was quite a job, two gallons of liquid, two bags of stuff. People were ever so kind. Somebody would take one and somebody would take another, another lady carried the Christmas cake and we laughed on and off the flights, joked and really it was absolutely wonderful as we went down the steps, or the gangways, off and on.

Well, our moment had arrived again, people were there right at my side to get me off with all my goodies, off the flight. As we walked through the places and bits until we were coming out into where the people were to meet relatives and friends, my silent prayer was, "Let them be there, Father to meet me."

We turned a corner and behind a barricade was the biggest placard, "WELCOME TO JAPAN."

This wasn't needed for I caught sight of them and amid shouts of "Rosie! Rosie!" tears were streaming down my face just to see them, and all the people helping were so happy for me, shaking hands and giving the things over to Margaret and Kay. Two more friends were with them, people wishing me all the best.

We got out of the airport and on our way to Mag's apartment. It had a very compact living room, two bedrooms, nice kitchen and bathroom. You actually sat in the bath and I mean sat. I don't mean you got into the bath and sat down. It was a 'sitty up' bath. It was very good. We talked and talked, filling each other in on all that had been happening.

The next day a group came to Mag's to pray before we went out on the first mission. They gathered together round the table in the living room and as one after another prayed, I was praying with them, my gift of tongues joining in to agree. Two can put ten thousand to flight. I was just in there, backing the prayers with all of my heart, when, suddenly, everything stopped. Everyone stopped praying. I looked, everyone looked at me. "What did I think I was doing? Tongues were to edify yourself." But at home, I was on my own. Father had taught me the power of prayer in tongues.

Not only did they not like my using my tongues, they did not believe in tongues. "O Father, what now? I have come halfway round the world and I am wrong for using the gift You've given me to use."

I went out of the meeting and went to my room. We slept on the floor, just as they did in Japan. So I got down on the floor. "What can I do Father? We are not in unity, how can we work together?" It was at this point that Father told me to go to the wall in the sitting room, put my hands on the wall and pray. So I came back out, went to the wall, put my hands on the wall and as I started to pray, I was coming against something evil. "You see," Father said, "When we don't know how to pray, the Holy Spirit prays through us," and this was definitely one of these times. It went on for a little while.

After I was finished, He then said, "Go back through, put your hands on the kitchen wall and pray again." Off I went. I did the same, put my hands on the wall and prayed with my gift of tongues. I was coming against something evil.

When I finished, I came back through to go back in the bedroom. A voice from the prayer meeting, the group, said, "What do you think you are doing?"

I said, "I'm obeying my Lord. He told me what to do."

With astonishment they said, "Where you placed your hands on the wall, in both rooms, there is a Shinto shrine that the people worship and bow down to, and bring presents to. They are in every home and on every street and if you want the gods to bless you, you must give to the shrine. The Japanese people live with fear in their gods." O how sad; Jesus was so wonderful to set us free from all that.

After this I was accepted back into the prayer meeting. Later we travelled to our first meeting. I was the speaker, now it was my testimony of what my Lord had done for me, but I found I was adding truths from the Scriptures. "We can't earn this, we are not entitled to it, we are not good enough to receive this, we don't get saved because of how hard we work." After the people at the prayer group had said about giving to the statue and not because we give anything. "Our Lord loves us the way we are, with all our faults, with everything. I'm not better than you because I'm saved. In fact, it makes me very humble that I am saved, because He loves you just the same."

Some came forward for salvation. Now my Lord was teaching me evangelism.

We had coffee and went on to the next meeting. "O Father:" my heart was singing. Sharing the Gospel, Jesus said. Our testimony was great, but His, the testimony of Christ Jesus our Lord, is much greater.

Our testimony is strong within us and no one can take that away from us. We know what Christ Jesus has done, but we should be growing all the time.

Now my heart was hungry for more of His Word to verify the Gospel, so I went back into the Bible to read and learn. I could not give to the people if I myself had not got revelation knowledge of what I'm talking about. (a) it would be second hand and (b) it would not be real to me. Like Rees Howells' book on prayer, because I was walking in intercession and praying in intercession, I knew exactly what he was talking about. Prayer was real for me. Now it is evangelism, so another learning plateau to move into, to preach.

"O Father, the joy to be going on to evangelism with the backing of intercession and prayer."

You see, there is no work done without prayer. What is prayer? It is our relationship with our Lord. The more you pray, the deeper your walk with our Lord, the greater intimacy with Him.

"More Lord, I need to know You more, so I'm not false or talking through a hole in my head. I need to know You better Lord so it is really You talking to Your people."

We came home in the afternoon to get our dinner and back out at night to a Bible study. I could not wait. For me, you see, I needed to hear the people and then hear my Lord to know how He wanted to help them in their situation. I would be praying into the night. The church was bringing the people to themselves, not to Christ Jesus our Lord. "They don't know You Lord."

Mag and Kate took me, in between meetings, to see places in Osaka, magnificent places. What magnificent things: "They are very clever people, Father, all of them."

It was so wonderful really, the things they had created. They took me to a festival and the figures were all made out of flowers, some wonderful scenes. They told the story with the scenes. You walked through from scene to scene, very skilfully done.

Mag also made me try the food the Japanese people eat, raw fish and sushi, seaweed. I could just manage a very little sushi, but the fish, this was an art of how to swallow it. I'm sorry, but the raw fish in my mouth was enough to make me retch, and to try to swallow it! The size of the piece that Mag took was about the size of a banty egg, whole in the shell. The piece I managed eventually to get over was about the size of a cherry and you put it on your tongue and swallow it whole. You don't chew it. To my greatest relief, I never had to do it again."

We went out and when we went to the people's houses we always managed to get English food, cooked differently, but English food. We went to the highest building in Osaka one day and had the most beautiful knickerbocker glories you ever did see.

There were lots of fun times, but for me my heart was waiting while Father was teaching me new things every day. My mind was alive to take in all He wanted me to say. One of these days was the children. We came to the underground - it was only seven in the morning - and as far as the eye could see were little children, no more than three years old with satchels on their backs. No nonsense, no sentiment, they had to learn and they would be at school till four in the afternoon. I was still nursing my bairns at three and four. They are still babies, but Mag said this was the rule in Japan. The next stage up would be out till six and so on. No time to play, no time to be children.

I was also taken to the biggest Buddha in the world. He was as big and as high as the temple. He was awful. I went round him praying against him thinking of David and Goliath. Nothing is too hard for our Lord. I had also prayed against the idols in the streets.

In the meetings every day, people were beautiful, and not a lot but one or two would come through, but the greatest victory was just loving them. Everywhere I went, Father said, "Love them," so love them I did. I put my arms out and they would come into my arms, crying, laughing or just in silence, just wanting to hold me.

Mag and Kay and Beth and Georgia, for we always went everywhere together, all said, "Don't do that." It would undo all the good that they had done. These people were very ornamental and did not touch each other. They bowed to one another in acknowledgement but never hugged. But all I could say was, "This is not me, this is my Lord, I'm doing it because I want to obey Him."

After a while, they gave up on me and I carried on, rather our Lord carried on. The women, like the children, did not know love. Father wanted them to receive His Love. It was all rules and regulations, no love. The men were very stand-offish. They went to work, then they went to their clubs and only wanted the women for sex or bearing children. No real communication, no talking, no relationship - their purpose just to keep the home, if you could call it a home with no love. Because these people were so clever, the home had every electrical gadget there is, something for whatever you are doing, so the women got through the housework, cooking, doing things in very quick time, no labour needed - but they were sad, unwanted, unloved, bowed.

At that time, Japan had the biggest and highest suicide rate in the world. How our Lord wanted them loved with self worth for themselves.

The prayers at night were as intense as the speaking in the day, to break the walls down, to let our Lord's love in.

I am not sure which Sunday it was, but I was asked by my friends' pastor to speak in church. Now the church was not a church as we know it back in England. We went to church in a hotel. I can't remember the name, but it was a big, big hotel. The room where the church was held was huge, massive, could hold one hundred or more people, so this was my biggest speaking engagement. Yet the pastor had said, "Five minutes," so I asked my Lord to give me what to say, but finish it in the five minutes.

We sang and praised our Lord. Beth and Georgia were the leaders for the music and Kay and Mag would join in to lead the church in worship. Then it was my turn. I stepped out, the pastor introduced me and gave me the lectern. My legs were like jelly. I thought people could see that I was shaking, but once I started I forgot about myself and concentrated on Christ Jesus our Lord. The privilege our Lord had granted me, the honour He gave me, favour that I was worthy to stand before His church of a hundred people. It was a sea of faces waiting with such excitement. You could have heard a pin drop. "Speak through me Lord. Speak through me Lord." He did, everyone wanted to shake hands with me. Everyone said I had said more in five minutes than the pastor had said in the hour he was speaking, and guess what? I spoke for exactly five minutes, not one second over. What a privilege, what an awesome privilege.

With it being Sunday we went out for lunch and some more touring, but my mind wasn't on the touring. My heart was singing, thoughts with me were just of Jesus my Lord.

We were invited to a wedding with a family from the church. It was like I had been taken into their hearts. The more and more people we met, the more and more we hugged and embraced. "The walls were coming down fast, Father."

I cannot remember much about the wedding; I seemed to be on duty in the prayer line.

The week progressed and on the days I was working, just about the whole time I was covering everything with my gift of tongues. I did not know what I was praying, but my Lord did. I would just set off speaking in my heavenly language. Whatever I was covering I did not know, but He was in charge. He just wants the willing vessel who is open to His leading at all times. Paul says we are to pray without ceasing (I Thessalonians 5:17), but it is not having to think of something to pray, it is total surrender to Christ Jesus our Lord, and He will give you either the words or the Scriptures to read or the tongues. Just be open to Him.

The dialogue was in Japanese for the wedding and the vows and the services and at the reception, so it was no problem for me to read a prayer from my Bible since I was not aware of the content of the conversation with the groups of people or at the table. So I sat being very pleasant to everyone but unable to join in. It was all very excited chattering, so "Praise Jesus," it was fun and joy all round. I was introduced to the bride and the groom who were able to reply in broken English.

The next week we were working from Mag's flat. People were coming a lot and it was discussion, laying foundations, opening things up for them to understand. But one of these days one lady, after hearing the Word and the testimony, coffee being served, came over to talk. She could speak very good English and was relating to me about her arm, her elbow really. The bone had been broken at the elbow and had not healed where she could use it. The bone did not bend up at the elbow, it lifted or bent down, like it was twisted a bit off beam and did not line up well. Christ Jesus could heal that so it will be perfect, so I asked if she would like to pray. If you remember, away back at the beginning, I prayed for a lady who scalded her arm under an electric water heater and helped her. She was shocked and surprised because I believe all the pain and heat went and the redness left. She was so aghast she practically ran downstairs and out of the shop. Well, then there was the baby in the café. A scald is a terrible thing and sometimes needs skin grafts, but with the baby there was no mark on the arm. The skin was perfect and a beautiful colour, no angry red or scar, so God healed her and here I was again. But this time was the first time openly the lady really wanted prayer. So we prayed.

After, there seemed to be no immediate change, but I knew when the lady touched Christ Jesus, the lady with the issue of blood who had suffered for twelve years, Jesus said, "Who touched Me?"

The disciples said, "But Master, the crowds are all around touching You."

But Jesus said again, "Who touched Me?"

Now the woman thought she was going to get wrong: but no, Jesus wanted her to know that her faith in touching Him had healed her, so He said, "Woman, your faith has made you whole."

In the story, the woman said, "If I can only touch Him, I know I shall be healed."

Well, this is what happened to this lady. I knew she had received the prayers, but not from me, from Christ Jesus. Something went out of me so I knew she was healed.

We finished the meeting, but later that night the lady phoned and she said. "I'm healed, I'm healed."

She could bend and straighten the arm like it was normal. She did not go hysterical, she wept silently unto Jesus our precious Lord.

I never saw her again, just like the young girl in Bangkok. God's appointed time.

Mag and Kay were all excited. The church had been practising for a while to sing in a choir for some festival that was special. I don't remember what it was but we all went. It was striking. We were all dressed in white and scarlet. Beth and Georgia were there as well. There were solos and the whole choir was singing. O, it really was beautiful, to see and to listen. I loved when the worship really praised Christ Jesus. It was like my heart was singing because He was singing too. I can feel it in my very being. For me it is like liquid love coming down and I wept with joy for my Lord because they really were singing in Spirit and in truth.

The weeks were flying by and we entered our fourth week, which Mag and Kay had booked in at the Y.M.C.A. in the mountains for all the people who had accepted Christ Jesus as Lord. I was introduced to a Barbara, who was a drama teacher. She was coming. We were going to pray, to teach, to do anything and everything we could to bless these girls and women, because then they would be disciples going out into Osaka to preach the good news. I don't know how many came, but the prayer was that Father would baptise them with the Holy Spirit: that would be wonderful. So it was worship praise. There was prayer for healing. There was dancing. There was drama. For me it was, "Come to Christ Jesus, just come to Christ Jesus. Just hunger after Him. Come to Him."

Some got baptised in the Holy Spirit, some needed a lot of ministry. We were working with them into the night: the pain and trauma, the lives of some of the girls. Breaking down barriers that we ourselves put up when we have been hurt. I don't want it to happen again. How we worked, building, building. One of the banners was a wall and the building bricks on it. We finished about midweek and travelled back to Mag's flat, but I knew that my time was finished.

It was time to go home. I could not, of course. My flight was not until the weekend, but it was like I was in limbo, couldn't settle. Mag and Kay had more places they wanted to show me and so we went here and we went there. Then, the last day, before I was to fly home, we sat and prayed together and talked of all that had happened. They both asked me, "Just what part or what place did you like best?" They had taken photographs of every new thing and there were lots of photographs, which filled four albums. I said, "Being flat out day in, day out with my Jesus; listening for His every prompting prayer before each meeting and being ready at every turn."

Mag and Kay were quite disappointed "Did you not like this, or that? Or wasn't something beautiful; didn't you really see the beauty?"

Everything they had done and the work they had gone into to bring it to pass for me to be there, was absolutely wonderful and yes I did appreciate it, but for me, I took very little in from what I saw or where we had been. "O Father! to work hand in hand with You was more brilliant."

We said our goodbyes amid tears and hugs and I was on my way home.

# CHAPTER 6

# Great works in the chapel and an end to the lease on the café.

*I* slept and slept on the flight home. When I got home everyone was there to see me. Everything had gone well in the café and the church - but I had changed. I could not settle any longer, I yearned for the mission fields.

All the work that had to be done in the café was awful. All the drive and initiative I'd had was gone. I was tormented. It was a headache. It was a heartache. I really did not know what I was going to do, or what was wrong with me. I had to do it. "Help me Father! Please help me!" It took me a long time to settle down. Father did bless me. As things began to happen at home, I was so low that my Jesus came very strong.

I wanted things to happen here, at home, the same as had happened in Japan. Father gave me a Scripture in my prayer time, Ezekiel chapter 4, the whole chapter. This was the beginning of learning to fast. I could not lie on my side as the Scripture said, but I could take the bread and water. I promised I would do it if I could find a barley cake bread recipe.

Nancy was our local lass. She was an extremely good cook, a great baker and the seamstress, so I asked Nancy if she had a recipe for barley cake or bread. To my surprise, she said, "Yes."

If you read the chapter, my cake cum bread was made of wheat, barley, beans, lentils, millet and spelt. I did this. I did not cook it over dung as it said in the Bible, but in prayer, it was the siege over Jerusalem. I was really coming against the principalities and powers of darkness over Jerusalem. I measured out my daily ration of bread and water then from time to time I would have it during the day. I was not impressed with the bread. It wasn't unpleasant but it wasn't lovely crispy, crunchy, crusty bread, but I could manage it. With all the pulse in it I expect it was very good for me; and water, but I did not really like water, but this was the drive and initiative coming back to carry on in the café.

Whenever I was in prayer, all I used, or whatever I used, was on a much wider scale. While I was in mid fast, my beloved Lord came to me one day. I was in the back shop and I turned and He was standing in the doorway. I immediately went down on my hands and knees with my head on His feet. He filled the doorway, so tall. No facial expression, but I knew it was my Lord, that's all I can say.

Then another day, He was stood in the kitchen door. So tall, again no face, but it was my Lord.

Then another day, He was sitting in front of the cooker, this time, His brow was on His hands and the pain was terrible.

Then, the last time, it was winter and the provisions were not getting through. I had no bread for my customers, so I set off with Edward's car, because it had front wheel drive, or whichever it is that is necessary, back wheel drive, or front wheel drive. I got through, anyway, and I was going along, praising and thanking my Lord for getting me through; when, like the kitchen, He came and sat beside me with one arm on

His knee and His head bowed on His hands. The pain of seeing Him in such distress, like this, was more than I could bear. I had to pull off the road. I wanted to hold Him, but I dare not. I sobbed and sobbed and wept uncontrollably for a while and then it was over and He was gone. I continued my journey in silence, just thinking of my Lord and what could be wrong for Him to suffer so.

I don't know how long I did the siege, quite a long time; I knew it was over. It was not like the Bible three hundred and ninety days.

After this, again the groups of churches would come, have a meal and share my testimony. It was Japan now as well and all the things my Lord was teaching me.

One evening a couple came in I knew from the fellowship at Hawick; they were close. I made them a coffee and a sandwich; one thing about the café, there was always plenty to offer people to eat. We sat in the café and talked. It got round to deliverance. After sharing things, he asked for prayer for deliverance, "Father, take over here, I don't know what to do."

I was concentrating, waiting for my Lord for we can do nothing unless Christ Jesus shows us. But Jesus only did what His Father told Him so "Show me Lord, show me what to do."

Because he asked again - Jesus said: "Ask in prayer, believing, and you shall receive" and "Whatever you ask in My name you shall receive" (Matthew 21:22, John 16:24). So Father, he was asking for Your help; he wanted to be free by the Holy Spirit from his torment.

I went to James 5:14,15: "Anoint with oil … the prayer offered in faith, if there is sickness, the sick will be healed … if there is sin, the sin will be forgiven."

I was praying all this back to Father. I was weeping and asking when Father said, very calmly, "Command the spirit to leave."

So, just like my Lord, I was not shouting, I commanded the spirit to leave. To my surprise, I saw with my own eyes the spirit, the serpent, a snake, leave this man's body. I stood frozen to the spot. I was standing behind him; he was sitting on a chair. It moved along the floor. I wanted it out, O God I wanted it out. So in my shock I repeated and repeated. To my surprise, I was still claiming, "In the name of Christ Jesus, get out! In the name of Christ Jesus, get out!"

I did this until it was out of the café door, not just out of the café, but out of the double front doors as well. I asked if he was all right and then I prayed for the Holy Spirit to fill the void so nothing could come back in. With the house swept clean, I asked God to cleanse him with the blood of Jesus. When it was all over, I asked again how were we doing? To which he answered he felt great. I then told him what I had seen. Both of them were amazed but left very happy people.

They were gone, but I was weeping again, "O Father, how we have moved into another part of my walk with Jesus." This was the first time of deliverance with many more to come.

In the service, one Sunday night, a man came in with another man. We went right through the service and, while we were having coffee, the gentleman told me why he had come. This man he had brought with him was possessed. Now here was a different situation. He did not look as if he really wanted to be here, and did not ask but was willing to go along with the man who was a pastor. I said I would pray and back the pastor. To my horror, he began to yell at the man, but not at the man, at the spirit in the man, to "Come out!"

I was standing just off the side watching and could see very clearly. The spirit in the man was mocking. I waited, and then asked my Jesus, "This is not going well. Father; what should we be doing?"

With this, my Lord said, "Go forward and love him."

I never hesitated, I put my arms around him and loved him. Within seconds he broke and he was crying like a baby. The more I loved him, the more he cried.

My Lord said, " Sit him down here. Be ready."

So I sat him down, still holding him, loving him and talking to him about Jesus our Lord, when he started to retch. I ran for the dish and the man vomited and vomited. I bathed him and washed his face and hands still talking about our Lord, but now, I was commanding very calmly, every unclean spirit to come out of him and away he would go again, vomiting. This lasted quite a while then I had the 'all clear' to pray over him, anoint him with oil and pray for the Holy Spirit to come. I asked if he had made the commitment and he said, "No."

So I asked if he would like to make the commitment now. He said, "Yes."

We prayed the prayer of salvation and I began to ask the Holy Spirit to fill every area which had been cleaned out to cover him with the blood of Christ Jesus our Lord; to put the cross between him and the world, to strengthen him, clothe him in the robes of righteousness, Your robes of righteousness Lord, in Christ Jesus our Lord. After it was all over, the man was so thankful. I asked him how he was. He said he felt as if he had gone through the mangle but he was ok, to which I said that he had received major deliverance with the divine hand of our Lord. "Do you feel clean, or is there still more to do?"

"No," he said, "Everything is gone."

I shared how we can let these things return if we open the doors. We make the choices to stay clean or to go back to bad habits, or so very carefully who you gather round you or what you allow in. We must be responsible for our actions and how we handle people.

After a while, the pastor came back again through the day. We went into the chapel on the same day. He brought a young lad with him, in his early twenties and the lad was possessed. So again I said I would back him in prayer. Now this time he started very well. I was aware things were fine, but he went down in the spirit and again I was aware our Lord was very much in charge; when, suddenly, instead of commanding the spirit out, the pastor began to talk to the spirit.

At this point I jumped in with both feet and stopped the man and asked Father what He wanted to happen. I commanded the spirit to come out and it was resisting but calmly I focussed in on Jesus and in the authority of my Lord commanded again. The lad rolled over and I ran for the dish and he choked and spluttered until everything was out. Now I knew Father was teaching me how to handle these situations.

After seeing to the lad, I asked the man what he thought he was doing. Our Lord Jesus never conferred with the spirits; that was very dangerous indeed.

The man came back again only once more after that with a young girl in her twenties, and as I prayed for our protection, I saw the girl, and as she came in it was like the disturbed mind was overwhelmed with being in the chapel. She was running around like a scared rabbit. I never waited to see what the man would do. With this lass, I was so conscious of the terror within her and if she might harm herself, I just kept praying to my Lord to take control. "Come Lord Jesus, take control," over and over again.

At last she calmed down. I was binding the spirit but loosening the girl, but all of a sudden, she gave in. I was able to come close to her and then hold her and begin to command the spirit to come out, which in this situation was fear. After bringing everything into perspective, still holding her, I began to explain all about Jesus our Lord. "In our own strength we can do nothing, but all things are possible to him who believes."

To my surprise, she sat up and began to talk normally and ask all about the Lord. The spirit was gone: "no weapon formed against you will prevail, no evil can come near your dwelling place" (Isaiah 54:17, Psalm 91:10). In all things Father was teaching me. I was amazed at His wonderful touch, such beauty, such love, such compassion.

When it was evil, I knew it was not the person, but the evil over the person. No two people were the same; no two ways of dealing with the spirits, no formulas. For every single one, we must rely on our precious Lord. If, and a big if, we take it out of His hands, it is detrimental to us as well as to the soul in trouble.

The problems were getting bigger and bigger. The next was a man up over the border. I was asked if I would go and help. I met up with a lady and we travelled together and she filled me in as we went. Now, again, this was wonderful because the lady was used as the intercessor, while I was doing the deliverance. She had the symptoms so as we worked, she could tell me how things were moving in the man's body. Time after time we thought he was clean, when something would kick in again and I don't know how many spirits he was delivered of but the quantity in the bucket was quite a lot and it was like green bile. Poor man, somewhere around five in the morning we all felt everything was done. Praying over him, he was born again, so I knew he belonged to Jesus.

A little time passed and I was invited back up to a meeting to hear some speaker, so I went. We had a time of worship, which was beautiful, when a couple arrived, let's say it was John and Mary. Mary came into the meeting and asked if I would help her husband. I went out into the kitchen where her husband was leaning over the sink. I immediately commanded the spirit to come out and the man was choking and coughing and retching at the same time. I was running my hands up his back, right up the back like you would with someone who was choking, when all of a sudden it was out. He was scarlet in the face and the neck. I sat him down and washed him while making sure everything was gone, then I prayed for the Holy Spirit to come to comfort and soothe the man.

After a while he was quite calm and free. He looked at me and said, "That was an animal. I thought I was not going to make it."

I missed the meeting, but I did not care. Doing what we were doing, learning by actually doing the work was far greater than sitting listening to someone talking about it. This is how Holy Spirit did teach because I had no idea what to do. I had to depend on my Lord, every minute of every day. And in helping people, it had to be my Jesus.

Father was teaching me; my focus was more and more on the church than the café. I went through the motions but my heart was still on the mission fields. More and more I was in the chapel. Father brought people to me. I never advertised, I never charged but they gave me a lot of money. We prayed over the amount so we both could get blessed and the words came, "Father loves a cheerful giver" (2 Corinthians 9:7).

And you cannot out-give our Lord. I've always tithed to Maranatha. Thousands came into the chapel and thousands have gone out to where I was told to send it, because my Father had shown me He supplies every need from His bountiful riches in glory.

Another lady came bringing a man with a heart problem. But before we came to Jesus and prayed for the man, the lady asked if I had any oil. "Of course," I said.

I went through to the vestry, got the oil and handed her the bottle. She asked if I would sit down. I did. She said, "Our Lord told me to anoint you."

Well how strange. She anointed me; my right ear, my right thumb and my big toe on my right foot. She said, "I don't know what this is for, or what it represents."

We prayed together as sisters. I'd never met this lady before but I was so blessed. After which, we prayed together for the man. It's a beautiful time to spend together in the chapel.

That week we were having meetings of Bible study with Keith and Mary and it was quite well attended. He was bringing a young lad with him from Poland who would be his guest speaker. Well, he was beautiful. We were finished, and teas and coffees were being served and I asked Keith and Mary what the lady had done, to which they replied, "Don't know."

Well, everyone went home and Mary and Keith and the young lad were the last to leave. I hugged the man and thanked him for his teaching and I queried if he knew what was meant by the oil on the lobe of the right ear, and the thumb of the right hand and the big toe of the right foot.

He began to laugh heartily, and so I said, "O! Come on! What is it?"

He then went very serious and said, "Go to Leviticus 8, verses 22 to 23."

This was the anointing of Aaron and his son as high priests.

"You have just been anointed high priest in the Levitical priesthood. Our Lord was their portion. When the land was divided up and given out, the Levites did not get any. Our Lord provided for them."

I was stunned at the time. I was always looking for the men to be the leaders, not the women. I still believe that the men must be leaders not women, but I am an intercessor which is one set apart to hear Father's heart and can carry it out just like the high priest in the Hebrew Scriptures (Old Testament).

"So be it Lord, You have anointed me. I pray, Father, for Your purpose. Don't let me be high and mighty, don't let me step out of line. Father, Your Word says: 'We are as the filthy rags - keep me humble. Only let me do what You want me to do. Keep my mind stayed on You and thank You for the privilege and thank You that You have called me and I only know that You will, for Your purposes, finish what You have begun."

The chapel was still doing very well with different ones coming in and people being saved. It was baptism in the river, and during such a service, a minister came and said I could not take the children any more because of what I was doing. The parents did not want me to teach their children.

I was quite shocked and said, "But I'm following the Scriptures. People, after making the commitment, were baptised into righteousness. Die to self, rise to Christ Jesus. And Matthew 3, verse 15, 'Jesus answered, and said to him, 'Permit it at this time for in this way it is fitting to fulfil all righteousness.'"

Then the minister said that not only could I not have the children, but I was banned from going back to the church. I was devastated.

A fortnight later, the same minister came back into the café. He apologised, laid hands on my head and blessed me and then said, "Rosie, carry on with your work for Jesus" but the damage was done and the enemy had won that round.

Then he tried his hand again. I was asked to speak at a young people's meeting at the farm of a brother in Christ Jesus. I went in Edward's car. The meeting was such a success. When we broke for coffee, because I was so close to a ladies prayer meeting, I asked if they would mind if I went to the prayer meeting. No one minded, so I said my goodbyes and set off.

I was only in first gear all the way down the farm track. I had reached the bottom and put the car into second gear to come out on to the road, when everything went out of control. I was travelling along the bank side. I repeated and repeated, "Jesus my Lord!"

Afraid at first of what could happen, I could not hold the car at all, the force was much stronger than I. After travelling the bank side only a short distance, the car rolled over on to the roof. It all happened so quickly.

I sat for a moment then realised that Satan was really having a go at me. Now I could smell petrol and was afraid the car might burst into flames. I began to call on my Lord again.

Being upside down, I could not open the doors. The roof was now flat which had jammed the doors. I started to come against Satan. After telling him a few home truths, I then asked my Lord to show me what to do. I was on the front side of the roof so I climbed over into the back and, to my joy, one of the back doors gave and I got out. I walked back up to the farm road and met Dale and Peter coming away.

The lads ran down the road and got the car on to its wheels. You couldn't drive it, so they pushed it back up to the farmyard.

Everyone came back inside and I related my story of what the enemy had tried to do for bad. Our Lord turned it round for good. They weren't hearing second hand.

The lads brought the car back; they were part of it so they had cemented their faith, seeing the state of the car, and the power of my Lord to save me. The lad at the farm gave me his car to drive home and to keep until Edward's car was put right.

Edward could not believe it. He said, from the state of the car, I must have been flying. The car was a write-off and he said, "The car, Mother, was out of control, and you couldn't handle it; that's what was the matter. That's why you were travelling the bank side."

I never pushed to answer any further; I did not want the bairn to worry that I might be in any danger, but here we were again, Father, at the beginning of learning spiritual warfare, and from then on I did not believe the enemy's tactics in war.

In future, as soon as I realised what was happening I would be straight in with Scripture. Jesus said, "I have given unto you all power and authority."

The enemy comes in as a dirty rotten liar. Master of disguise, a thief and a robber, but and a capital B, Jesus Christ my Lord is a Mighty, Mighty God. The enemy would torment my mind day and night, so I would end up speaking out loud in my heavenly language, my gift in tongues until I had drowned him out. He would give me peace for a little while then he would start again. This went on and on but Jesus was with us. "Resist the devil and he will flee from you."

The battle was for my mind but he was not robbing me. I belonged to my Lord. He was my husband, He told me so just after Jim died. People would come and say, "You'll marry again. You're too young."

But no, the Lord gave me Scripture, Isaiah 54, "For your husband is your Maker, Whose name is the Lord of Hosts; and your Redeemer is the Holy One of Israel, Who is called the God of all the earth," (verse 5) - the whole chapter really. And in my spirit, I knew this was true so I received back into myself my Lord as my husband now.

As you may have guessed, Edward, bless him, would not allow me to drive his car ever again after this calamity.

With the different ones coming in and all that was going on, the Methodists came back to me to see if they could bring their speakers, but I said I would have to ask Father. Well, I did; I asked my Lord and He said, "Bind."

"But what with, Lord?"

After a time, I was given a gift of fifteen hundred pounds, so again, whenever I needed, Father would supply. This was brilliant.

We had a young estate agent with us, so when I shared with the fellowship what had happened, this young man, being an estate agent, valued the building at fifteen thousand pounds. I rang Mr. Wright and said, "Father told me to buy the building." We were to stay non denominational.

Mr. Wright said, "We will do our best for you, Rosie. But it would have to go through the proper procedure."

Well we sent it to the estate agents and they valued it at fifteen thousand. Next it was put in the papers to sell but only for two weeks and it was stipulated it had to be Christian. The young man, after we all met and prayed said, "I would offer what we had, fifteen hundred."

So we did. All the negotiations, I was praying like mad, very hard, covering every aspect of it; and 'Praise be to our Lord' we got the building for fifteen hundred. O my Lord, how wonderful. He will supply all my needs from His bountiful riches.

Apart from the people who came in on a Sunday night the main callers were very close. Ron preached, I preached, we took turns. Roly and Liz were our music ministry and Tony joined them and sometimes Fran. Fran and I met regularly on a Tuesday evening for prayer. She was extremely faithful in prayer and we used to cover a fair amount of prayer requests for our families or things very near to us.

As people came on Sundays, all I wanted to do was to pray for them and pray that they would stay. The vision was for rooms, so if they were in difficulty they could stay and so on and so on, but I wanted them to meet with Jesus. If only they could meet with Jesus, I knew they would be all right. So we were praying either to build on to the chapel or to change it.

A couple came in who were in such need. Tony constructed a partition the size of a bedroom off the chapel and the vestry could be their sitting room and there was a kitchen as well and outside, a loo. So we had the availability for this couple to stay. The fellowship kept them and paid the electric bills, the heating and so on and the food. The chap got a job at Otterburn Hall as a kitchen porter and they paid off all their debts. I used to go in and work with the lady. We would talk and talk and pray - such a damaged soul. Just for her to share the problems was a major breakthrough. We had lots of happy times.

They stayed seven months, but problems arose, so I felt it was time for them to move on. I went to Betty and Jean and shared about this couple and Betty and Jean thought it would be a good idea if the couple went up to them and worked with them.

By now it was coming up to the five years for me to move out or buy the café, but I did not want to buy it. I felt my time there was over, we would move home and the bairns would move back in. I stayed on until nearer the time to finish everything off and to do all the organising. I really cannot remember much about leaving, but another chapter was closing.

# CHAPTER 7

# The call to Israel and my experiences there

*I*t was wonderful to be back home. My time was over in August, and Roly and Liz were going to Israel for a wedding and asked me to go with them.

I prayed about it and received the o.k. So we left Newcastle by bus and flew out from Heathrow. It was very exciting. We travelled from Tel Aviv by bus to Jerusalem. We went into a hospice right opposite the Damascus Gate.

Now from the time of the plane's touching down in the Holy Land the heaviness was like a vice over my head. For three days I was under this grip. When in doubt, do nowt. Well, I certainly was in doubt. I just had to wait for my Lord to show me what I was under. Well, three days went by, then my Lord showed me. Every spiritual force of evil was over our God's People, on God's People and in God's Holy Land, so praise Jesus, I was now to go in spiritual walking, which I did.

Roly and Liz went to their wedding. I stayed behind to pray. I asked the lady where one would go to find the temple for this was my starting point.

She thought for a while and then said, "Solomon's temple?" which is the Wailing (Western) Wall. This I received as right, so I proceeded to find it. I headed off to find the Wailing Wall.

I went through the Damascus gate, down to old Jerusalem's narrow streets. Every part was taken up with stalls on the roadside. Actually, it was cobblestones on the streets. The places you would go and into. I was praying all the time I was walking. Everything you could mention was being sold. I walked on and out into the huge red courtyard or square; it was massive. As you walked out, there was the Wailing Wall on the left; the only wall left of Solomon's temple. The stones in the wall were about two foot by two foot and there were trelliswork partitions down the middle.

The men go to one side, the women to the other, and I went down to the wall and stood for a while. You could see where people had pushed pieces of paper in between the huge stones. It was awesome. This was Solomon's temple. The stones were beautiful. All over Jerusalem it was white. You would think it had been scrubbed and washed. Scrubbed like a white wood kitchen table, bleached white.

There were some chairs so I sat down and then Father would give me the Scripture. I would pray back to my Lord, stand up, wail, weep unto the Lord with my hands on the wall, like other times and then I would stop, sit down, write my Scriptures down and Father would give me the next Scriptures with the same thing. I would speak it out, pray it back to Jesus, wail at the wall, finish, write up the Scripture and sit down. This went on for four hours.

When I was finished I backed off the wall, you don't turn round and walk away till you are a long way back. I got to the end of the trelliswork and then turned. There was a lady sitting. She spoke first, "Have you finished then?"

"Yes," I said.

"Well, our Lord has had me sit here and cover you in prayer for protection. You've not been aware of the women who have been all over you. You see, they know the Scriptures, 'Call for the mourning women to come, let them make haste and raise a wailing for us,' Jeremiah 9 verses 17 and 18. This was the subject of all our prayers for Israel and Jerusalem, for the people, for the hurt, the harm, and the evil. They know about it, but you are the alien and they did not like your doing what you were doing: what they should be doing and know what to do, but don't do."

I said I was really unaware of anyone being here, I was so in the Spirit with my Lord.

She then said, "Is there a man in your life?"

I said, "O no."

"O, sorry," she said, "You're a widow?"

I answered, "Yes."

Then she said, "Every prayer you have prayed will be answered. Your husband is with our Lord and your children will be saved."

She came back with me and met Roly and Liz. She herself was a Jewess.

From that day, I never prayed for Jim again. To know he's safe in Christ Jesus, that we will be together again was such a joy. The Bible tells us there is no marriage in heaven, but it was wonderful just to know he was there.

Roly had brought his guitar and in the evening we would have times of worship and testimony. What a time!

Through the day we were visiting lots of places you would read about in the Bible. I believed that for me, the next prayer line was to walk the walls round Jerusalem. You could go up on to the wall and walk round the old city, so Roly and Liz would come with me. At different points on the wall I would stop and Father would give me the Scriptures to read out aloud over the Land or whatever part I was looking at; then I would pray and cover again in spiritual warfare, as far as the eye could see.

We went to the garden tomb. The whole garden was just grief.

We went to King David's palace. We did not go in the palace, which was an extremely posh hotel, but we went into a building opposite which was a college and lecture halls and I could feel the beauty and the peace.

Then we visited a special church with acoustics that were extremely good. Roly said the singing in this church would be magnificent.

We had a prayer time in all of these places and then went back to base.

We had become extremely friendly with a young lad called Troy, and a Japanese man, and sometimes they would come with us as we shared our food, and spent many hours talking with our Lord.

We went right up the Mount of Olives one day. I struggled; it was very steep. It was wonderful up there, the view was right out of this world, right across the whole of Jerusalem. The prayers again were to cover the whole of Jerusalem. "Come Jesus."

We visited the 'Japanese.' This was a little café in name. O, real fellowship in there, a whale of a time of sharing - and there was a massive church there called Christchurch. We prayed in there.

We went back down into the city. We walked the steps to where they said Jesus was crucified, but the 'place of the skull' was on the other side of the road. I was quite upset. The whole place was packed, commercialised, selling everything to do with our Lord but not recognising our Lord.

We went with Troy and the Japanese man to a church on Sunday. We were in a tent, it was beautiful - all believers. Shabbat was something too; from Friday night through to Saturday night everything stopped - and I mean everything stopped. Cars were left, buses just stopped; the silence that came over the city, they would not strike a match. The meals were prepared on a Friday for the Saturday. No-one made anything on Shabbat. It was incredible to see.

After we had explored everything in Jerusalem Roly hired a car and we then set off to go to other places. Father directed our path every night. He would tell us where to head next day.

When we arrived, He would give us the Scriptures to read out and the prayer to pray. Our first was Bethlehem.

To our surprise, our Jewish lady was there also and we went round together to see all the places where Jesus had been or was. We met up with a lady all dressed in white. Now she was an old lady but she knew our Lord. We talked and shared. In the conversation she shared how she was going away for three or four days with her priest. She asked what we were doing.

We shared, "We are going through the Holy Land; our Lord wants us to be praying out over every situation."

Immediately she said, "Stay at my place, while I'm away."

I was thrilled, but the Jewish lady said, "O no."

She was going back to Jerusalem. A little conflict set in. She really had taken to us and wanted us to go with her. She anointed me with oil on my lips and said like Isaiah chapter 6 verse 5, all about 'Woe is me,' but read right through the chapter: 'The seraphim flew to me with burning coal on his hands which he had taken from the altar with tongs and touched my mouth and said, "Behold this has touched your lips and your iniquity is taken away. Your sin is forgiven." I heard the voice of the Lord say, "Whom shall I send and who will go for Us?" Then I said, "Here am I. Send me, Lord." '

The whole chapter spoke to me but I believed that was it. I must go on to where my Lord wanted me to go.

To our greatest joy, Roly and Liz said, "Well we'll go together," so the Jewish lady left, peeved a little, but Jesus had spoken.

So we went home with our lady all in white. Would you believe it? The little house was called 'The house of prayer.' It was so exciting, one big room with a beautiful domed ceiling, a single bed and a double bed behind muslin material, curtains to separate the beds from the room and separate the beds from each other. We went down steps to a shower, toilet and a kitchen area. She opened the fridge and the food was all ready cooked and prepared for four meals. What a mighty God we serve. She hugged us then departed.

We sat dumbfounded for a little while then we worshipped our beloved Lord. "All my needs from His bountiful riches in glory."

The days just flew past, seeking the Lord facing every day with prayer. All for what I believed our Father had shown us. He guided and led us whenever we went through the Scriptures, for four days.

At the end of the days our lady came back. Her mission had been successful and we believed ours had too, for we were praying for so much, what our Lord wanted. We gave to the old lady for the beautiful food and our beds and we left to journey on to our next destination.

I'm asking you here to bear with me because some of the places may not be in the right order as Father led us - but He did lead. Only my memory may not be quite accurate of which went where throughout the book. Really the Holy Spirit is bringing everything back to me and to my remembrance, so they are just in the right place. Everything did happen maybe not just as I thought but it is coming as He, the Holy Spirit, is revealing it to me.

We travelled to 'The Beatitudes,' which overlooks the Bay of Galilee. Up on the mountain or hill, whatever you like to call it, which was open. We went right up. We travelled up and up to it until we reached the top and were looking out through a beautiful church building. This was where Jesus gave the sermon on the mount. The Scripture says, "When He saw the multitudes, He went up on to the mountain. After He sat down, He began to teach." In another Bible it says, "Jesus gave the beatitudes." Matthew chapter five. We were up the mountain and I used the beatitudes for prayer.

We were looking right out. It was a magnificent sight. It was so right to use our Lord's Words, "Blessed are the poor in spirit, for theirs is the Kingdom of Heaven."

I was crying again. " Blessed are those who mourn, for they shall be comforted."

What a promise for His people everywhere, for people of every colour and every creed were coming here to see the church. "Meet with them, Lord, reveal Yourself in this beautiful place. Blessed are the gentle, for they shall inherit the earth - bring it to pass heavenly Father."

"Blessed are those who hunger and thirst after righteousness for they shall be satisfied." Every word is blessing that He wants to pour out on His people.

"Blessed are the merciful for they shall receive mercy." Again, what a promise! He has done it all: He is pouring out His love on His people - out upon us. "Open our eyes Lord."

"Blessed are the pure in heart for they shall see God." Purify our hearts, Lord, purify our hearts.

"Blessed are the peacemakers for they shall be called the sons of God." O precious Lord, let us have the peacemakers for they shall be called the sons of God. Bring in Your sons, Father, we need Your sons, men made in Your image, formed in the likeness of God. Men with compassion, men with love. Real love directs and loves with such a zeal to see the people like You, Lord.

"Blessed are those who have been persecuted for the sake of righteousness for theirs is the Kingdom of Heaven."

Persecuted for the sake of righteousness. Job said, "Though He slay me, yet will I trust in Him" (chapter 13 verse 15).

Habakkuk 3 verses 17-19: "Though the fig tree do not blossom, nor fruit be on the vine, the produce of the olive fail and the fields yield no food, the flock be cut off from the fold and there be no herd in the stall, yet will I rejoice in the LORD; I will take joy in the God of my salvation. God, the LORD, is my strength." Nothing, but nothing can compare with knowing You, Lord.

"Peter do you love Me?"

"Yes Lord, You know I love you."

He said to him, "Tend My lambs."

He said a second time, "Simon son of John, do you love Me?"

He said to Him, "Yes Lord, You know that I love You."

He said to him, "Shepherd My sheep."

Then He said a third time, "Simon son of John, do you love Me?"

Peter was grieved because He said to him the third time," Do you love Me?" He said, "Lord, You know all things - You know that I love You."

Jesus said to him, "Tend My sheep."

You can see now that I am quoting from John 21:15-17. Jesus led Peter through an experience that would remove the cloud of his denial. Peter had denied Him three times. Three times Jesus asked Peter if he loved Him. When Peter answered yes, Jesus told him to tend His sheep. It is one thing to say you love Jesus but the real test is willingness to serve Him. Peter repented, and here Jesus was asking him to commit his life.

Peter's life changed when he finally realised Who Jesus was. His occupation changed from fisherman to evangelist, his identity changed, he was forgiven and he finally understood the significance of Jesus' words about His death and resurrection.

"Persecuted for the sake of righteousness." What can compare with our Lord? He bends over backwards for us to grasp what He really is teaching us. He never gives up on us till we grasp what He really is doing in our lives, so we may see Him as He really is.

"Blessed are you when men cast insults at you and persecute you and say all kinds of evil against you falsely on account of Me. Rejoice and be glad for your reward in Heaven is great; so they persecuted the prophets who were before you."

After praying through verse by verse, as I looked to the left I was looking over Capernaum, so I went to the side and sat down again. Father gave me the Scriptures to read out loud then pray.

Capernaum was my next visit. We walked all round the building which had been dug out like excavation work so you were looking down into the village of Capernaum and again you walk up to what was left of the temple. Compared with the little houses in the city the temple was huge - no roof on, but the pillars and the size of the main hall. We sat in the temple and prayed.

Next to it was Nazareth. Father had given me a picture, where you opened two glass doors and you were looking over the whole of Nazareth. It was like the balcony was suspended in mid air with nothing underneath, again very high up. So we travelled up and up and right on the top where it levelled out, we pulled into what looked like a monastery.

Roly knocked on the door. A nun came to the door and said the monastery was closed now; they did not take visitors any more, so Roly thanked her and came back to the car. We were pulling out of the grounds and I said, "Let us go back; this is the place."

Roly turned the car. I knocked on the door and the sister came. I said, "My Lord had sent me to pray over Nazareth."

I described the balcony. The sister took me along a passageway, opened the glass doors and there was my balcony. They then greeted us, welcomed us in, took us right to the top of the monastery and gave us each a room, and bread and water. She said after the sisters had said evening prayers we could go into the chapel and have our prayer time.

This was perfect. The place was empty of any comfort at all. Like the supper of bread and water, bare necessities. It was the dedication to our Lord, the self-sacrifice of themselves, very plain fare, but nothing mattered as long as they were obedient to Christ Jesus. They came and got us when they finished prayer. We had to sign the visitor's book and then we were shown into the chapel. It was void of comfort but Father was faithful and gave me my Scriptures to read out and pray over. Roly played a bit and we sang; another good day, and tonight we had a bed again.

In the morning Liz and I went out on to the balcony, Roly played and sang while I read out loud over Nazareth. Then I prayed, mostly in tongues. This time I was not impressed with Nazareth; it was dirty, with rubbish all over the streets; it was a dark place, unclean and unkempt. I would not want to stay. After we finished we shook hands with the sisters and left.

Our next place was Mount Carmel, where Elijah had been. We travelled through the valley and up again to a monastery, where we stayed for one night again. It was a paying guest house so we had good food; both dinner and breakfast. Again we sought our Lord for the Scriptures and prayed them out.

After this we travelled to Tel Aviv. We called at a hospice there too; we sang outside in the garden. This was our last port of call before we were to head back to the airport and home.

It had been a trip of a lifetime, preaching at every port of call, praying at every port of call, seeing where our Lord had walked, seeing where He had lived. The magnificent beauty - and yet everything about His life and His death was commercialised. Everywhere we went was tarnished as man had turned it into a way of making money. It had been exciting to be going but it was always a thrill to be coming home, each time we touched down back in our land, England. It was such a joy.

# CHAPTER 8

# An enlightening public speaking engagement and preparations for Romania

*D*o you remember the Jewish lady (who gave me Isaiah 6 "And whom shall I send? Lord, send me")? Well, this was the situation: I went on one mission after another and at this point I should like to bring in my friend Sylvia to 'The Pathway of Faith'.

Sylvia came in one day to the café. She was very distressed. We sat together in the café and she shared the pain in her heart. We prayed about it but, as always with Jesus Christ, when you meet people it is more of the family of God (and this lass is wonderful). Our spirits just felt that the Spirit of the Living God within us is one and the same and Sylvia just loves Jesus my Lord. We just loved each other.

We kept in touch quite regularly; you see how wonderful our Lord is? God's love and healing come as our Lord takes us each one of us individually through the wilderness, through the pain, through the deliverance of dying to self, getting rid of self. Paul said, "It is no longer I who live but Christ who lives in me." We have to want the changes.

It was one of these times of prayer. Sylvia was a hairdresser; I could go to her shop and get my hair done. I had been asked to speak at Consett 'Women Aglow,' so I accepted. Sylvia had given me a piece of worsted gents tweed, which I took to Nancy to make me something. Nancy said there was not enough for a suit but it would make a nice edge-to-edge coat. It was black with a very faint stripe in it. Well my coat was ready. Josephine brought a square of scarlet lining from the mill, and I hemmed it, to make the shawl drape over the shoulders, which was all the fashion then.

So I was set. I went to Sylvia's first, then Sylvia said, "Let us go to Linda's." Linda is Sylvia's daughter and she was a beautician. I had never worn make up since Jimmy died, but I knew Father was in charge so we went. Linda did make up my face; it was beautiful, I looked like a lady from one of the women's magazines. Sylvia was coming with me and so she would drive and we set off.

We arrived to a very good turn out; the hall was packed. We went in; I was invited into the prayer room, before the meeting, and we were praying our hearts out for all who were present. We then came out and went up to the top table. Well, the ladies were along the top table - all the official people - and my seat was on the end.

Now Father, as you know by now, always gives me the Word, but it was always subject to change. As the Holy Spirit takes over I would be led off His way and what He wanted to do and say. Well this was one of those times. I love it really, for the Holy Spirit is so in charge. I believe we sang something first, then we all sat down and the ladies on the top table began first, and then another programme, reports, financial reports and so it went on. I myself was thinking how very efficient they all were but Father had something else in mind and I began to cry. All through the reports I was sobbing and sobbing; the more efficient they were, it seemed, the harder I cried. The ladies were very embarrassed and did not know what to do about this woman sobbing at the end of the table - and this was the speaker.

Well can you see the picture? This beautiful face, that Linda had done, was now streaked with black eye mascara. I must have looked terrible. Eventually one of the ladies got to the point of introducing me. Well I stood up and stepped forward and began by saying "Thank you for asking me to speak," and I went on how I had my notes of what I was going to say, but our Lord had other plans. I shared how, through my sister in Jesus, my Lord had given me the beautiful material and this was my new coat: how my daughter had brought the scarlet lining from the mill, how my sister had done my hair and on top of that Sylvia's daughter had done my face. How we can dress ourselves up in our finest regalia and look like a million dollars on the outside, but our Lord is looking at the heart.

I took off my beautiful scarlet scarf and my black coat, I called it my 'Joseph's coat' - it wasn't many colours but it was from my Father and it was beautiful. Underneath I had on a gent's very plain beige cardigan, clean on. I took that off and under that I had a dress I had made to go to Japan and because I had worn it and worn it, holes were now under the arms. The body bit was all right but quite worn under the arms. I put my cardigan and coat and scarf back on and said we can hide all the bad attitudes, we can hide all the falsehood; we can hide what we do at home from people but not from our Lord. He sees everything.

Now it was the ladies who were weeping. I then asked if anyone would like to pray. I cannot remember if anyone gave her heart to Jesus but a lot came forward for prayer. I was well through when this lady came forward and I asked her what she would like Jesus to do for her? She said, with tears running down her face, "I just want to hold Jesus." I was so blessed; we stood and loved each other, holding each other, and we were both crying again. This lady knew my

Lord - it is just so beautiful to meet up with those who love Him.

Sylvia and I left.

We had lots of times when we would come together and it was always God's appointment. She would come to the chapel, or I would go and visit her. Again I went with her, this time because she felt she was to go to Africa and work with two lads she had tithed to for a long time; so I went over to go with her for support, as she went for yellow fever jabs and all the other things one has to have to go to Africa. Well, I was sitting in one of the waiting rooms and Father was so close to me, and I said "What is it Father?"

Nothing, so I just prayed and waited. After we were finished we went back to Sylvia's and she was making us a sandwich and coffee and I felt Father telling me to encourage her by telling her how close Jesus had been with me in Israel and some of the things He did. Then I asked Sylvia if I could have something belonging to her so as I was in prayer for her she gave me a pair of gloves, which she herself loved. I was holding the gloves and she was in the kitchen and Father said I was going with her and as she came through we looked at each other and both spoke: Sylvia said "You're coming with me?"

I said "I am coming with you."

We laughed at that and I think Father was bringing us even closer. It was getting late, so we hugged and said our goodbyes and I set off with all the things racing through my head. I would have to arrange for my jabs now, which I did. I just went to my doctor and he did everything. I had to wait in between some, then they were all done. Now Sylvia and I met up and went to book our flights. We each paid a fifty-pound deposit - it was so exciting. This was booked for the second of March.

Well, when Father wanted me to go anywhere He paid, but nothing came in. We were quite upset. We lost our fifty pounds, but we had jumped the gun, we were running ahead of our Lord. It was a hard lesson but we repented of what we had done.

Sylvia was now going out with Richard, so I was to go through to meet him. Well, poor lad: he said, quite openly, after we first met, he was scared of me. He was so wonderful with Sylvia, showing her how to do things, just like my Jimmy used to do. As Sylvia went to him absolutely up to high doh, Richard would just calm the whole situation down and show her what to do and how to do it. O Father, love was so beautiful to watch as well as experience.

We drifted apart for a while, as Sylvia was more and more going with Richard. My path was more and more with my Jesus. Now Eddy came into the church and was telling me about Russia. There was an appeal for people to go to Russia, St Petersburg. We applied to a Mr Ian Campbell in Edinburgh. Eddy wanted to go with me. We applied and had to send passport photos for them to get us visas. I was off again.

# CHAPTER 9

# My experiences in Russia and Romania.

*I* travelled with Eddy. We arrived at Edinburgh. There were people from Stornoway, Glasgow; we were the only ones from down over the border. It was good meeting the team. There was a conference on in St Petersburg for Jews. There was music, dancing, singing and drama. We had to welcome the people in at the doors and after the meeting we had to get the ones who had made commitments and get names and addresses for home visits.

We flew out from Edinburgh and as we got off the plane we were put on a bus and taken straight to the stadium where the conference was being held. This building was massive, with great wide steps up to the building and an entrance, just like the mall to Buckingham Palace, stretching out from the steps.

This mall was full of people coming to hear about Jesus; it was like Japan. I was putting my arm out and they were coming in as hard as they could come. I was sobbing in the Spirit at what my Lord was doing and these people were a good percentage Jewish. "Father" - how I wept with sheer joy. When Father moves, Father moves.

We had to stay on the top of these steps till nobody was coming, so we were there a long time. Then "Praise Jesus" we could go in and watch. It was magnificent - in Russian but I could enjoy the music and the dancing and prayer. Then when the appeal was made they were going forward in droves. O my, my, Father, this was wonderful! Then when it was over we had to rush back out on to the steps asking everybody if they gave their hearts to Jesus, and if they did we asked them if they wanted a home visit. Then it was names and addresses.

It was very late when we finished and our bus would take us back to our digs. Now digs was a huge building but very dilapidated; a broken down place with the rats running riot. We were up on the third floor, half the rooms you were not allowed in. The plumbing was something else. We did have a bathroom in what looked like a flat; bathroom, kitchen, two bedrooms and could be a living room. There was a shower if you got down on your knees in the bath and it was an art to get it to work. I think it depended who was using the water somewhere else in the building. Anyway it was adequate. The beds were army beds; someone said it had been army quarters at one time, but "Praise Jesus," it was a bed. There were three ladies to a room, maybe ten of us in one flat as the living room had beds in too. The only plug to work a kettle was behind my bed. The dining room was downstairs and we would eat together.

The food was not spectacular so the lads would go off to McDonald's to buy more for their suppers and take the couriers with them. There were maybe twenty of us on the team altogether, and about ten couriers: two of us and one of them. All the lads would buy the meals for the couriers as well, and the couriers said what they bought for one meal would last the couriers all week. As for me, Father asked me to fast again so I only went in for drinks.

The second day we started off with prayers in another big room on the second floor. It was wonderful; then we were free till it was time for us to go back to the stadium at night.

Now the rest of our team were going sight seeing in St Petersburg but Eddy and I just stayed behind in conversation. We were told of the thousands of people who died in the making of the underground tunnels for the trains.

Eddy had also bought a little book on the building of the underground and the human suffering that had occurred. Also, we learned about the mafia, the fear the people lived in and the poverty of the ordinary people. The women have to work as hard as the men, in some of the most awful conditions you could imagine, and for a pittance, while the mafia and hierarchy lived in such luxury. Having read this book, we were both in intercession. I was weeping again; crying out for the bloodshed, innocent blood, weeping uncontrollably for the human suffering in Russia, here in St Petersburg. We were in prayer the whole afternoon till it was time to meet and eat before we went back to the stadium.

We travelled over. I believe we walked the second and third night, because we had free time in the afternoon. We had plenty of time therefore to get there on time plus we actually travelled on the underground. Then we walked so we were seeing the city and the underground that we had been praying about.

The same as the first night: the mall, as I called it, was packed with people and again they just came into my arms, tears streaming down their faces and mine. The Holy Spirit was really bringing these people in.

The third day, Ian had asked if I would lead the prayers on that day, and preach. Father had given me a word and "Praise Jesus," it actually fitted in with what we were doing and where our Lord was taking us. When I finished, the Holy Spirit moved so in one girl's heart. So I worked with her all afternoon with Ian until again it was time to go back to the stadium.

I think one of the girls had put the kettle on and I was not aware and I leaned over my bed for something and the kettle spilt over and scalded my arm. Now Ian was very concerned and would put dressings on and bandages and such a fuss because of where we were and I had to go and have it dressed every day. So again I was coming against the devil trying to stop us succeeding. I was not fooled or distracted or duped into giving in or giving up. He had tried his ways once too often and I knew how he worked so I prayed all the harder. Everyone was saying my arm would be a mess, I would need skin graft, the lot - but I knew I would not; my Lord would see to that, which He did. By the time our stay was over my arm was perfect and all it had done was take the freckles off in the place that was scalded.

Now the fourth day and every day after that for ten days we were put into twos, with a courier to interpret for us, and then sent out. We had so many house visits to do in a day, which was quite hectic and we did not have the same ones every day but our couriers knew where we were going so it was on the underground, off, into trams and then walking. We travelled in come cases quite a long way out of town but for us it was terrible. Some were flats up flight after flight of stairs and the stairs stank with people using them for toilets and when we got to the flat it was whole families living in one room from grandparents to babies. It was awful because they lived in one room. The kitchen and bathroom, they had to share with other families living in the same flat, but another room. It really was poverty if ever I saw poverty. The man I was with at the beginning knew his Bible. Wow, he was good; he could share the Scriptures and Father would give me a turn and I could come in. They just received the love and whole families were coming through to Jesus.

The amazing thing was, after they prayed the prayer of salvation the first thing they asked was how did they get home to Israel? It was the same every time.

The wonderful thing was, we were to invite them to a place on a certain date and the authorities would be speaking to them about how they could go home. It was a very humbling experience going in. These people who had nothing made us something to eat and drink and, like the courier said, they themselves had nothing. They always wanted to give us something. One lady gave painted wooden spoons and another lady gave me chop sticks and painted something that was pretty - some they liked, something that meant so much to them but because they were so grateful they wanted us to have their treasures - something that meant so much. It brought for them a moment of joy, a moment of sweet peace. "O Father, bless Your people restore, precious Jesus, what the locusts have stolen and let them run to you. Let them receive Your salvation. Let them see their Messiah."

There was joy because as the whole family came through everyone would come, and again my arm went out and we hugged each other and wept together. As I said it was very hard, walking, travelling from home to home, leaving the last home, praying to my Lord not to forget a detail of the pain in the homes. I must not forget anything, because as soon as we get to the next home everything went, because you know a whole new set of circumstances, a whole new heartache of pain and suffering as one saw how they were living. "Please, Lord Jesus, please let them receive, for, with Him, our Beloved Lord, He will take them Home to freedom in Himself."

The conversations were all the same at the table, utterly, utterly inadequate, "Father have mercy."

We would come back in with the joy that ours were saved, and at night as I lay in my bed I would pray, "Come back Holy Spirit so I can yet again tell you all about these beautiful people, worn out, aged, wrinkled, faces of pain. Thank You, Lord, thank You that You are their Healer, that You are their Messiah."

At the end of our time we all went to the meeting where everyone would come to hear the last meeting. It was in a cinema. It had a stage with such colours of beauty. The stage was decorated with flags and banners; it was stunning. We sang, the lights went down and again it was all in Russian but it did not matter, you were there, it was electric. It was breathtaking as the speaker and singers and performers of the conference came out on to the stage and people who had received our Lord were still coming. The seats were filling up as they crept in, in the dark. I was so overcome with joy seeing them coming in - why in the dark? Was it shame or was it fear? Not really, realising that Father had really set them free. No one standing with a big whip to knock them down, no one going to break or crush their spirit, but people all around who wanted to get them home. What a wonderful end to our time in Russia.

When everything was over and the lights went on the place was full and, as we saw people we knew, we were waving like mad as we made our way out, for our job was over. We were hugging couriers and hugging people saying our goodbyes and still they would push things into our hands. One old lady gave me a little blue book, very, very old. But for her it would be a treasured possession she just wanted to give.

After we got back to digs we were all sharing about the different people we had met. Ian our leader came in and told us that because we had worked so hard, we were being treated to a night at the theatre. Well we were thrilled and so our last night we all went to see how the other half live. We were taken to the theatre - we only had to walk along the street and the theatre was wonderful. O it really was beautiful, plush and the painting and the décor velvet. The arch was dripping with rich velvet curtains, the carpets you sank into as we walked along; it was breathtaking. It was a block booking so we were all together. The show must have been a variety show as there was no theme and every part was different, no carrying on of a story or whatever from the scene before. We all enjoyed it; we talked about it all the way home.

Eddy had managed to slip away sightseeing and after we came home, when he came on Sunday he had photographs too, so he gave me a great pile. We travelled home from Edinburgh nearly in silence.

We both were thinking and going over in our minds everything that had happened. We had only been home a few weeks when we were asked if we would like to go to Romania.

Well, we went, though I travelled to Eddy's and he took us to Ross and Belle's house where a meeting was held every week to pray for Romania and to encourage if there was interest for people to join the team again. I knew Father was encouraging me to go and Eddy wanted to go so we put our names down.

There were no flights to pay for as we were travelling overland. So it was money for the kitty to pay for petrol. There was no accommodation to pay for as the people of the church we were going to work with were giving us accommodation but we had to take things.

One of the things was medicine for the mental patients; I wanted to take that. Well, when I shared I was going, Avril, Edward's partner, got Josephine and Beverley, and she baked herself too, and she and Edward sold all the home baking on the main street in Bellingham. I cannot remember what they made but it paid for a good supply of the medicine we wanted.

Next Ross, our leader, wanted sweets for the children of the orphanage. Avril's sister owned a shop that sold sweets; so she landed with cardboard boxes full of little bags of sweets, weighed up and everything, just ready to hand out to the children.

Next it was biscuits; Avril again landed with two or three packets of biscuits per person.

Mrs Davenport gave me money. I went to Andy's at Scots Gap to buy the big drums of paint and Andy gave me so many tins, four or five.

Lastly we wanted little combs or small items to put with the biscuits to give as presents to the old men and women in the old folks homes. We were buying shaving cream, after-shave, hair oil, anything in that line for the men, and soap, talcum powder, nice smells for the women. Well, I took all my provisions and then a call came for a doctor who used some ancient tools for his equipment, so we decided to have another whip round and buy him some. We got a stethoscope and something else, they were very ordinary things but as Ross said, when you have nothing to work with it would be heaven on earth. At last, everything was ready, all present and correct.

Peter came to see us off, we travelled together, again Eddy was such a quiet lad but it was wonderful to see him coming out of his shell laughing and talking to the men. There were eight of us on this team so away we went. We were travelling in an ambulance. The men took turns for driving, and the talking in the back. Ross and another lady who had been the year before pointed out the route and navigated through the cities and over borders and so on. There were checkpoints on two borders with soldiers with guns and we needed our passports.

On the previous year's trip they not only stopped them to check them out, but they had to get out and take stuff out as well for the soldiers had to look through. Father had me praying in tongues at both borders and yes they checked our passports but to Ross's surprise waved us on. The whoops and shouts of glee because they could be stuck at the check-point for hours, yet Father got us straight through.

As we travelled through Romania to where we were going it was mountainsides and valleys. The scenery was wonderful and now and again we would slow right down and drive past a donkey and cart. A tiny little cart would not carry much, but I suppose it was better than walking for the fellow sitting on the side of the cart.

Our destination was Albania. We arrived at the church and the pastor greeted us then it was getting us all into our digs. Three of us were to go to one house, so I was to go with Ross and Olga. Well our digs were great, it was a huge room with twin beds and a bed on the floor and just outside our door was a shower room and toilet. The people again to our joy, or my joy, were from America. His firm sold trackers to Romania but the work they had done was wonderful to hear. They were as pleased as we were to hear the tongue you could understand. I forget how long they had been in the land but o we did talk. We sat till very late, just talking and talking, very obvious they were overjoyed with having us for fellowship.

After a long time we said our good nights and we went to bed. Everyone picked their bed, I asked if I may have the one on the floor, no problem. It was a double size mattress and two mattresses one on top of the other. It was well-padded, with a new mattresses, so quite thick, really very comfortable and like home. I could have my books, daily readings and my Bible notebook on my bed.

Ross was our leader but I felt I had to take the lead in prayers and the things for my Lord, while Ross planned where we would be visiting first. On previous trips they had painted and decorated a room out at a hospital or children's home or the mental home. This year it was to be the hospital up in the mountains, so we were up early next morning and we all were to come together at a friend's house before we would set off on our mission. Well, the people again were a beautiful people but yet again in such poverty.

We gathered round a table with a canopy over and started our day with prayer and thanks-giving. If there were needs or hurts among us as a team Father was dealing with us first, there was repentance and brokenness within our group so we prayed for healing and forgiveness and it spilled over to the family in whose garden we were in. "O praise Jesus," what a joy to see Father setting the captives free.

Our first morning took a good part of the morning to see people released when we were ready to move. We drove up some of the most beautiful scenery till we came to our doctor. Well the doctor was just so lovely, he was young and I bowled him over, we gave him the presents we had brought for him, he was so grateful and unloaded the paint. One of the lads, or two, I am not quite sure, said they would like to take on the painting, meaning they would not go round visiting; we could do that and because they could settle to do the painting without interruptions they would work all day. Brenda, I think it was, said she would work with them cleaning the walls and the ceiling and get the preparing done, scraping walls and washing them down.

I have to say I thought the monastery up in the mountains of Nazareth was sparse but this was ridiculous. There was absolutely nothing, the kitchen sink was out of the ark and to get the water to wash your hands you used a pump. There was a table and three or four chairs of sorts. The machine to sterilise the equipment was ancient. In the doctor's room where he saw the patients was one solitary cabinet with objects which were really for me unrecognisable. How on earth did the man look after his patients? The room to paint was totally empty. I was hoping this meant they had cleared it because we were coming. Two ladies curtsied to us as if we were someone special. O my, Father, if this was the beginning please prepare me for the next. The doctor had a horse and buggy, he would give me a ride. I think the reason was to take the ladies home. So I got up into the buggy with the ladies and the doctor was up front. The team followed behind in the ambulance.

As we turned a corner going through a little mountain village there was a funeral. The coffin was in the old-fashioned glass carriage with horse, beautiful black horse with red plumes, the headdress like you would see in the Wild West.

After we got to the ladies' home the doctor decided to travel with us in our ambulance back to his home. It was good banter back and forth as all of us were asking questions about the hospital and his practice. We were nearly back to Albania when I got my opportunity to ask him about himself - if he was saved? It was really good, he came forth with good points of the whys and wherefores and we shared lots of different things from all of us. I think if we had had to go a little further we might have made it and he would have received his salvation but as it is, Father, we sowed the seed.

I think that was all for that day except we were going out on the streets to sing with the young people of the church. Now this was glorious; we sang together, the young people in their language and we in ours but the miraculous thing was they chose all the songs but they were our songs too and it was wonderful. We drew quite a crowd, people stopped to listen. We stood quite a long time, maybe a couple of hours. When we stopped we moved in among the people shaking hands, giving them hugs even a kiss with some. What an end to a perfect day. We were quite excited really so we were praying and talking and sharing till one and the other fell asleep.

We were up next morning bright and early for our time together. Before we set off for our day we prayed and sang, praising our Lord for everything. The day before, the work at the hospital had gone very well so the boys would go themselves today. So Brenda would come with us. We covered everything, then set off; today it was the mental hospital.

We got there and were ushered into the offices of both the doctor and head of staff. We sat and listened while Ross talked to them; she being a nurse knew all the medical terms and the jargon. After a while they would show us round. The doctor and head of staff were extremely pleased with the medical things we had brought, as they themselves were unable to get these special drugs.

Now the place was sparse again, but for a good reason. This time nothing with corners or sharp edges or whatever the inmates could harm themselves or each other. We were not allowed to see the bad cases, and the wards we were taken round were clean and the people were clean, no nasty smells or urine smells. All in all I was praising Father; as we went along the ward they would come for a hug or a cuddle but you could see they were looked after.

We came away from there quite happy and next it was the orphanages. It was a beautiful day and all the bairns were allowed out on the grass. We spent the whole of the afternoon there. We sang some choruses and they joined in and that was how it went; we sang and entertained them, then the children sang and entertained us; the man in charge and the staff, for everyone was there, no one was left out. We then started to give them their bags of sweets - enough for everyone. What a joy to see the little faces light up with something so small.

After this we were taken round the orphanage and again we all thought it was great: clean - there was a huge shower room with individual cubicles and it had just been washed down and the smell was so clean. The dormitories also were like children's bedrooms at home, things dropped and left but that was surface. Underneath again was clean - they didn't know we were coming.

After seeing some of the children's homes on the TV I have to say I really was not looking forward to going but my heart was singing when we came away. There were some beautiful children; when you see such situations your whole being says, "Thank our Lord for our children and grandchildren at home."

We came back, had our evening meal with our hosts telling them all about everything. Then the word came that the Pastor was so impressed with what had happened on the street the night before he asked if we would go again. The young people were going into the next village and were singing in the church tonight and would we like to go just to support them, which we did.

The young ones were a choir tonight and there were one or two solos. It was like Russia; we did not understand it but the young ones were loving being able to sing. When it was over we followed them back to the church and had teas and coffees. It was good fellowship again; one or two who spoke English kept the conversation going between us all. We travelled home, as we prayed and covered everything of the day making sure all was well. Then lights went out and sleep.

Our next day was the old people; this was not so good. Some were still in bed, others looked a little afraid with all of us trooping in. Our young doctor joined us, some of us were handing things to the old people while some of us were sitting on the beds talking to them. I don't think they had received presents before - they seemed not to know what to do with them. One old man was having a go at eating the soap not the biscuits. We went forward and opened the biscuits and took the soap off him as we wanted to talk with him. Our young doctor did the interpreting and we began to make progress.

We went round all day and by the time we got round wards, and then to the ones that were up and going about again, we felt it was a day well spent.

We travelled back to digs and again word had been left where we could go singing to a different part of the town; so we all went. Being a different part there were very few people so we decided to have fun ourselves, just praising our Lord and singing to Him.

This turned out to be great and the young ones wanted to talk and it turned out to be good teaching and sharing as we were getting to know one another; roads ahead were being opened up.

The next day was not quite so exciting as we went back to places that the team had been in previous years and Ross was catching up with all the news, while we just sat. Never mind, it was still nice to see other parts of town.

We went back to our garden with Ross's friend, there to find the Pastor who had come looking for us. The bairns had enjoyed the night before so much the Pastor had decided we should go for a church picnic. The next day they would provide the food, we could play games or talk, just a fun day so, we accepted there was no singing that night. We travelled back to digs and we decided we would have an early night but pray for openings and more breakthroughs on the picnic the next day. We eventually dropped off to sleep.

The next morning we were up and ready and raring to go. The first stop was our garden, where we shared our hearts and how we had prayed the night before so our team were all going on the picnic.

The lads had finished the hospital room. I guess for me I was disappointed that they had been coming for some time to the same church, the same pastor but very little witness. There had been more openness than ever the night before, the night we sang to our Lord and shared to get to know one another so "Father we need real breakthrough."

Today, it again was lunchtime before we finished but I felt we had brought every thought captive before Jesus so He was going to be in charge. We travelled to the church, met up with the Pastor and set off in convoy. The chatter was good - everyone was in good spirits. It was good to have the lads with us now they had finished the painting. We travelled miles up and up into the mountains, the weather was perfect, the sun was shining - a real picnic day. Well we seem to come over the top and come down a valley and of course it was a perfect picnic area. We pulled off the road and there was a good flat area and a stream; it was not deep enough to harm the little ones and the space was a real good stretch for games. The only thing was three great big bullocks with huge horns came wandering into the picnic. Fortunately they were very docile creatures and were very interested as to what we were doing. They ambled round us with one or two chasing them away; anyway they must have been satisfied and ambled away themselves. The bairns played, the lads joined in. I think there was football at one point.

While this was going on we spread out the food. When the game was over everyone came to eat, I am not sure if there was a campfire, and we began to sing. It was so relaxed, everyone doing his or her own thing. Some were sitting in groups, and conversation, good testimony, sharing, really talking about salvation. It is so easy - Father really was in charge. Even the Pastor started to ask questions; real discussion was now coming with one another. The young people were joining in: "Keep it going Lord, keep it going."

Because I was really not in with those who were translating and those who keep going asking more and more, I was praying, covering all sides, aware when English was spoken. It was heading on the right track, a little more depth, Father - people were opening up like flowers; barriers were coming down. The Pastor was really catching the fire. It was getting dark by the time people started to pack up and even then they did not want to go. We all packed back into our vehicles and headed home.

That night Ross and Olga were full of it, so again, Father, although we just did not get right to the point of commitment, they were happy with how everything had gone. For me, just like the doctor, we would have made it but maybe we just had to sow the seed and Father would send in someone else to water it.

The next day was Sunday and we were all ready again in prayer for the service. The church was packed and our team had to sit right at the front, as we were to sing in the choir. We were starting our return journey on Monday, so this was our last night. All went well. As always the goodbyes are very hard - you just get to know them then we are to leave them. We left the church but were to come back Monday morning to say our final goodbyes. We thanked our hosts and hugged them and set off for the church and people turned up from all ends and sides to say goodbye.

Around mid-morning we finally got on our way home. The ambulance was empty now and all the way home Brenda crocheted shawls to sell for more money to give to charities. We ourselves had got to know one another very well and so again real testimonies and sharing were being done all the way home.

# CHAPTER 10

# A mission in Otterburn, a trip to London and a Jewish period

*I* love going away and Father really was blessing me and sending me out on the mission field. It was lovely to be back to catch up on all the news. The chapel was fine and things had been champion while I was away. Ron and Roddy and Roly had carried on.

Now Keith phoned to say he could bring a Mr Bob Walker down to see me, to which I said yes.

He arrived and began to tell me he had come to work with some Americans who had come over to Scotland a while ago, and now he had come there really seemed very little to do. We discussed it and I said, "Why don't you come and we can do a mission in the village?"

He was thrilled at this and it was arranged. He would come for a fortnight. Periodically, Father had me come right down the valley, knocking on every door and I felt it must be time again. So the lad came and stayed with us and really it was wonderful.

You never know everything and even now I am all these years down the road, and yet I know nothing, but somehow it was like my training was well through and my next training was to give others the opportunity to learn. This was what I felt with Bob.

We set off every day to knock on doors and while Bob was doing the talking I was doing all the praying. He was a very confident lad, knew his Bible and knew the lessons. Out of the whole village five or six gave their hearts to Jesus our Lord.

We would come back in at teatime and then go along to the chapel at night. I was very pleased and I think he was pleased too. After the fortnight he was going back up to his friends in Scotland. We arranged he would come back and spend Christmas with us.

More and more people were coming in. Pat and Jimmy and their little ones would come every week. Pat was a tremendous loving and giving lass and Jimmy played the drums and was a very good singer and the little lad was four or five but such a good bairn.

Tony, who played sometimes with Roly, had two bairns to Christine his wife. They travelled in every week.

Marion and Tommy used to come periodically and bring her mam.

John was a wagon driver who pulled up on the lay-by and came in.

May and Harry have a fellowship in a church in Biggin Hill just outside London and after we had such fellowship, they invited me down to stay with them. Now, Harry is, or was, a builder and had built this church. It had everything: the place they could fill for baptisms, so many rooms off the main hall, and a lot of people attended, so away I went down to stay with Harry and May.

I travelled down by the bus and May and Harry met me off the bus and showed me round. We also visited their daughter and the grandbairns. Through the week there was lots going on. I went with them to women's meetings, and all three of us went to all the prayer meetings. Then we visited South Church that May and Harry belonged to.

While I was there, there was a baptism service. It was wonderful to be welcomed in to such a big church. I was praying over and people also prayed over me. At one point, as the big church made the decision to support me monthly, I was absolutely thrilled. By Thursday, it was six o'clock; there was a prayer meeting in the morning and after it we were to go to the bus station to confirm my bus home. I remembered and reminded Harry about this and Harry said, "Yes," but didn't.

We drove home. Now I shall tell you, Harry owned a big building business. There were offices and office workers and the top brass of the company all had company cars. When we got home, he took me round to the end of the house and covered my eyes. He led me a little way on. I opened my eyes to see the most beautiful car, a red Rover. He opened the door and amidst tears of joy he said, "This is for you."

I could not speak for joy. She was so beautiful. "O Lord, thank You, thank You. Bless Harry and May."

We went back to Harry's daughter's and I wanted a flag, so Harry's daughter drew a flag, like you see on the president's cars and drew the Holy Spirit; then embroidered over what she had drawn and it was wonderful. The only thing we could fix it to was the wireless aerial. When it was time to come home, Harry drove in front and May sat beside me and I drove my new car, but Harry brought me all the way home, such love, Lord, and care, right to the door.

The bairns were gob smacked. This was my car. O I was so thrilled; my own car and a red one too. I loved red. She was wonderful to drive and the comfort and luxury of the inside. I was so blessed. I had the car for a long time.

I always take my cars to the garage for service, M.O.T. and tax and one day I took the car for a service. At the same time, we had another young lady staying. We had been praying through things and I went for my car and drove home, and because the young lass were doing really well, she wanted to go home. So after prayer and thanksgiving, we packed everything into the car and away we went.

It was incredible, really; we got as far as Belsay, just on the outskirts, when the engine burst into flames. I was horrified. We both got out and I got everything out of the boot, all her things. We were standing waiting, at the side of the road, either for the explosion or something else to happen. I wanted to stop the traffic in case someone else was involved, praying to Father as to what to do.

An A.A. man came along heading for home, finished work for the day. He stopped, got out, took an extinguisher from the back of his van and put the fire out. When the smoke died down and he got a look at the engine, he said it was the electrics had caused the fire. He phoned for the truck to come and take it away. He also phoned for Roly to come and take the young lady home. I came home in the breakdown truck.

Would you believe it? The car was a write off. Richard did everything for me to get the insurance money. By the time I got the insurance money, which did not seem long, Harry and May were back up on holiday. They organised a man to get me another Rover. I had it, it was insured, taxed and M.O.T. and I was back on the road in double quick time.

Again, what the enemy did for bad, Father turned around and everything was back on course, even to having the Rover car. What a mighty God we serve. All this happened and Father has supplied me with a car ever since and Harry and May still come for holidays and we still keep in touch.

The church supported me for about a year, which was again so generous and just at the time I needed support. Now, because of so much happening in the chapel, things were changing. You see more and more people were coming again, not for the service, but for ministry and I think our core was being moved on.

Ron and Jill left.
Roddy and Katie left.
Roly and Lizzie left.

Right at the beginning, on receiving the chapel, Father showed me to focus on the first church at Antioch where the people met in their homes and I never had to count heads, because like the vision, people would come for as long as they needed to and in God's time, and then they themselves would be moved on to fulfil the calling on their own lives. So, it would always be a passing through process. People would learn their gifting and move to where Father wanted them to be.

Like Jenny: I was told about Jenny, who at the time was living in a caravan in Bellingham. She stayed with us for somewhere about a year and a half before she said, one day, she would like to go home.

I said, "That is wonderful. This is what our Lord would want."

She went home and came back to tell me everything was fine. She would like to give to the work.

I said, "Yes, that would be wonderful. Give it in to our Lord's work."

She said, "Yes, But this is where I have received. This is where I want to give."

There was another young lad, extremely clever, picked our phone number out of the phone book. He came for a year or two and then went back to Germany. He sent money from Germany. The tithes all were coming in.

Because it was changing, we still gathered on a Sunday, but more for prayer. It was the house of prayer to all nations. Things requested and things for prayer from near and far. Tony had taken Roly's place, as music and the gifting had changed. It just was so wonderful; as we were praying, Tony would take off with the worship. Again, some would pray, some would bring psalms, some would worship, the pattern of the first church. Jesus said, "My Father's house is a house of prayer."

Now a lady came and asked for deliverance, so we made arrangements and the day came. She came into the chapel, very nervous. We had gas heaters to warm the chapel and a little corner with armchairs for comfort, so our corner was all ready. I'm not sure if we had coffee, but we sat and talked, very relaxed; and I just kept asking pointers. So she talked about herself. Well, it was wonderful. She just poured her heart, till I had all the information to do with the deliverance. Father then said, "Command it out."

So with no hint of making the lady aware, I just calmly commanded the spirit out. It was so taken aback by surprise, it went. She sat up and knew. She said, beaming, "It's gone."

I said, "Yes."

"But," she said, "I was terrified. When I have gone for deliverance before, it was so frightening and such a frightening experience."

She asked again, "Is that it?"

I said, "Yes, you are clean and clear."

Then I prayed for the Holy Spirit to come and fill the temple again, because it had been swept clean so that no spirit but the Holy Spirit would enter and fill the void. "We praise You, Father, for the way You are."

She was thrilled. She then asked if I could say a prayer for Israel, so I said I would ask and see. She left a happy, happy lady. We would be in touch so I made enquiries of what to do, how to do it and who I would need to be in touch with.

I phoned Ray, who said I needed to get in touch with Laurence. Laurence is a Messianic Jew and he was delighted. We made arrangements. I phoned all around to everyone I knew.

Tony would come and play and we were all set. Laurence came, and the lady, and Tony and myself and no one else.

We introduced ourselves and then Tony set off to lead us in praise and worship, but stopped and I knew too. We had to hand over to Laurence and let him tell us what Father wanted us to know.

Well, he started by blowing the Shofar (the Biblical ram's horn). I was on my face on the floor sobbing yet again. When he had finished blowing the Shofar he then began to talk. I was still on my face before my Lord. The whole time he spoke I was crying. He laughed about it, but I found it very profound. It was nothing like I had heard before. O Father, it was like strings flowing to my ears. So this was now the beginning of learning about God's people. I was hungry to hear it. I was like so overawed. It was like a window to heaven that had been opened with fresh understanding, with much deeper revelation of the Scriptures, which speak of Jerusalem, and all the time he too preached for two hours. We were so thrilled, I had never heard preaching like it. I was still on the floor, the whole time he preached. I knew that this was something so different and I was crying the whole time as the Word was coming forth.

The next thing, because I had met Laurence, he phoned to tell me of Messianic meetings in John's house the last Saturday of the month. So I went and attended quite a few and met Peter who was a Jewish man. So they began to come on a regular basis to the chapel on Sunday evenings. With learning so much about the Jews and the teaching, we then kept Shabbat (Sabbath). I would light the candles on the altar on the Friday night and sat with prayer. This was Shabbat.

Now Eddy went to the Messianic meetings too and when it was the festival we would have a big meeting in the chapel. For instance, Easter for us is Passover for them and Laurence came.

We invited fifty people, set the tables up in the chapel with all the things, so we all partook of the Passover as Laurence preached about it. And again, when you hear how

it all fits together, the whole Passover, it really is incredible -
how wonderful to hear in detail every significant thing bit by
bit as it was explained to us. I then had prepared a meal for
all of us and we ate and shared all we had learned.

The Jewish wedding is another special significant set of
events which so make sense when you hear, in real life, how
things are done in the Holy Land. Every part of a wedding is
very important when it is explained.

Eddy then asked if we could invite Jacob Prasch to speak
to us so we invited him to come. About fifty people again, on
a Saturday. We provided the food. Avril and Edward did the
catering for me.

Next it was a man from Nottingham who was Jewish and
it was on a Saturday.

With all these meetings going on, this was when I met
Peggy. Now Peggy just loved Jesus, just like Sylvia. I cannot
explain it but we loved each other as if we had known each
other all our lives and it was just so dovetailed. To pray with
Peggy was heaven. We used to come together when Jesus
wanted us together, like Sylvia and Marian.

Well we continued to keep all the Jewish festivals.
Laurence came each time to teach us our Jewish roots. For
the Feast of Tabernacles, I made the booth in the church.

He came and taught us. Then, the Feast of Trumpets, then
the Feast of Hanukkah. Each one was teaching us, and our
brothers and sisters in Christ Jesus, to get to know all these
wonderful things. I really say to you to ask your (believing)
Jewish brothers to come to your church and teach you. If I
tried to explain, it would never come forth right as it should.
Believe me, we need to know, because our Heavenly Father
ordained it that way, so that we have our Jewish brothers
to teach us about it. In the Bible it says, Zechariah 8 verse
23: Thus says the Lord of Hosts, "In those days ten men
from all languages and nations will grasp the garment of a
Jew saying, 'Let us go with you for we have heard that God

is with you.' " The church of Christ Jesus will be Jew and Gentile, side by side working together.

After our Hanukkah meeting, a week or more later, I lit a candle on the altar and the glass holder just smashed. I knew Father was showing me that the full year of learning about the Jews, the apple of God's eye, was over. We did not have to copy them. They are Jews, we are Gentiles, but we are one in our Lord. So this was now the end of learning about God's people. The Bible commands us to keep Shabbat, but after a full year of seeing the truth from the real Hebraic perspective, there was no longer need for us as Gentiles to keep it in a legalistic way - because we are free in the Lord - in church - we could keep it at home; it is a matter of loving and honouring our Lord.

# CHAPTER 11

# My trip to Africa

*N*ow that Christmas was here, Edward gave me the most beautiful picture of a tiger - a mirror surrounding the mother and her cubs. Well I was thrilled but I realised that Father was showing me I was still going to Africa.

If you remember earlier, Sylvia and I booked our tickets to go to Africa and we lost the money. Two years later, to the day, I flew out to Africa on the second of March.

Now all my other missions were ten days to a fortnight, except Japan which was a month. This could be three or even six months. Receiving the picture I was praying every day for Africa. A lady came to see me as she heard I was going, and she actually said, "I wonder if it is to do with the blood-shed of the Mau Mau at the hands of Britain?"

Not being very well up with my history I really was not sure I understood, unless it was the repentance in Britain for what she had done. Remember the weeping of the suffering and the death in Russia was innocent blood, but Father would show me. Well, in my prayer line, I lined up with Bridget who was out in Kenya teaching English and as we had kept in touch with one another I shared that I was coming.

I also wrote to Joseph to make arrangements to meet up with him. Joseph was a pastor out in Kenya to whom Sylvia had been sending tithes and was one of the two men she had tithed to for a long time.

Bridget was absolutely great. She would meet me in Nairobi and we would work it out all together. Well, you see, my flying money came in then - I was not even asking. I was praying for Africa because of Edward's picture. When I had moved, God moved. We trust Him implicitly so I booked my flight. His timing is perfect - all we do is obey.

Now this time it was different; I thought it would be six months. Leaving the bairns for such a long time - I guess I never thought about it when it was only a fortnight or ten days at a stretch. Josephine was absolutely great. She was such a little worker and could keep the lads going. She was, and is, like my sister Joan, so organised. She did all the work in the house and the washing and the ironing and made all the meals. I loved to get her letters.

My heart was breaking coming to say goodbye. Edward wept. It was like I was going away forever. I was in torment. I had left the bairns too much. Was it fair to be doing my own thing? I wanted to serve my Lord. I chose to give my all. I chose to give them up. Like every mother, I loved my bairns dearly and no matter what anyone else said to me they were the best. After Jimmy died I tried to be mam and dad and I gave in a lot; but in the café I knew Father was teaching all of us, and everyone had to work.

After we came back home from the café, we were more like friends than mother and children. They were adults now and so we talked like adults. Our generation was not allowed to go to pubs but our children's generation was all changed. I tried to restrict them to protect them in my way, but of course I caused such heartache.

Edward was a fine lad. He was powerful and was a great big lad. I was very afraid he might hit someone, being full of drink, and would kill them. One of the hotel managers came to the shop one day and said how grateful he was for

Edward. The army lads had started a fight in the pub and Edward had stepped in and sorted them all out - but I knew nothing about it.

Another time, a brawl had started outside the dance - and the same thing. Edward had stopped it and I don't know how many more.

David was so easily led. Now my fear for David was, yes, too much drink, but getting into bad company; and yes he was brought home in the wheelbarrow one night legless. Again I knew nothing about it.

My fear for Jo was, again, that she would not come to harm by the world and its ways.

I had finished at the chip shop one night and received a phone call to say they were all stuck at Wark, so I had to go out and seek them.

I guess I would make lots of mistakes in the house. Like all families, we rowed and you could cut the air with a knife at bad feeling and I did not correct as I should, but really they were marvellous.

Well, it was time for me to go, so I left. I travelled by bus to London to meet up with Mag and Kay who were back from Japan and living and working in London. All the way on the bus and I was praying for my bairns, when Lord gave me the Scripture, Matthew 10 verses 34 to 39, "Do not think that I came to bring peace on earth. I did not come to bring peace, but a sword. For I came to set a man against his father, a daughter against her mother and a daughter-in-law against her mother-in-law. And a man's enemies will be the members of his household. He who loves father of mother more than Me is not worthy of Me and he who loves son or daughter more than Me is not worthy of Me and he who does not take up his cross and follow after Me is not worthy of Me. He who has found his life shall lose it and he who has lost his life, for My sake, shall find it." I am quoting from the Life Application Study Bible.

Jesus did not come to bring the kind of peace that glosses over these differences just for the sake of superficial harmony. Conflict and discouragement will arise between those who choose to follow Christ and those who don't. Yet we can look forward to the day when all conflict will be resolved for the other verses on Jesus as peacemaker. Christians' commitment may separate friends and loved ones. In saying this, Jesus was not encouraging us to disobey our parents in conflict at home, rather He was showing that His presence demands a decision, because some will follow Christ and some will not. Conflict will inevitably arise as we take up our cross and follow Him. Our different values, morals and goals will set us apart from others. Don't neglect your family, but remember that your commitment to God is even more important than the family is. God should be your first priority. It was comparative, really, because my faith was so strong that if I obeyed Him, He could come and would do more for me, for my bairns, than I could, and teach them through the conflict of life.

Mag and Kay met me off the bus and we went back to their apartment. Because my flight was not till the next day, Mag and Kay would show me round London. This was my first time in the capital. It was beautiful. I saw the changing of the guards, I saw Clarence House, Buckingham Palace, The Mall - we walked it. Actually to be there, not just seeing it on television. As usual, we had so much to talk about and catch up on, so we laughed and talked until the night.

Next, they took me to the airport. Here we are again, once more hugging each other and saying our goodbyes. "Well Father, what will You have in store for me this time?"

It was a good flight with no problems. I was talking to my Lord all the way there. We touched down in Nairobi, and after getting my luggage I had to go to the immigration desk, where I was asked, "How long are you here for?"

"Six months?" I replied.

"I think not," he said, "You have to be back here in three months and we will check out again to see if you need to stay another three months."

I came out into the crowds of the faces of the people meeting loved ones and there was Bridget. I was so confident now; I lifted it to my Lord, but I knew He would have everything just right. We travelled across Nairobi to Bridget's boyfriend's family house where we were to stay until we travelled up to Liansa district to meet Joseph.

I wrote to him right away to say I was here. The house was a council house, not unlike our council houses back home. Father, big sister, seven brothers and a little lass about seven belonging to the sister. They welcomed me into their home and I had a room to myself. I don't know where everyone else slept. One of the brothers was saved so we had lots of conversations about our Lord. The sister too would join in and spoke very good English. We got to know the neighbours. We would go and talk to them.

On Sunday we went to church on the compound; it was really good, but then I believe there was something operating halfway through the service, but the minister took authority over the spirit and it ceased.

Every day I was listening for my Lord to see what our work would be here. A different culture, I already perceived their knowledge of the spiritual forces at work, whereas at home you would think the devil and satanic worship did not exist, but here is quite different.

"In the conversations in the home, be still and listen"; so I was being still and listening. We went for a walk one day and one of the brothers came with us. I was so aware of the agitation in this lad, such fear in his beautiful big eyes. He was very disturbed and after a while asked me what I thought I was doing coming here. "Why could we not leave them alone? Why push our culture and our ways into them? How dare we bring our religion to Africa?" Then he went on, " People have come here for centuries and pushed their ways, their lifestyles on the African people. Why can't they leave us alone?"

He said, "We like our ways better, where grandparents teach us the old ways of doing things, how whole families lived together right down, and they teach us what we should do and how to do things the old ways."

I was quite sorry for the young man. He really was zealous for his country and his lifestyle. I prayed all through everything the lad had said; he was so troubled. Now, like Japan, these people worship their god, but from what I was seeing and hearing, there were no idols to worship. It was all very secret, where the witch doctors very much held the people in fear of the unknown and the voodoo and the spells, or whatever - they were very superstitious.

We stayed about a fortnight then it was time to move on to Nakuru. Bridget and I went for our bus tickets that would take us right up country. I am not sure, but I think about four hours journey.

Now at Nakuru, this is where Bridget worked in a school for young pastors entering the ministry. O Father! We arrived at Nakuru and got another bus out of town to the outskirts. We got off the bus and then set off walking to the school. When we arrived, we came into the compound. Down the centre was a big building. Church was held in this building, and the school. Down the left hand side were the sleeping arrangements for the boys. There was a building at the bottom, which was kept locked. This was the principal's quarters and he was there at this point. I should add that the principal was either the leader, or one of the leaders connected to the church we attended in Nairobi.

Standing by itself was Bridget's little house. One main room with cooking and sink off to one side. A little room was off and this was her bedroom and just along the side of the kitchen was the toilet cum shower room. Very compact, very small but very adequate. She insisted I had the bed and she made a shake down on the floor for herself. So this would be home for a little while. Also, there was a similar little house, just up from Bridget's, which was the library.

We arrived on the Friday and on the Saturday there was a conference for the boys all day. The principal was there. We went to see him, just to get permission for me to stay with Bridget until I had made contact with Joseph. There was no problem; that would be all right.

Next was to write again to Joseph to let him know I was now as far as Nakuru and I would wait here until I received word from him. Next, the principal asked if I would lead the seminar, so it was into prayer. Bridget said I could use the library if I needed my space to pray or whatever. So I took her up on that and while she was making our meals, I went to the library.

It was dark very quickly in this land all the time. Not like home when we turn the clocks back for winter and move them on for summer; and so the huge gates are locked as it begins to get dark, to safeguard the school and everyone in it. So I was in the library listening really to the sounds of Africa: the crickets that never stopped, the birds screeching. There were different sounds all the time. I thanked Father that we were safe and had arrived safe and, as usual, went through bringing back to Him every event.

I had written to Joseph but we had to travel back to Nakuru to post it. You see, they are given a box, or maybe you pay; I never asked; but there was no delivery of mail in Africa. So all Bridget's mail would go in this box and you posted your mail over the counter. I think I would write home too to let them know I was safe, that I was still in limbo till I met up with Joseph, so no fixed address.

I prayed for the boys, to prepare their hearts for the next day and on and on. "Show me Father Your plans while I'm here. Guide me in detail every step of the way."

I felt I had covered everything and brought everything captive before my Lord, so I left and crossed the compound to our little house. The sky was breathtaking. It was so hot through the day but very cold at night.

The night came in and we had our dinner, supper, or whatever you would call it. We then settled down to pray together and Bridget opened up and shared lots of things in her heart and in her family. We prayed back things, repentance of wrong choices in things. We covered the ground then we retired to our beds.

Next morning it was Saturday, seminar day. "Well Father, what do I bring?"

Straight away I was given I Corinthians chapter 13, all about love, "If I speak with the voice of men and of angels but do not have love, I have become a noisy gong or a clanging cymbal. And if I have the gift of prophesy and know all mysteries and all knowledge, and if I have all faith so as to remove mountains but do not have love, I am nothing. And if I give all my possessions to feed the poor and if I deliver my body to be burned but do not have love, it profits me nothing. Love is patient, love is kind. It is not jealous. Love does not brag and is not arrogant, does not act unbecomingly. It does not seek its own, is not provoked, does not take into account a wrong suffering, does not rejoice in unrighteousness but rejoices with the truth. Love bears all things, believes all things, hopes all things, endures all things. Love never fails. But if there are gifts of prophesy they will be done away. If there are tongues they will cease. If there is knowledge it will be done away. For we know in part and we prophesy in part, but when the perfect comes, the partial will be done away. When I was a child I used to speak as a child, think as a child, reason as a child. When I became a man, I did away with childish things. For now we see in a mirror dimly, but then face to face. Now I know in part, but then I shall know fully, just as I also have been fully known. But now abide

Faith, Hope and Love, these three, but the greatest of these is Love."

Well, as my Father had shown me, I took this passage of Scripture and related it to the boys, verse by verse, with cross-references to explain the real Love of God: God's Love is unconditional Love. The Life Application Bible quotes, "God gives us spiritual gifts in order to build up, to serve, to strengthen fellow Christians."

Paul offers a glimpse into the future to give us hope that one day we shall be complete when we see God face to face. In morally corrupt Corinth, love had become a mixed up term with little meaning. Today, people are still confused about love. "Love is the greatest of all human qualities and is an attribute of God Himself" (1 John 4 verse 8). Love involves unselfish service. Service to others gives evidence that shows you care, and the content of God's message. Hope is the attitude and focus; Love is the action. When Faith and Hope are in line, you are free to love completely because you understand how God loves. As we walk through our daily walk with our Lord, coming through difficulties, dying to flesh, learning from our Lord at every turn, we live our life with Jesus Christ our Lord. We look to Him, we trust Him, we believe Him.

Paul said, "It is no longer I who live, but Christ Who lives in me". We lay our lives down. At the end of the day, we were praising our Lord, thanking Him for all He was teaching us, because when you are teaching or preaching, Father is speaking to you. It was a fabulous day.

Now Bridget was out teaching through the day so I was alone. And right enough, being alone, my precious Lord brought the bloodshed of the Mau Mau up front and I was repenting and weeping for the bloodshed. My intercession would last so many hours while Bridget was out; then every day six or seven of the lads would come with Bridget and we would sit and talk and talk to these young lads training to become ministers to our Lord. It would be late every night with questions, but praise our God, we could answer them all.

So it was intercession for the time Bridget was out, teaching, coming to pray with the lads when her time was up, not always the same boys, for they had come to do work and they had work to do as well. This went on for another fortnight.

We travelled into Nakuru at the weekend for mail and provisions and to church on Sunday. One Sunday we were invited to the pastor's house for a meal. We had a wonderful day. The fellowship was wonderful. It was this pastor who'd said where I was going and for what. So I shared, I was meeting up with Joseph to work with him in the Nyanza district.

When I had finished telling both him and his wife, they both said I must not go. The last party to go to the Nyanza district had been murdered. Only one man got away and returned. I said, "Father has not brought me here to be murdered. I will go and I will accomplish what He wants to accomplish."

The next week my letter came from Joseph, He would meet me off the bus. Bridget, bless her, would not let me go alone; she would come with me and stay overnight and travel back the next day.

We went for our tickets. The journey was another four hours. We boarded our bus saying goodbye to all our boys. They actually set us off to our bus then left. I was so thankful to Bridget who spoke the Swahili language fluently and for such a spelk of a lass she was so strong and identified more with the African people than her own people.

Joseph had told us where to get off; our stop came and off we got. We were dropped off at the side of the road in the middle of nowhere, there was nothing. We waited and waited and prayed.

Joseph arrived, walking with a young man beside him. Joseph could speak very little English. We greeted each other. The other young man could speak good English and I learned that he would be my interpreter when I preached on all our journeys. I also learned that Father had given me this young lad as my protector, my everything.

We set off walking to base as I called it, base because we would be out on mission all week and come back to base at the weekends. It was miles, no wonder he was late. By the time we reached base it was nearly dark.

We arrived and Joseph's brother's wife was there to greet me: his mother, his father, his wife and all his children. I don't know how many, but born one a year, which I was to find out was the norm.

A meal was ready, and I don't know what it was but we ate and the chatter was good as Bridget carried on the conversation with the whole family, and then would tell me the gist of what was being said. We turned in late.

The toilet was down away from the house, the kind of toilet we had before flush toilets were invented. So you just sat on a board. The house was his brother's house, nice size living room; there were toilet, washbasin and shower in the house, but they did not work, and a kitchen.

My bedroom was just off the living room. Where Kenneth slept I don't know, but as I said before, he was a very busy lad and my bodyguard.

Bridget and I were in the same room and we did have a prayer time before we settled down for the night.

Joseph, his wife and family lived a little way off. His mother and father lived up behind our house and his sister-in-law lived away in the next village.

The next morning, straight after breakfast, we set off to take Bridget back to catch her bus to Nakuru. We had to go to Kisumu for Bridget's bus.

After seeing Bridget off ok, we then got on the bus to Ogus. We travelled quite a way before arriving in Ogus.

We had prayers and then Joseph wanted to show me his dress-making college, as he called it. It cost eighty shillings a month to rent an empty building and I mean empty. There were two sewing machines, one lady who had been to school and taken a sewing course and two young girls. Here we were again. My heart was sinking at the dreadful poverty after seeing this so-called college.

We went on to visit widow Knight. We went through an alleyway into what looked like a square with rubbish everywhere. There were houses all around; houses built with blocks like we put on the inside of our houses. This lady was a widow with four children. I really was uneasy, things were not right.

Neighbours began to arrive and so the little house was full. Then I was asked to give a word. Joseph prayed in Swahili and Kenneth said he was ready. Well, I had nothing prepared, no warning that I would be preaching and no time to ask my Lord for the word, so my silent prayer went up for help. My word came immediately, 1 Timothy 3 verses 1-4, "It is a trustworthy statement if any man aspires to the office of overseer. It is a fine work he desires to do. An overseer then must be above reproach, the husband of one wife. Temperate, prudent, respectable, hospitable able to teach, not addicted to wine or fornication, but gentle, un-contentious, free from the love of money. He must be one who manages his own household well, keeping his children under control with all dignity."

With Kenneth speaking after me, I took the Scripture verse by verse. I was surprised at the Scripture but aware of the truth our Lord was bringing forth. My uneasiness of something not being right was now verified and I was very aware something was not right. The blank faces in front of me revealed that something was not right.

I carried on. My next Scripture that came was even worse. I Timothy 5 verses 1-17, Father was really teaching right standing with our Lord. Now these verses were all about widows. As I went down my Bible verse by verse it was real instruction for the widows. I finished, waiting to see if any more came. No, this was the end of my word.

Joseph prayed to end the meeting. After the meeting it was more relaxed and everyone had to introduce themselves to each other. We had an evening meal after which we left to walk miles to another house where Joseph and Kenneth and I would sleep.

We walked in silence and when we arrived there was a huge stone built house, out again in the middle of nowhere. Toilet again away from the house and the same as ours back at base. Kenneth and Joseph had put up the mosquito net over my bed. Because it was so dark now, I couldn't see anything so I was shown to my room and where the bed was and I just went straight to sleep.

In the morning, I woke early so prayed back everything: from setting Bridget on the bus right up to getting into bed and praising and thanking Him for my night's rest. I got up and had a look round. It had been a beautiful house with big rooms. I went to the bottom of what had been the garden to the loo. On returning I could see the beautiful house derelict, empty, not cared for or maintained. Coming back inside every room empty, no furniture, nothing. The room I had just had the bed.

I bumped into Joseph while I was exploring and again, Father, I prayed for my protection. I loved him with the love of Jesus Christ my Lord, but he is shifty. Even this early in the morning, being together, everything he says and does, I feel, is a sham; no depth to him, very little truth and the Scripture I was given yesterday seemed to apply to him and Mama Knight. Kenneth is, on the other hand, so innocent, so clean; his beautiful eyes just gleam. Thank You father for giving me Kenneth, for he does not leave my side and we can communicate. I have never felt so isolated.

Seeing all the black faces yesterday, some beautiful, some devious, some angry, some worn and tired and weary, some sick and you are unable to communicate, and you don't know what to do or how they are thinking or how they are responding. I knew my message was for Joseph and Mama Knight. God was speaking to them, but did they know or did anyone else pick it up? I must just keep handing Joseph back into Your Hands, precious Jesus.

Kenneth came and we were to walk back to Mama Knight's for breakfast. Wonderful really as I could cover all yesterday in prayer and put a start to the new day. As I went, it was daylight so we could see.

When I was a child I did have a terrible fear of the dark. When I switched off the light I would run and jump into the bed afraid someone or something would grab my legs. Well, when walking in the pitch black, the night before, I could not see where I was even walking. With every step, every shape of the night and the eerie sounds, the enemy was going to have a field day but, no way, I stopped him in his tracks, confessed my Lord Jesus over us as we walked and cut him off immediately. No monkey tricks from him, Lord. We are walking in the power and authority of Christ Jesus.

When I stepped off the plane, Father gave me the Scripture: "Claim every place on which the sole of your foot treads. I have given it to you, just as I spoke to Moses," Joshua 1 verse 3. I prayed, "Listen to that, satan; get off my back."

After praying through awhile, walking, I then started to praise Him, "Glory to God, we worship You Lord Jesus." Lift up the name of Jesus and He will draw all men to Him.

Joseph had gone to the post box for his mail and there were two letters for me. O how blessed to get a letter from home. One was from Tony and Christine and the other one from Dorothy. I just had to smell the paper and hold it. I was touching home. "O Father, how I was blessed - my bairns as You promised You would."

Before Bridget and I left Nakuru we had bought airmail letter papers. I had brought some from home but had used them so I topped up in Nakuru.

We got to Mama Knight's house and the men sat down to eat. I don't know what the heat of the day was - food was the last thing I wanted - but drink, I could have drunk the sea dry. I could drink the chai, which was tea, but an awful sickly substance. I took it not to offend but if I was asked, I just took boiled water.

After breakfast we went out and crossed the road. Not a road like our road - flat dirt track, quite a width - and one man was bringing his cattle. Now the cattle were like the cattle you see in the Bible times with huge great horns. We waited till he was past, then crossed.

There were cars, buses, wagons and trucks but very dilapidated. Every one was like a rust bucket but it went. I guess in this country it would be a Godsend to travel from place to place.

We headed for the dressmaking place, factory as Joseph called it. Well bless him, Lord. "I want to give the girls employment and make the clothes today." There was a board outside with "Rosalind Hindmarsh's Factory," written on it.

It wasn't there yesterday, Father. There was no sign of this board yesterday. I was not impressed. My mind was working overtime. You see I was thinking of Sylvia and the two other ladies who went out to work to send money to this man and I believed it was for the hospital. "O Father; don't let me go down that track. If I mistrust the man, this is only day two of being with him."

I had prayed that the five hundred pounds which it cost me to come might have been spent better by giving it to Joseph. Could it be given for the poor and the needy? Another thing that Bridget warned me about was that because we are white people, and from Britain, we are rolling in money according to the black people, so my warning bells were ringing again about the notice board.

Next after speaking with the two girls at the factory we would visit the hospital. "Father, please forgive me, I must not judge this man."

We walked and walked in a desert-like land after leaving the village. You walked for miles on a dusty, sandy, soily, barren land. We walked to climb uphill and passed a couple working in their shambas, which is their land to grow their crops for themselves to eat. I was to learn that the women did all the work planting and weeding and hoeing. The men did nothing. I was not impressed. Just like Japan, the women were downtrodden baby-bearing slaves and it was a child a year. O my Lord, the women have such misery. The women have nothing, but this couple were working together. Thank God, not all men are alike. They called out "Hodi Carabuyu" which means 'welcome'. The tribe I am with are called the Kikuyu tribe and Joseph's district is called the Sare-Awendo district. Both Joseph and Kenneth called back (I'll have to spell it because I can't even speak it) "Habariyako". How you ever manage I don't know, but everybody would shout "Hodi Carabuyu" for "Hello", and this (Habariyako) was then like the answer, meaning "Everybody is well." So we kept going, up and up.

We stopped and Joseph pointed to a rickety old haphazard fence round a square piece of land, a little patch really. I didn't like it. My awareness of something wrong just got stronger. These ladies had been working for years sending out money for the hospital, and this is it? He then said he had just put the down payment. I took photos and walked the boundary of the fence. When I came back to Joseph and Kenneth we then walked across country to the next village and to visit a chief. I thought, " This should be good, what next, Lord?"

We duly headed off across the country. Again, we walked and walked. I was praying all the time, for Father had said, "Every place you put your foot I have given to you."

I received it, Lord.

We arrived at the village and I was introduced to the chief. Now this was great, we got on like a house on fire. We talked and talked. I was sharing all about my Lord. He shared he was in England in 1984. He spoke very good English - having been scared stiff of my teacher in my youth I never learned any languages at all. After quite a long time, he then asked if I was part of this hospital plan. To which I answered, "No, I'm only visiting." We shook hands and we left to trek back to Ogus?

We called again on the girls and I took the photos. We then took a bus to the 'Hall and School proposals Faith training college,' Joseph called it. He really had a vision, this man, what with the hospital, the factory and now a school for boys. He wanted to be able to get them to learn carpentry, metalwork - it was wonderful, Lord. He had no keys so we could not go in and there was no other body there, no boys.

We travelled back to Ogus and went back to Mama Knight's house, where tea, chai, was now being made. Mama Knight asked if I would like anything else because I really did not like this chai. I was about to say, "No," when she held up a tin of 'Milo.'

Well, I thanked her so much for it and accepted the Milo which was good, and after discussions among themselves we were on the move again to go to John Okeld's home where we would have prayers and I would speak. So Father gave me the Word.

We arrived, I was introduced to John and everybody, and we started. Well Father, my heart was singing, this people knew my Jesus. They sang their hearts out, no shifty eyes, just pure joy, loving Him, loving me. What a time we had. The clapping and the praises went on and on. This is what I had envisioned. It was like when I was a little girl at my aunt's. I had a chorus book with Negro Spiritual songs in it and I would get that book out and sing. In the front were the beautiful faces of the black Negro children with such joy and the eyes were shining with love for our Lord. O how great.

I don't know what Father gave me to say; I was so overjoyed being with all these people who worshipped Him. After, I did ask if anyone needed prayer but, no, they wanted to talk to me, so Kenneth did overtime that night. The questions were coming thick and fast. It was great; it was like being back at school with the boys all sitting on the floor round my knees eager to know more and more.

Our meal was served and "O Father, help me" to be able, like Arthur Blessitt, who took what was set in front of him, Lord. And, like the chai, the meal was ogali which is like a porridge but very thick, and you all sat round the table and took with your fingers so much ogali and then another plate of sukum iki which was boiled cabbage. Now, as in Japan, this is the staple diet. Fine, I was ok.

After supper, I was shown to my hut and like the films it was a small mud hut with a thatched roof. Would you believe they had got a bed in this tiny hut for me to sleep on and a mosquito net, and Kenneth (bless him, dear Jesus) never left me. He lay across the door, curled up like a ball. Sheets and blankets were on this bed too. Because I had no privacy through the day, I would pray about things that bothered me, but here I prayed all things back to the Lord through the night. I was over and over things. I was not sure about where we had been or everyone in the fellowship at John's, but I prayed into the night, covering everything. It is not for me to judge, but to bring everything to my Jesus.

Next morning, like setting of the sun, the dawn is equally as magnificent. You never saw such skies in your life. I rose and went out. I was shown the toilet, a hole in the ground with a bric-a-brac screen around it, and my wash room was the same: like a screen round a little corner with the box with the water and a towel. Much later on our journey, I discovered Joseph put these up for me everywhere we went.

After breakfast, Joseph, John, Kenneth, Samuel and I went for a walk to the next village, so "Every place that the sole of you foot treads," I prayed it back.

We came to another compartment and another compound. Two widows whom Joseph helps both wanted prayer. I just walked round behind the men and, as I did so, I was told when we got there. I laid hands on one of the women and prayed, then went to the hut of the next girl. Her baby was sick. More and more I was seeing such sickness with children. After tending to the sick in prayer and talking to them through Kenneth, we turned around and walked back.

We walked back to John's village. We were to have a service. Now they call it mass, so I was seeking from Kenneth what this really meant. Were they catholic, or what was the answer? No, it was my joy, they called it mass to impress me. Normally it would just be a gathering, so I found myself explaining all the different religions, but only one Lord Jesus Christ. We asked again if anyone wanted prayer? A young girl came out weeping and shouting and knelt down in front of me, so I knelt down too and took her in my arms till she calmed down. I then took her away from everyone and, through Kenneth, asked all manner of things, which she confessed. I then prayed over her and we came back. John is the pastor of this fellowship and he had plans to build a church, so I walked around and claimed the ground. The people were so hungry for You, Lord Jesus. The men went in to John, but I sat outside, just talking to all the people, about Jesus Christ my Lord and reading passages of Scripture to them with Kenneth.

After a while they dispersed and Kenneth told me we were having another meeting later, so I wrote another letter or two. About half six, people started coming in so we sang and praised and I spoke. Joseph made an appeal and people came forward. He took them through the prayer for salvation then he handed over to me again to pray for the sick. Everyone came forward for prayers for the sick and I was not doing this. Our Lord was the picture; I was not the one who was doing it.

The more people I met, the more I could see how they had been used and abused. Every false thing you could imagine was operating in and through these people. Poor people, every denomination was present, every teaching was present. As long as they got the people to follow, they cared not what was being taught. Emotional blackmail, if they followed catholic, the pastors there would give them medicine; if they followed Church of England or Methodist or United Reformed they would get food; if they followed a Jesus Group or Adventist Group, they would get clothes. So the people were like piggies in the middle and they were so poor, so sick, they needed everything.

We had our evening meal, ogali and sukum iki and a drink and went to bed, back to my hut. I could not sleep, I was coming against every evil in the book, every exploitation, man's inhumanity to man, going back and forth breaking the chains of slavery, breaking chains of poverty, breaking chains of control, breaking chains of religiosity. "O my Lord, they have come into this land and brought everything but the love and peace of Christ Jesus as Lord."

I prayed into the night then lay down and slept. Next day, I awoke feeling quite released, after being able to see what my Father wanted me to see, but I couldn't let up - must keep going to get the real breakthrough in the Heavenly. Leaving nothing to chance, once you have the breakthrough and your peace back, you have reached our precious Lord and He will do the rest.

We met and talked. It looked like we were moving on, so it was goodbye to John and Samuel. I could hug and pray for them to teach and preach the truth.

We walked a very long way, probably about half way and then a matutu came. Now this is a bus but, like the films, the chickens and everything else you could name were on the bus as well as the people and you were pushed and pushed in it. It did not matter if you got a seat, people were sitting on top of you and if you were standing, you could not stand up straight for the bus was not high enough. Some people were hanging on the sides with arms hooked round the windows. It really had to be seen to be believed.

We arrived back at Ogus and Mama Knight gave me a fresh cut pineapple. How refreshing; it was like nectar, so juicy. After Joseph and Mama Knight had discussions we went back to the matutu and we were taken back to a place called Rangwe.

We all jumped off and set off walking to the pastor's hut. When we arrived, the people were already there. It was like bush telegraph. I was so thirsty. The pineapple was good but caused me to be more thirsty than if I had had the water. Now this was different, they wanted to talk, to learn from the Word. This was wonderful Father, lead me on - and He did. We went from Scripture after Scripture, just reading the Word - it could not be better. Father really wanted them to get the Truth of the Gospel. Back and forth, reading right out, the Word was going forth. As I read, Joseph would not read, so I read and then Kenneth read. Dear Lord, I was so excited, I could see what Father was doing, proclaiming the Word of God, the Truth, out over the land.

We broke for supper - our ogali and sukum iki - and, lo and behold, the pastor's compound was full of people who heard a visitor had come. They set off singing and clapping and I continued to read out loud from the Word. Man, what a breakthrough - "Praise Jesus!"

Joseph gave the altar call and the prayer of salvation. I hope it was salvation, I never asked Kenneth what he was saying. Then I always asked for prayers for the sick and everybody got up again. I was just allowed to go along and lay my hands on their heads and pray. It was midnight when we finished, but what a day. "Lord, the breakthrough is coming."

Again I was taken to my hut and Kenneth, once again, lay across the door. I really was thanking Father for the blessings into the night, thanking Him for everything. I slept like a baby.

The next morning dawned and I was up washed and ready. The pastor's wife came with all her children, seven, one a year. "O Lord, bless this woman." I prayed James' prayer for Mama and her children, and anointed them all, praying against the sickness.

The pastor came and asked for prayer, so I anointed him, praying for healing, wisdom, knowledge and understanding. "Bless this man, Lord, with Your Anointing." His heart was reaching out to You Lord. I was weeping in prayer over this man and his family. I shared with him what Father had shared with me, stepping off the plane for Africa. Joshua as promised, "Every place on which the sole of your foot treads, I have given to you, just as I have given it to Moses." This pastor, like John, just wanted to serve You, Lord. He said he wanted to come with us and take Africa for Jesus.

Kenneth told me we were headed back to base for tonight so we set off again. I had a spring in my step. "Thank You, Father, I receive Africa for You."

We had not walked far and we stopped for a matutu to take us back to Sare-Awendo. We got off the bus at the bottom of our track and it was virtually straight uphill to Joseph's family's land.

We parted at the top of the hill. Joseph left for home and we went on to Joseph's brother's house. Kenneth began, straight away, to prepare our evening meal. He told me we were having potatoes, cooked rice, meat and gravy which they call soup, greens and fresh fruit to finish.

Joseph, his wife and the children arrived for supper too, so we washed our hands, said prayers then ate. It was ok, quite nice really. I'm not quite sure what meat it was but it tasted quite good. When we had finished we left the table and the children sat down for theirs.

After supper Joseph's children sang to me, and his wife and his mama from next door came in. The man from up the road came in and his mam and dad arrived and they asked me to read to them. "How wonderful Father! Here we are again."

I read out to them the Word going forth. I read about Joseph's coat of many colours. I stopped and Joseph's mother asked me to read on. I was only too willing. After reading for quite a bit of the story of Joseph, Joseph asked me to pray for his eight children. Again I was anointing with oil and praying again for the sickness. Everyone seemed happy with this and we hugged each other and said our goodbyes.

I went straight to sleep that night with peace in my heart, just talking everything back to our precious Lord Jesus.

A new day dawned; it was Sunday. Kenneth and I set off to meet up with Joseph at Sare-Awendo, so we sang and talked all the way down our track to the main road to get the matutu to Sare-Awendo. We got off to wait for Joseph. Joseph came and we headed in another direction. We walked for quite a while and then we were picked up on a truck - I guess one of Joseph's friends.

We travelled a long way to a crossroads. What I mean is, no road really, just this flat dirt track, and when we came to the crossroads you could see quite plainly the different directions the roads were going, because it was flat and very wide.

This crossroads was our stop and we got off. I never knew where we were going or what the plan of the day was - no one spoke of it.

We started to walk away. We arrived at the village and everyone came running to meet us. The pastor came first to greet us. He took us back to his hut and asked for prayer for his sons and then he told me, through Kenneth, a young girl was very distressed. She was unable to carry her children full term; she got so far then lost them. She would become very ill in the stomach and of course the husband was very cross and called her a barren woman. In Old Testament times, a woman who was unable to bear children was a failure. Her barrenness was a social embarrassment to her husband. So like Sarai in Genesis, Sarai sent her servant girl, Hagar, to be with her husband to bear children for her. Now in this instance, childlessness was a cultural stigma (Genesis 16) so in praying, at first I was to break the curse from the girl and the anger and bitterness of the husband's words of his shame, and then ask for the healing of the womb. This I did, under our Lord's instructions. I also prayed for the cleansing of the home, the past, binding of the spiritual forces of the past, but loosing the girl into her rightful inheritance for the future. I was quite satisfied all was done and all was well. I always gave the man a ticking off, through Kenneth, for his attitude putting the whole blame on his wife, and that maybe it came down his line of the family, because later she did conceive, so the girl was not barren. A curse over the girl caused the baby to come away early in the pregnancy, making her unable to carry it full term.

Another young girl came with her baby, very sick, so I anointed the baby and prayed the prayer of faith over the baby, and one by one, more and more came. I was about to go and find Joseph when another girl came running to ask for prayer for her children. I did pray, but because Joseph was busy and had allowed time for me to talk to the families of this pastor, I was really pleased, as we were able to get in a bit deeper. Now I know Father has it in hand anyway and His way is bigger than all of us, but I was thrilled that Kenneth and I could get in a little closer and talk to the families about Jesus Christ and bring them to Him. I also was so aware of some of the curses over the children of these families. The children were so sick, so I prayed around the place, speaking out the Psalms over the land, breaking the curses, as in Deuteronomy 28.

We were offered some refreshment and these people had taken me into their hearts. While our fruit was being prepared, I was allowed to nurse one of the babies. I was honoured; this was a big step to allow me to hold the children - much progress, Father. One of the girls came and could speak quite good English and knew and could understand my breaking of the curses over the families and the children. Now we were able to go in depth about our Lord, as she understood. I asked if she would not start a prayer group for mothers for toddlers; now she really wanted to know how and she was firing me with questions. "Father, a real breakthrough."

Joseph reappeared and it was time to go. We hugged each other and we set off walking again, I was praising because of the inroads Father had made. As we walked, a few drops of rain started and Joseph said, any minute the heavens would open and we would be soaked. I stopped and prayed, like Elijah, to "Stop up the heavens, Lord, till we get home."

I also asked for a lift and, lo and behold, along came a truck. He took us right back to the main road. It turned out he'd travelled to Britain every month to Aberdeen, also to Switzerland. At this moment he was visiting his parents. We got right back to Sare-Awendo and we travelled out to the sugar factory. This was where Mama Beldine lived. She worked at the factory so she lived on the compound; the house we stayed in was her husband's house on his parents' land - her husband was Joseph's brother.

He was a teacher, but lived away, where his job was - so Father, need lots of prayer here. We arrived and it was lovely to see her and we greeted and shared with each other. Now this little house had a proper loo and a shower, so Beldine suggested I might like a shower. I jumped at the chance. First shower since arriving in Africa, and a loo you could flush - what a bonus. It seemed we were here for the rest of the day so I wrote another letter to Frances and Robert and Joan and Noel.

By this time supper was ready. After supper Beldine's children and others came in and friends of Kenneth and the children and they sang for me and we sang together. A story was asked for so I was reading 1 Peter 4, "Living for our Lord." So I launched out on that very chapter. Now this was great, what with Beldine speaking a little English and Kenneth and one of Joseph's bairns - it came into a good Bible study, and the questions were being asked from Beldine as well as the children and Kenneth's friends, so good ground was being covered and understanding, real truth which he had never had, it was so good.

It was late. Mama Beldine started work at seven in the morning, so we had to go to rest. In the morning we were up early, the children up for school. The owners of this plantation had the houses and the school for the bairns - it was good, Father. At the factory, the siren went, and this was the changing of the shifts, "I'm impressed, Father. These people have a life; they are taken good care of with the families, everything you need and protection."

We left the home together, with hugs and kisses, and we all set off down the track to the matutu, Beldine to work and the bairns to school. I was praying hard all the way, so as not to forget anything of the day before, and to my surprise we got to the matutu at the bottom of the track, but back to base. We could have the day off - wow!

After we got back, I got my breath back, first day off. So, what to do? Well washing to do, and other things so I set off to get clothes washed. I had one dress, but it was great, you could rinse it through one day and it would be clean and, smelling so clean, be ready for the next day. I had taken this one in with me all the time. I could rinse it through at night and put it back on in the morning, which was brilliant in this heat. I washed all the things to get them all out on the line. When I came through, Kenneth slept all the time when he was not speaking after me. He was like a small child, who runs and runs then just flops and is all out for the count. After speaking, Kenneth would sit down, curl up and be sound asleep. But today he was sitting on the veranda. I asked him what he was doing. "Watching de clothes."

"Watching the clothes?" I said.

"Yes, de cows eat de clothes."

We had such a good laugh and I left him watching 'de clothes'. I went through to write home again and, as always, thanking our Lord for Kenneth. It was not that we talked a lot, but he was there with me all the time.

Come teatime, Kenneth and I were invited to Joseph's house for tea, dinner, so we set off to walk up and up over the top of the hill and across and down the other side. The land all around I think, but am not sure, was the family's land, so there was quite a bit of land involved. Joseph's mother tilled, sowed and weeded a field out the front and I remember thinking how hard this woman had to work; this is it, an old lady.

Joseph seemed in a good mood and after supper we sat out the front and talked. His house was a big house, stone built, but nothing finished inside. There were no doors on the rooms, no floors in and the walls weren't finished. It was in quite a state for them actually to be living in it. Joseph told

me about his ordination and his work. It was a real privilege
to work with this man. I was still praying because something
was wrong and I knew it was as he told me this work was
down on the coast after his ordination. He had been there
for two years but did not like it so he had come back home
to work with the church in Sare-Awendo. He travelled a
lot to all the areas and knew all the pastors. He showed me
photos of ceremonies of him preaching. He was a very good
preacher and believed only to preach salvation. This is good,
Father - he is not like a Catholic or any denomination so we
agree on lots of points.

Now our work together was done. In the service he then
handed over to me. Because the salvation message was so
important, he wanted to do that part, to call the people for
salvation, but then he proclaimed that the anointing was on
me for the healing and so called the people for healing. He
said that Father has anointed me for that. I really enjoyed our
talk together, getting a little more information to work on.
"What has happened, Father? Show me what to pray; what
Joseph is about and what went wrong, so it can be put right."

It was time to go, so we set off back up the hill thanking
Joseph's wife and the bairns for such a lovely evening,
having time and relaxed days. I had a good long time resting
with my Lord. "O, how blessed to be at such peace in His
loving arms and aware of His presence, His comfort and
encouragement to me. He is telling me just to be confident
in walking with You Holy Spirit and to open myself up to
trust whatever my faith is in. To believe for great things that
He has given me north, south, east and west, like He gave
Abraham. My joy Lord, thank You, thank You, Lord, I'll
receive Your promise."

Next morning, with the bags packed ready for the next
mission we went up to meet Joseph, singing. We seem to be
going a long way. "Praise Jesus north, south, east and west,"
Father said last night.

We were waiting for a matutu and others joined us. A chap came next to me speaking good English, such a joy to be able to talk to someone. A truck arrived and we all piled in and he took us off. It had rained a lot through the night so our beautiful flat wide roads had turned into clarts and potholes. We seemed to go quite a way and all the way little villages were dotted all over the horizon.

We arrived at our destination and we piled off. Joseph asked the driver if he would pick us up next day.

We set off up the hill. Kenneth told me we were going to the tobacco factory and to the plantations. We trekked right up and up and came over the top and down into the village. Now this was beautiful: well kept, nice flowers, patches that were like little gardens round the huts were set out round the compound. It was surrounded by a fence with gates, as a deterrent to keep out predators. "O I liked it, Father."

It was clean and nice, and around another part a hedge was growing, cut and kept, and the huts were different. We were greeted and taken to the guesthouse. The doorway was very low, you had to bend down to get in. I bent down, but not far enough and banged my head on the plinth, but once inside it was quite high so you could actually stand up straight, see quite a lot and much lighter too. Though it was a thatched mud hut, it was more like a guesthouse. Rooms went off from the main centre and it was quite different from what I had seen so far.

We were given water to wash and fresh cool drinks, very, very good, and then came back to the centre room and it was lunchtime. A table had been set up and a meal was cooked in another hut and brought in to our guest hut. "O my, Father! Help me, please help me!"

It was chicken stew, but everything had gone into the pot, guts, head, feet, the lot. No sukum iki here, they were giving me their very best. Ogali was served with it. I was thinking of Arthur Blessitt again and the other missionaries who ate what was put in front of them to prove God's power.

One such story was that the stuff had been put into the meal; the person did not know and ate it but our precious Lord kept them safe. Because of that case many came to the Lord. "So Father I need Your help."

You had to fish into the pot and get something out. I took my turn to fish in the pot. To my greatest relief, I fished out the liver. I was so thankful; it was something that I could eat. Like Japan, I could never have got it over if it had been the head or the intestines, and I took my ogali, praising Jesus. From this time on, if we were given a meal like this, Kenneth would get me the liver before anyone else got it and I was so thankful.

After our meal, people were arriving for our meeting. Joseph opened the meeting then handed it over. Today, Father said, "John 3." I went back and forth through how we must be born again into salvation. Joseph made an appeal for healing and six came out, so I prayed over them and we broke for teatime. Mine was Milo; if I said I liked anything, Kenneth would get it for me every time. I was pleased about the Milo.

No one would move; they asked question after question. We went through John 3, back and forth verse by verse. "They are so hungry for You, Lord, so hungry for Your Word."

By the time we had finished and had to start again another lot of people had come for an evening meeting, so we started again. I stayed on the theme of salvation. Joseph made the appeal and prayed for them and asked again if anyone wanted prayer for healing. Some came forward but they wanted to know more and more so we just kept reaching out and preaching out of the Word, then talking about it.

Supper was served but they wanted more and more of our Lord, so I kept reading and answering the questions. I learned there were three pastors present so I wanted to pray for them, Peter, Shem and Dominic. I enthused and enthused, "We must give the people Jesus Christ our Lord; not man's words but God's Word from the Bible. Only through the Word can we receive healing and salvation. Where the Word is preached, signs and wonders will follow."

By the time we had finished it was very late and an old man came up and wanted the Holy Spirit, so we prayed for salvation again first, then the baptism of the Holy Spirit. Now this was what I wanted the pastors to do, and praised Jesus. Because the old man had done it they saw what happened, they asked too, so the pastor came through to Jesus our Lord and we prayed for baptism. I also then talked about water baptism, "Die to self, rise to Jesus Christ. Bury the old man, rise the new man."

The next day Joseph and Dominic had to go to another village to pray for a man who was a cripple. Kenneth was agitated because they would have to cross a river up to their necks. "Please would I pray?"

So we prayed for them while they were away. To Kenneth's greatest joy, Joseph and Dominic came back. They had had a great prayer time and had not needed to cross the river, so Father, "We praise and thank You, Your holy Name."

The arrangements were all changed and another meeting was arranged. While we waited for the people to come, a storm broke, sheet lightning and very heavy rain. You would not believe the people still coming from all ends and sides, six more pastors and all their people. This time it was "The sermon on the mount."

Everything was going well, like we had stepped up a gear because again, all the prayers were for salvation and healing. The shouts were coming from every side with questions all about You, dear Lord. They were soaking in Your Word, Your truth; very late but still wanting more. I prayed over all the pastors, all received salvation, and then prayed for baptism in the Holy Spirit. I was so excited as if the air, which was electric with the storm, was electric with our precious Lord. I found out that these people had walked all day to get to us. People just slept where they were. I was taken to my bed by Kenneth.

Next morning people arrived again for more, so we set off again in the Scriptures. I so wanted them to know our Lord for themselves, labouring the importance of knowing Jesus Christ, "You can do nothing without Jesus; all things are possible to him who believes." I was telling them the importance of prayer, getting to know our Lord from every side and every situation. Joseph was getting impatient, wanting me to move on, so I finished with prayer and praying over all of them. I prayed for the valley and the plantation, praying the blessing.

We set off walking and they all came with us. We walked a long way and one by one they dropped off and headed for their own homes. We arrived at the bus station and the hugs and kisses of farewell. I was weeping, "Father keep them safe. Let them have received such an anointing to encourage them and set them up for life."

A truck arrived already loaded, but they made room. Dominic and his sons were the last to say goodbye, and bless them, Father, all young men gleaming in the presence of our Lord. As we waved goodbye, I turned round to see our truckload of people and, lo and behold, they could speak English. So to my joy, I set off again, teaching them the Scriptures, while we travelled; again, not religion, but Jesus Christ. They took it all in.

We arrived back to Sare-Awendo and caught the matutu back to base. "What a time Father, such a joy, seeing Your hand at work."

I prayed back all the way up to the base. Joseph is changing, no longer shifty eyed. He is changing, "Praise

Jesus we are hitting the mark, Lord! We are hitting the mark. What a time Father, fulfilling His promise."

Back at base, I just wanted more time to myself, so I went into the Word to study and read, Father - and He was showing me not to get into myself thinking, "I don't know enough." Faith and understanding are what He wants, not intelligence. Quite often, the Holy Spirit, our Lord and our faith are different. It is the commitment to one person, Jesus. It is not works or service that matters, but intense spiritual reliability, expecting Christ Jesus at every turn. The special mark of the Holy Spirit is boldness. "Attempt great things for our Lord and expect He will do them."

Well, really, Father was moving in front - I was not expecting great things but He was doing them, great things, anywhere and everywhere. I just had to keep going. The expectancy of what Father had done at Dominic's was great and, "More Lord, more."

While waiting to see what was next, I washed again and sat on the veranda, watching 'de clothes', so the cows would not eat them. Clothes dried in the heat quickly, so I decided to go for a walk. Mulling over, it was a rich land, but in such poverty so I prayed to break curses of the generational bondage over the land. Next, sickness, terrible sickness over the people, so I prayed through that, there and then. Such corruption in the government so I prayed that back to the Father too. The promise of the north, south, east and west of this land, the bride of Christ, for Jesus.

I came back in as thunder and lightning split the heavens again. I joined in as if I were not singing in the Spirit, I was shouting with the lightning and the thunder, praising our Lord. He was rending the heavens and it will break forth over the earth. What a time of prayer!

After the storm, I went to pray for Joseph and his family again, then covered everywhere I had been. The peace was so still, not a bird or a squeak, total silence. "What a mighty God we serve!"

The next morning, we were all up, our bags packed and down the road at half past seven. We took the matutu to Kisumu where we were to meet Joseph. It was a good journey and we arrived safely. Kenneth and I waited on the top of the steps. I spotted Joseph coming with Mama Knight and Samuel. I found out we were going to the tea plantation. It was a long journey. I praised Jesus north, south, east and west. The bus moved on. The people had actually to pack it before it moved off the stand. It had to be heaving, bursting at the seams and we were off to Kericho, (how to pronounce these words, I don't know.)

We travelled a long way. Now each tea plantation ran into another and on to another and they are massive. Each plantation has a whole valley of workers and so built houses and schools for the children, just like the sugar plantation. They really worked hard and they really looked after their workers. Of course I didn't know how much they would be paid.

We were taken straight to the canteen where the meetings were being held. The message was given three times, because this was a different tribe and so Kenneth interpreted just one sort, then the next man picked up from Kenneth and so on, and Joseph made the appeal for salvation and a lot stood up and prayed after him. Then he asked for healing and everybody came forward for that. I just had to go along laying on hands and praying the prayer of faith as there was no time.

After we finished we were taken to the pastor's house for refreshments. Joseph was allocated to a certain part of the plantation by the pastor. As it looked so long and so vast, he wanted to go into every valley of the plantations, but the pastor was having words so he was really getting agitated and dictating to Joseph.

We went back to the hall for the second meeting and everything was fine, Father, everything in hand; the same pattern, two men giving the interpretation. I found I had to concentrate, so I would not lose the thread. Father was doing a lot. Time came for the salvation, but everybody came forward for the healing.

We finished again and an evening meal was served. I got my chicken liver again; bless Kenneth.

After supper, Joseph wanted another meeting, he was so pleased with the outcome of the first two, and the hall was packed again. The same pattern was repeated. We finished at midnight and went to sleep, praying into the night with all that was going on.

I woke early and went for a shower. O, how refreshing you feel, so clean. Kenneth brought me my Milo and I was taken all around.

The children wanted to touch me. We walked around through the estate; it belonged to the Brooke Bond Tea Company. We came back to the pastor's house and I looked at photos. We had a meal round about eleven. I was told we were setting off on another long journey. The pastor asked for prayer for the church and for himself. It was incredible, all these pastors receiving prayer and I prayed and anointed with oil and prayed everything I knew to pray over these lads.

We set off walking and walked miles through the tea plantation, on to the next one, on to the next one and we were stopping at the third one and the children ran to greet me. It was wonderful to see such good clean healthy bairns happy. We had our meetings, left and travelled right on back walking, then up and on to the road for the bus to Kisumu.

We got off at Kisumu and Mama Knight and Samuel were travelling back to Ogus, but Kenneth, Clement, Joseph and I were going on to Rangwe. We missed the bus to Rangwe so followed Mama Knight to Ogus. We arrived and Mama

Knight made us ogali and sukum ike. After this, we set off to walk to digs right out of town. "O my Lord, what a joy and all the happenings at the tea plantation." I prayed it all back and fell asleep.

The next morning we got up, packed and Kenneth brought my Milo. We set off and arrived at Mama Knight's where she made the men something and, through Kenneth, wanted to talk. She made a living for herself and her children by going to Kisumu market. She would buy there and bring it back to sell at Ogus market for a small profit: what a hard life. She asked for prayer. Again, I anointed with oil and prayed the prayer of faith. Because of what had happened here the first night, I knew that there was sin, but what I didn't know was how or in what area. I prayed again in everything I could to cut her free from it.

By this time, Joseph was hopping again; he wanted to be off. I was taking too long, but I carried on anyway. We left and we got our lift to Rangwe.

We travelled a different way, quite a way, we were dropped at Rangwe and set off walking to Clement's hut, another pastor. We did not stay at Rangwe, we went on to God-man Mountain, but Clement came with us. We walked two or three hours and arrived at God-man Mountain. We set out over and up.

We were sharing everything with our host. Tea, chai, was served and Kenneth brought me my Milo; it was refreshing after the walk uphill all the way. Refreshed and blessed, it was time for our meeting.

Father gave me '1 Peter 1, verses 3 to 6.' I was preaching the Word, reading out loud, then taking it verse by verse. When I finished, Joseph made the appeal and everyone came forward for salvation. We then asked who would like prayer for healing; same again, everyone just kept standing.

When we finished, we broke for supper and after supper people were collecting for a second meeting. Joseph started.

A pastor said he would like to give testimony. This was the first time this had happened. The man said that he had been a servant of God for twenty-one years but had never ever experienced the power he received in the prayers. He said as the laying on of hands was done, he burned from the top of his head to the soles of his feet. He said he was having great difficulty in talking, as he just wanted to be with God. He said he wanted to meet the servant of God from overseas. He wanted to stay, but wanted to go just to be with Christ Jesus. He said his goodbyes and then he came to me, taking both my hands, and indeed the power of God between us was such that I was weeping with joy. I had such an encounter with this man.

He began to prophesy and gave the Scriptures of Psalm 50 verse 10, "For every animal in the forest is Mine and the cattle on a thousand hills are Mine." He began to praise and speak with his heavenly language. I believe that Father had baptised him with such an anointing of the Holy Spirit that he had never experienced this before.

He left and we started our second meeting. With a testimony like that, I knew that all the people were with me. The expression on the faces had changed. The expectancy was there and they were holding every word. I used the same Scripture but went on to explain the baptism of the Holy Spirit. Joseph then made his appeal for salvation and everyone came forward. Then the prayers for healing; everyone wanted prayers for healing.

After we finished, it was around midnight, but one after another wanted to tell of healing in the body. The rejoicing! I left as they talked and shouted and laughed among themselves. I lay down and sobbed into the pillow, for the privilege. Father was keeping His promise of doing great things; but for me, I was so humbled for I knew that He, and He alone, was doing all of this. I went to sleep.

The next morning I got up, washed and dressed. We prayed together, that morning, giving thanks for everything from the day before. People had just stayed that night sleeping just out in the open. Wilson, our host, took me walk about. He told me his father had built a church on this mountain. We walked the land and I shared Joshua with Wilson so we prayed, receiving Father's promise. He showed me his cross.

We came back and shared again. I was saying that because Wilson's father did have the church on the mountain the Lord was blessing because of the prayers of the people who were faithful before. This was purely Jesus Christ at work and the land was holy; it was consecrated to Him. Wilson asked me stay; he wanted me to stay on the land. He would build my hut, he said, and I would be their Mama. "We need you. We need you to stay, or we shall die - but keep coming into our Lord with you staying and being present with us."

By this time, Joseph was ready for us to start another meeting and the people just kept on coming. All received prayer for salvation and prayer for healing. We had a short break then on to the next meeting. Something our Lord was pouring out over this land. We had supper then started again; they just kept on coming. It was midnight again and I was speechless. I went to bed and wept and wept. "Praise and glory and honour are Yours Lord Jesus."

The next day we were moving on, but Wilson wanted the place where the church had been to be blessed. Joseph read Psalm 127 and he asked me to pray. We left amid such joy and headed back down the mountain. Wilson and Emmanuel wanted to be baptised so we headed for the river again. This had all been discussed. The river was running high so we chose a cul-de-sac where the water had swirled inland. Joseph changed; I just took off my shoes. Kenneth begged me not to go in but Father was with me; I had no fear. I waded in and turned round. Joseph called for Wilson to come first, but a shout went up from the bank side. Wilson came and made his confession. After taking him down under the water he came up and I prayed for the baptism of the Holy Spirit. Next was Emmanuel. After I came up out of the water, I asked Kenneth what the shout was for. He said, "There are snakes." But again, Father was so with me. It confirmed our Lord was with me, for them.

Wilson pleaded with me to stay but I said I couldn't, it had to be Father. I had to know it was the Lord Who wanted me to stay. "I would know without the slightest doubt, but you, Wilson, have been baptised, and I said I think our Father is raising you up to follow in Father's footsteps."

We got back to Rangwe and then we were going back to base; o how wonderful, just to sit with my Jesus. We caught the matutu back to the main road then the bus on to the place of our base. The peace was coming over me, the noise on the bus was quite something but it was as if I was quite oblivious to it. I shut off the noise and was at total peace with my Lord.

We climbed up and up the track to base. We arrived and had to sit for a while with the heat and the climb. I just rested in my chair. Kenneth, bless his heart, brought me fresh sliced pineapple, so refreshing and tasty. Joseph had gone home. Kenneth went to see if there was any more post from home. I got up and did my washing and hung it out and so we sat on the veranda and watched 'de cows don't eat de clothes.'

I wrote up my diary but just wanted to sit with my Jesus. Usually I am praying and praying but no words would come, only total awesomeness of what He, our Lord, had done on this trip.

Much later, Kenneth arrived back; one letter from Bridget, none from home. Kenneth made our supper, I read my letter from Bridget; she was asking about my coming back and how we would meet. I gave it all back to Father; everything is in His Hands anyway. He knows His plans - "Let everything come as You want it, Lord."

We were just sitting in silence when Joseph arrived. He asked for prayer; he was thanking me for coming. He also was overwhelmed at our precious Lord, what He was doing. He was saying he had always worked alone; now, because I had come, all the churches were joining with him and were catching him. They wanted his vision, they wanted what he had striven to do for so long on his own: for the boys, for the training college, for the hospital, for the girls, for the work in the college of sewing. I find it so humbling and an honour to receive such praise from this man of God. We were off that morning but Joseph came to tell me that he would go ahead to get things ready, so Kenneth and I waited just until lunchtime.

The time came to go; it had been raining heavily but, praise the Lord our God, when we went down the rain had stopped. We travelled up to Sare-Awendo where we met up with Joseph yet again and we piled on the truck. We travelled out again another way off the track and then we walked. We walked and we walked to a place called Agougo Nyamasare. We sat and talked. The father had died and the church was now was in the hands of his son. The people were arriving so we prepared ourselves.

My word that day was the greatest commandment, "To love the Lord your God with all your heart, with all your soul and with all your strength." (Deuteronomy 6 verse 5). The meeting lasted till very late. By this time we got through all the prayers, but I was troubled for this son. I prayed into the night.

Next morning, I washed and dressed and went in search of the man, found him and we sat and shared and shared till I believed he got everything out into the open. Once he got the trouble out and confessed, our Lord showed me "Consecrate this man."

I asked him to commit his life to Jesus Christ our Lord; he was only too willing. I anointed him with oil, prayed over him Psalm 127, then got some water, prayed over the water and consecrated the building, using Solomon's Scripture, 2 Chronicles 5 - the whole chapter: Solomon dedicated the temple, sprinkling the water everywhere. We finished and the lad was so pleased.

We prayed together then we went to move on to the next village. We walked for miles. We entered the village and, to my surprise, I was told by Kenneth that the man of this village had eleven wives. So each of the huts held a wife and he himself was away getting another wife. We entered the master's hut, it was huge, and this was where our meeting was to be held. It was full, but they all wanted prayer, no Word; Samuel persisted.

I just prayed with my heavenly language. How does one pray in a situation like this? They received the prayers and left, but some more came and we held our meeting and praised Jesus. He was so gracious and was blessing as I prayed. Father knew that I was sore troubled and did He bless the wives? They came forward for salvation. I was jumping inside, "Praise God!" The wives made us supper and what a spread, quite a number of dishes. I was very careful what I chose, but everything was fine. We had to leave straight away as it was a long walk back and I wanted to make it before dark. This place was called Barackakech.

The next morning was Sunday. We started by praying for all my fellowship back home and my bairns, tears flowed as I missed them. It brought it so close again; when you are so busy and you are out on the field your concentration is so strong, but when you have the time the bairns come back in. The Holy Spirit came to my aid as I prepared for our service here in Samuel's church.

This was the church I had dedicated. A bell was rung and people were walking for miles. How they put us to shame. There were no musical instruments but a choir of girls. The singing was beautiful; o how our Lord was blessed. They sang from their hearts and the glory filled that place. Samuel spoke before he introduced me and he was saying they needed money for instruments. When I stepped forward, I shared with the girls on worshiping in Spirit and in truth. I said, "You don't want any instruments when you can sing to our Lord like that; your faces beam."

How we like to know when we are pleasing our Lord. Joseph made the appeal and a lot came forward, but when he asked for healing, everyone came for healing. We had a meal and then it was time to go.

Samuel walked with us for miles and miles. We got back to a place called Rapoliji. At this point Samuel would go back. We said our goodbyes and o how Father had blessed this young pastor.

We travelled on and on and came to another village. We were taken to the headman who invited us in. Chai was served but Milo for me; o how grateful I was, "Thank you Father." There was difficulty here, I didn't know what, I just prayed and sat quietly. Supper was being served; I sensed tension. A young lady came and asked if I could dedicate her week old baby. "Father, what a privilege!" So I dedicated this tiny bundle to Jesus Christ my Lord. I prayed for the Holy Spirit to cleanse the mama and I also asked for the bad feeling and the disquiet of the spirit that was in the home settlement to be released, so that the Spirit of our Lord could come in. I also prayed for the mama after her confinement. Then we were prepared for the meeting.

The place was full and still they came. Here we were in a situation where there was more than one tribe so the message again was given three times; it was interpreted by three people. The appeal was given and many came, then the healing, all came with people telling of their healing. Some asked for the Baptism of the Holy Spirit and wanted to be baptised in water. Midnight came and I was shown to my bed.

I lay thanking Father for all He was doing and woke up at five in the morning; the husband was going out to plough in the shamba. I was so thankful and turned over and went back to sleep. I woke much later needing the toilet and had to walk out into the bush. There were no washing facilities either, so I just had to do without. The husband came back from the field and asked for the baptism of the Holy Spirit.

As we prepared to leave, he put twenty shillings into my hand. I prayed over the hundredfold return and the husband set us to the transport to our next destination and, while walking, I glean that he is a headmaster - what a lovely man. I gave the twenty shillings to Joseph.

We walked on and on until we came to the place where the trucks come. We sat by the wayside to wait a long time, but a truck did finally come, fully loaded with timber, but they squeezed us on. We travelled quite a way then we got out to walk again. Joseph said we would not be staying so we left our bags at a wayside home and off we went. We were nearly there when we came to a swamp, the river had burst its banks. Joseph and Clement waded through and went to see Shem to see if there was another way while Kenneth and I waited. Joseph and Clement returned to us. There was no other way. They brought some plastic slippers with them for me to put on and save my shoes. We plodged our way through. We arrived and Joseph and Clement found Shem sick, but they prayed over him and he got up straight away. Shem's place is called Ombo and as they talked I saw Shem wanted us to stay and have a meeting. After a while it was decided so Shem's eldest boy and Kenneth were sent for our bags. We were served drinks and sat in the shade of some trees round his compound, so very pleasant. The people from nearby walking past to see Shem were all invited to our meeting.

An old man came past, bent double, sat down beside us and conveyed to Joseph that he would like prayer for a very bad back and right down one leg. I talked to him about Jesus our Lord and how He came to heal and deliver. The old man listened very intently. I then laid hands on him and on his back and began to pray. When I was finished I sat down but he sat down, stood up, sat down, stood up, sat down, stood up, shook his leg. He turned to Joseph and said his body was healed; he was going home to tell his family to come to the meeting. He set off straight away and as he was going down the road he kept muttering all the way, "I-I-I-I-I." Joseph and Clement set off laughing.

We all went inside for our supper, after which we went over to another place and it was packed. I was praying the Holy Spirit would lead them to our Lord, speaking through me. Clement led the singing, then it was my turn, John 3 verses 3 and 5 - preaching "salvation, baptism of the Holy Spirit, baptism in water." Joseph made the appeal and everyone came forward, then prayers for the sick. We worked until midnight again.

On waking next morning the compound was still full, so we set off with another meeting, prayers for the sick. When we finished, Joseph was champing at the bit again to move on so we gathered our things together and set off again amid cheers and goodbyes. Some came running to ask if we could stop on our way to pray for the sick, much to Joseph's disagreement, but Clement pushed it, "We must go and help." So we redirected our steps to another village to the sick.

Father was telling us to build up the faith so they will reach out to Him and receive. I set off with testimony of the people healed at Shem's, but the Holy Spirit was showing me it was demonic, so I told the story of the man with the legion of spirits, when Jesus commanded them out they went into a herd of pigs. The lady who was sick came and knelt before me confessing and confessing and weeping as to what she had done. Clement was telling me all she was saying so I said for her to repent before our Lord, so she did. Then I took the authority over the unclean spirit. The woman got up and went outside and was very sick. When she came back in I prayed over her for the Holy Spirit to fill the temple. She then testified to all who had gathered that every unclean spirit had gone.

At this point, a man stepped out and pleaded with us to go to his wife who was dying - very, very sick. Our Lord showed me to tell the story of the centurion, so I told him that he must have faith like the centurion and that we would pray for his wife and she would be healed. He knelt down and I laid hands on him and we all prayed for the healing of his wife. We left and walked back to where we would get our truck.

We sat by the roadside till the truck came along. We piled on and we were going to base. When we got off the truck I did not feel good and struggled to get home. Shem's place was the worst place I had ever been for the sickness. The children had matter seeping out of their eyes and noses and were in a terrible mess. My heart went out to these children and now back at base, I had the symptoms. My head was pounding and my body was wracked with the pain. I was burning up. I went to rest but lay all night in agony praying to my Lord.

The next day the pain was worse more intense going through my body. Joseph and Karen his wife came to pray for me. I told them I was not sick, this was intercession for the sickness of the land. I had nothing to eat or drink, lay all day, no change, just praying to my Lord. The pain was so bad that by nighttime Joseph decided to take me to hospital, but I still tried to get him to understand it is the intercession

He waited another day, no change. The pain and pressure were unbearable, Joseph was now, very worried. He would not leave me and made the decision I must go to the hospital. The doctor said, "Malaria," and gave me seven pills, which put me out completely. I slept all night and wakened feeling much better, no harm and no pain, "O thank you Lord."

Kenneth had slept at the bottom of my bed all night. I could drink now too, I could not drink properly, just sip. I still continued in the intercession all night, praying for the things Father is showing me. The next day I was feeling much better, the pain had gone completely. Joseph and Kenneth decided I could go home. By the time I was checked out the dispensary was closed so I could not get my pills and had to go without them. We were not able to get the pills as it was Easter Sunday and Monday was a holiday, so I had to wait until Tuesday.

By evening, the medicine had completely worn off and the pain and pressure back. I suffered all Sunday night and all Monday. Gabriel, Joseph's brother, came with Beldine, his wife, and family. Through the day it was not too bad, I could bear it, but night was just terrible. My strength was getting weak, I had to abandon myself to my Lord. I still could not eat. Kenneth gave me my pills, but all the time Father was telling me, "It is not finished."

I knew this was the sickness of Africa. Kenneth returned with my pills. The pain was intense; my body was burning up, starting to vomit, and diarrhoea all day - no change. I tried to eat for their sakes; Joseph was really worried. My nose started to bleed, I was passing out, everything was going black, I must keep awake, giving it to my Lord. Gabriel got me to the bed, the pressure lifted and I slept. I had a good sleep - thank You Father.

I got up to talk about Jesus my Lord but Gabriel came in the afternoon. We drank a little but by suppertime I was in intercession again; coming against the sickness of Africa. Praising and praying, I had another nosebleed, the pills were doing no good, I was just interceding, no change. Friday came, I prayed all day, another nosebleed, went to bed, the pressure lifted; I kept praising, thanking my Lord. I fell asleep, woke midnight but quite comfortable so I just prayed all night.

The next day, Joseph and Gabriel decided I must go back to the hospital; they said it was too big for them to handle, they must get help. I told them that when we got to the hospital they would find nothing; for this was our Lord, it was not my sickness. I packed my bag and, with one either side of me, we headed down the hill for the matutu to the hospital. Only my Lord got me down the road, the main road; I thanked Him and sang all the way. We got on the bus; what a journey, "Help me Lord, strengthen me Lord."

We had to change buses so I had to sit down by the road. I sat until the bus came and gave my strength back to the Lord. The bus came, I could not see for pain, my body was very weak, "Help me Father, I must stay awake, I must continue to pray. My mind is on You Lord, I must pray."

We arrived at the hospital and the place was full. Joseph wanted me to see the doctor right away. "No, I must wait my turn."

"No!" Joseph said, "We must go straight to the doctor."

I still had the symptoms of malaria, but my Lord confirmed to me it is not my body suffering but was intercession for Africa. My temperature was taken, guess what? It was normal. Joseph would not take me home. He insisted I stay, that the doctor must care for me. I was sent to the ward. My heart was tested and it was strong. They tested my blood pressure; it was normal. They took a sample of blood; clear. I lay and waited - no change. I looked to my Lord. I was left alone, no medicine, no medication, nothing. I lay and waited, still unable to eat. As the pills were brought round for the other patients, I was looked at again. They decided to give me something for the fever burning up my body. Some liquid was dropped on my tongue, so many drops. The light was put out and I lay and prayed.

The babies were crying in the wards. I prayed for someone crying out for help. It was very late but the nurse and the lady doctor came back to look at me. Again, by now, sweat was pouring from my body. She asked me all my details again, including details of prescription I got three days later. I was sure Beldine had put them in my bag but I could not find them. She gave orders for pills to be given and I received them. It was all quiet again, I was still burning up, pouring with sweat but still in pain.

It was very late when the nurse came back to check. She was very concerned at my condition. She stripped me, took the blankets down and just covered me with sheets. She kept checking my body did not get cold, but kept at an even temperature. There was still no change but, as things seemed fair, she left me again. Dawn came at last. My thirst was terrible, if only I could have a drink. I struggled for water. After a while, I felt sick, felt I must make it to the bathroom. I got up, very unsteady, but made it, crumpling in a heap, but thank You Lord, I made it. I sicked up yellow mucus and was unable to move.

There was lady in the next bed, whose daughter was sleeping with her, so she came to help me. She helped me back to bed. It was after five now. They came to take temperatures and my condition was still the same. My body was still burning up, but not bad. I just lay.

Mid morning, it was the doctor's round; he was very good with me. At last the pain and pressure were subsiding. He put me on a drip, my body was so weak. He and the sisters were in and out all day and watching all the night. There was still no sleep for pain in my body. The sister came to offer me tea. I struggled but no food.

As the day went into night, the doctor was still checking and giving me little words of encouragement and telling me it would be all right. The nurse was the same, telling me I would be all right.

"I will, I know I will!" I thanked them and praised my Lord and I was telling them about Jesus. I still had no sleep, but things were getting better. The sister took the drip away and I was served breakfast, prepared by the sisters. "O Father!" There was beautiful real coffee with plenty of boiled milk to go with it, a boiled egg and bread and butter and jam. O, it was so good.

I really enjoyed my breakfast. I was a lot stronger and could sit up. The doctors came round and were so pleased with me, shaking my hand and talking about England. It was good to be alive. He popped in several times. I took five pills three times a day. The visitors would all come in to have a word with me. With the ones who spoke English I could have really good conversations and we talked about work, being a preacher of the gospel and they would say, "God is really with you."

By night, I had slept a little but I was wide-awake, praying all night. I was praying for the victory over the spirit of sickness over Africa. I was getting stronger; I could wash myself now and could wash thoroughly. There was a shower and having the use of this made me feel so clean, washing off the sweat was like washing off all the sickness. Day by day I was able to concentrate on the visitors coming to talk with me.

The lady in the next bed was coughing a lot and told me she was bringing up blood. I laid hands on her and prayed. After the doctor had been round she could go home.

Another lady came in who had been in hospital for months; she had malaria and was so weak. I prayed for her and laid hands on. There was no change, but I continued to pray in the secret place.

Tuesday went and at night I prayed against the spirit of death and, as I prayed, Father gave me a vision of the bodies wrapped in the grave clothes, but as I intensify the praying the grave clothes were cut off from the bodies and He raised them up and they lived.

Morning dawned again and I was then able to walk about, going outside, so I was asking my friend in the next bed to come with me and, praise the Lord, she did. She also seemed stronger, "Thank You Father" - there was answered prayer.

The hospital was Catholic, enclosed with high fences against predators, human as well as animals. Life was taken so lightly, man murdered man for very little. A simple argument could end up in death, so my friend told me, and that was why everyone was so suspicious of everyone else. We walked right round the compound, which was really a mini village. All the staff lived on the compound so one whole area was given over for staff and accommodation. The houses were quite nice looking, reasonably clean and newly built. It must have been such a blessing to have all the mains electricity, water, showers and toilets, but I suppose, when one lives in the bush, what one has never had, one will never miss. It was a beautiful area around the hospital, all planted up; the gardens were magnificent with colour, exotic trees and plants. How our Lord's creation is in such variety in every part of His world. We sat outside and watched the activity of all the people. I didn't understand, but I loved to watch people and, after a while in the afternoon, my friend wanted to rest, so I took her back inside. As she lay down I prayed over her again.

Night fell and I could hear all the sounds of Africa; it really was such a privilege to be here and listen and see. After the evening meal, the doctor came to tell me he was on duty and would be just down the corridor. I think he wanted to talk, so I asked Father to keep me awake to share His Gospel with the doctor. Father kept me awake, but intercession that night was poverty and unemployment in the land. My friend was so sound asleep I could talk to my Jesus and read my Bible out loud to break the curses off the land.

I was doing fine when the doctor came in. He opened the door and wanted to know why I did not sleep, so I thought, "Here goes Father."

I shared my work on intercession and shared the gospel with him. It went down like a lead balloon. He changed the subject back to me, he said I was fifty-one years of age but my body was like that of a woman of thirty-five. He said I should go out as much as possible walking, to get my strength back then he left.

"I am so sorry Father, maybe I jumped in too quickly. Please forgive me if I got it wrong." There was such a quality about this man so wanting to help his own people.

The next day I obediently went walking the compound again. In his rounds in the morning the doctor told me that my friend, if she continued to make good progress, could go home that Saturday. Joseph came with a letter from home: "O thank You Father."

I told him I had asked to come home, but the doctor said he wanted me to stay at least another week. Joseph only stayed a little while then went, so things were not so good.

I opened my letter and it was from Keith and Mary. I read my letter. O, Keith had filled it with lots of news about everything back home, but my tears were flowing for myself. You see, I knew my Lord was with me in every step of the prayer line; they were His prayers for His people. He was telling me what to pray next; but the intensity of the pain, the bleeding, the blackouts and the high fever were severe. As long as I was conscious, I could fight, but I was a little worried that the enemy was going to win and take me right out. Joseph was so upset for me and the work had come to an abrupt halt. Then it was the fellowship back home and my bairns; might I never see them again? To block out his tactic of fear I would pray in the Spirit. Right at the beginning of each letter was, "Did I know what an honour our Lord had bestowed on me and how much He loved me?"

I knew that everyone wants to know that our Lord loves them and they are His. I needed to know it too and because Keith had written it in the letter; I had not realised how weak or low I had become, and all at once my strength came back full force. I was not going to die out here. I had not done wrong and my Lord still loved me. "True love casts out all fear" - how I needed that, just someone to tell me I was doing ok, someone who cared. That someone is my Jesus.

I wept and wept. I was so thankful and I knew He was blessing me with such luxury, such lovely food and the rest. It was Jesus who wanted me to rest for another week. He wanted me to have the peace and tranquillity of this place, because the moment I go home, Joseph would have me on the move again, so I was not to spoil the work. O, thank You so much my Lord! The blessings that flooded my soul were so wonderful. I set off again to walk and found the chapel. I went in but no-one was there so I returned to my room. With the peace in my heart, and the knowing His Love, I fell asleep. I slept quite a long time, late, until lights out. "So Father! What will the prayers be tonight?" - but it was over.

I slept all night, wakening up, next morning, so refreshed. I took a shower and felt so good and clean. I waited for the doctor's round to tell him of my sleep, how good I felt and so blessed. He said very little, but was pleased; I could tell. So that day I could walk and walk; new strength, knowing my beloved Lord loves me. "O how I love Him so much."

This relationship with Jesus is my life; I cannot live without Him and I need Him so much every hour of every day. Life was surging back into my soul and my heart was singing through and through me again. My friend was going home tomorrow so I helped her to pack. She was very excited; she had eight children and was so eager to see them. The doctor came in and signed her off, everything quite right. The night staff came on, lights out - what a day! My heart was singing; the joy with the intercession finished, so I turned over and was out and slept like a baby all night.

Such hustle and bustle and rushing here and there, my friend's family came to take her home. I was introduced to her husband, her sisters and her brothers, who all came to take her home. After all the goodbyes off she went.

I could not go out that day; a storm was raging. Outside thunder and lightning were splitting the sky and the rain was pouring down, cold water coming down in sheets, but for me it was heaven on earth. My roommate was gone and I was alone. No one had been brought in yet to take her bed; I could lie back on my pillow. The storm could rage but I was alone with my Lord Jesus. I could talk out loud to Him again, I could pour out my heart, I could pray back every prayer, but out loud. I could tell my Lord Jesus anything and everything. I knew He understood me. I am not afraid for the wrong words in my prayers. He could see in my heart anyway and if I got the words wrong He was not going to get at me for what I have said because He would put it right. I was not afraid to pray in case I prayed for the wrong people or the wrong thing. I was praying to be heard; I was not afraid to pray to my Lord. I didn't want to be heard for the sake of being heard or to show off or to look as if I could pray. No, none of these things mattered; it was enough to be with Jesus and I could tell Him everything. Everybody could call me for doing what was wrong or right, but He would not; He came and I loved Him and could pour my heart out to Him. He heard every word and He loved me back. I was never alone for He would never leave me nor forsake me. He never would fail me but would teach me through all things. Just the touch of His Hand was like the word in Keith's letter. He loved me and my heart was bursting to go on again. My heart was bursting then, to thank Him and cover everyone and everything. I could cry to Him and He could bless me with joy when I was finished.

The storm was over and it was night; you see, when I am with Him, the hours pass so quickly. The doctor came in to see I was not lonely and told me he was on duty again tonight, so he would call back later. I just rested in such peace with my Lord. The doctor came back in. He sat on my bed and studied me awhile. There was just silence between us; I was not sure what was coming; I was praying in the Spirit in my mind. Then he began to tell me; he had monitored me day and night and had not seen anything like me in his life. He had gone to Germany to study medicine and when he had qualified all he wanted to do was come back home to help his own people. So he studied and studied to go further than just a doctor. He wanted to specialise in every field of medicine that he would need to help his people. He told me, "You have had the symptoms of every disease there is in Africa. You suffered the pain, you had every symptom."

He said he had treated me for everything and before he knew, it had changed to something else. He said he had had such difficulty to know what to give me next; what was he treating now? Then he said, "Your recovery is so remarkable."

The tears slowly ran down my face. I told him all about how I knew that Jesus was in with me: "The pain was not my pain but His pain for you and your people in Africa." How, at night, I was praying through all the different things at His bidding. Not what I thought, but what He wanted. I shared my letter from home and the encouragement written in it; how my Lord loved me, and this had been my turn-around. I had been tired, weary and weak, but I had known it was my Lord speaking to me, through my brother in Christ, and my strength had just risen up within me.

He listened then, very intently, but did not want to make the commitment to the Lord. He said he worked with catholic nuns but did not want their denomination either. I was sad, but Father is the One who saves; I just have to go and tell. He stood up and left. I was disturbed because he had the proof, Father, of what You had done. There was no explanation other than that You protected me from everything. I knew Father had reached out to this doctor.

The morning came and it was Sunday. Everyone just did the necessary today so I made my bed and tidied up the room. There was still no one in the other bed. My breakfast came and I had a new friend, Sister Margaret. She could see the grace of our Lord as the nuns tended the sick.

After breakfast I went into prayer. Father, it was a joy and took me all morning. After lunch, the doctor brought in a magazine to read about the hospital. To my joy, I read how they are seeking for the Catholic Order to receive salvation and to be baptised in the Holy Spirit. I was thrilled and excited, reading all about it. The sister came to see me and sat and opened up to tell me how long she had been here. She told me about the place, school and how the primitive African people were and how they still killed over argument - she was so troubled. She left, but "O Father," the information to pray was wonderful.

He led me through everything, praying for the nuns, the doctors, the teachers, the children, for the Catholics to receive their salvation, for the place, the compound and everything. I finished with the lass herself; her heart was aching, she needed encouragement, Lord, just encouragement. I asked the Lord to bless her.

By now the day was well through, but what a day with my Lord again, "Thank You, thank You." I went back to my magazine to read again, just in case I had missed anything for prayer before the night and sleep. I was doing my chores when breakfast came, such blessings; the smell of the fresh coffee is so beautiful. "How great Thou art, dear Lord."

The doctor came in and I asked, "If anyone comes to visit today may I go?"

He was very hesitant to gave his consent, but if they didn't come I was to go on Wednesday, so we agreed. He came back to bring me the paper to read. I went for a walk then packed my bag, but to my disappointment, no one came. "So Father, we are not finished yet."

I contented myself and prayed until nightfall. Today was the first of May and another holiday so many of the staff were off, just those for emergencies on duty. My visitor for that day was Sister Margaret. She came to pour her heart out to me again. She wanted to show me around and talked to me all the time, about the convent and then the chapel and many other things. She showed me then the ark of the Lord and talked as though this was where He stayed permanently. "O my Lord, I am so grieved."

I tried, very carefully, to tell her, in love, of our Lord with each one of us. She did not appear to understand. She had to go back to her duties and I was left very perplexed. I hurried back to my room and took the details back to my Lord. Night fell and a storm raged outside again. I saw a very watery rainbow coming stronger and stronger. "O! Thank You Lord. Your promise to Noah. Lord I thank You; I receive that promise for Sister Margaret and the doctor, and every prayer that has been prayed for this place and the intensity for Africa."

Wednesday came and I could go home. The morning went with prayer and, as I was already partially discharged, the doctor passed me by, but he called to see me. He said I must return for a blood test in a fortnight and wished me good health.

To my joy, Joseph, Beldine and Clement came to take me home without delay, but at last I could go. Beldine took me to the matutu and we travelled home. We arrived and walked up the hill. When we arrived, Gabriel greeted me along with the bairns and Joseph's mama and papa. This day was the third of May and it seemed as though I had been away for a long time. Beldine prepared our evening meal and we all ate together, then we prayed together, giving thanks for everything. Joseph and Clement returned home. We talked about the programme then we retired.

I didn't sleep, my burden for Joseph returned. I prayed; I did not judge, "Father, please have Your way in this whole family. With Gabriel I can see the love for Jesus, I identified with my Lord in him, but with Joseph I do not. Have mercy Father."

I woke early feeling fine. Joseph and Clement came around to discuss the programme. Gabriel wanted everything out in the open - "Praise our Lord. Do it Lord."

They went to discuss and after a while it was decided to hold the first meeting there at Gabriel's that night, so I had time to prepare at home. Father always has given me time to rest, and then the Word. It was late before we got started, but all the family were there. The children sang, it was good; then it was my turn. The Holy Spirit came upon me in power. After I had finished Clement invited people for prayer. Everyone was on their knees; some wanted salvation and the rest wanted healing. Our Lord was there in such power, greater than I had ever experienced and yet I was so weak.

When we had finished, the meal was served and we all ate together. My supper was pork sausages and chips; I could hardly believe it, what a blessing. How they managed to get sausages and chips I don't know, but we laughed and laughed. What a reputation we have for our chips; what a wonderful night of fun and joy, no one wanted to go home. We broke up eventually and we all went to rest.

I woke up very early, got ready, met with Gabriel, had breakfast, then we talked. He was displeased as he was going back to school, Beldine back to work and the children back to their school. Joseph was taking me back to the areas we had been in; yet Gabriel said he would not allow it, this was not of the Spirit. The mother church had been founded here yesterday and we must put things right here first. Clement had gone back to his home to arrange for me to go back there, but my Lord was showing me Gabriel was right. Gabriel opened up and began to tell deep troubles of how things had gone wrong, how the brothers had fallen out and gone their separate ways. As we talked and shared, I realised that all my fears about Joseph, since first meeting him, had been right. I praised Jesus; they were going to be put right. So I said to Gabriel that we must come before God and put everything right; the work could not prosper until everything was put right. A meeting was called for the next day.

"Gabriel is a good man, what a beautiful man of God. He loves You Lord. He wants everything right for Your church." We shared our evening meal and then prayed through everything back and forth, covering all manner of things, past and present; it was great. We worked until late then went to our beds.

I could not sleep, kept bringing back Joseph.

Next morning everyone arrived; Mama, Poppa, Beldine, Gabriel, Kenneth, Joseph and his wife. It did not start very well. The men were in a heated discussion, so I just went into tongues - without unity the work would not prosper. By and by, either Kenneth or Gabriel would tell me what was happening, what was being said, so I could keep up with the discussion. All my fears were then confirmed and one of the main reasons why had come. Joseph then told of a deal he had had and the Holy Spirit showed me the meaning. The family were quite taken aback as the truth was being revealed. The Holy Spirit gave me Scriptures, of Ahab who violated the Temple of the Lord and Hezekiah who consecrated the work again. A lot of repentance and redirection came through the whole family, weeping, repentance and seeking God's forgiveness. The church had been birthed afresh, clean, whole, and the family of brothers, wives and parents were reunited once more with our Lord and each other. The meeting was brought to a close in joy and peace.

We continued to talk about our Lord all the rest of the day and on into the night. We all ate together and then went to rest. I slept like a baby that night; all was well.

On Sunday Joseph came around and it was discussed, then decided, to hold a service where the church was started many years ago before everything went wrong. We all got ready; I put on my yellow dress and court shoes, and while we walked to the church I picked wild flowers. I laid them on the altar table and my thoughts were of the bride coming to the church. It was a beautiful service. I spoke twice, but not the sermon, Joseph did that; my work was finished. I knew my work was finished; I had such an affinity with Gabriel, so I was praying for Gabriel's replacement to be there at the school, so Gabriel could come home to his wife and family. We talked and shared until later then we retired. I was praising and thanking my Lord for so many things.

The next day, it was goodbye. The bairns and Beldine were going back to work and school, and Gabriel going back to his school. The goodbyes were said and everyone left. Even Kenneth went with Joseph, so I was alone and spent the day with my Lord.

In the late afternoon, George returned with a letter for me from Christine. "Praise my Lord." She was moving with my Lord and was growing. She was sharing Scriptures. Father had given her for me Isaiah 61, Psalm 23 and Isaiah 60, in that order. Also, a word; I wrote it out as I could not get all the words, "Rosalind My daughter, My child in whom I am well pleased. Fear not, for I am with you; I will never leave you nor forsake you. No evil shall befall you, for you have My angels, and the host, guarding you in your work, your servanthood for Me, your Lord. Do not worry, you will never go hungry, you will be fed with manna from Heaven. For I love you in the Spirit, for I will lead you into all truth.

I see your deeds for the people whom I love. Show them My love in the ways I showed it while I was on the earth. Imagine My body walking beside you; reach out and grasp My hand and it will always be there. I love you, My precious one. Take heart, arise and shine for your light has come and the Glory of the Lord is risen upon you. Meditate more upon My love for you, receive more of My love for you My child, My daughter, for the mouth of the Lord has spoken."

"O my Lord, thank You. I do love You so much."

Kenneth arrived home and began supper and we talked until 9.30 then we went to rest. "O Father, what a wonderful day." Because I was finished, it was preparation to get me back to Bridget. I went to rest and my mind was working overtime with everything, but I dropped off eventually.

The next day, I was up, ready, washed, did my washing, wrote my letters and brought my diary up to date. I spent more of my day in prayer. Kenneth came home and made chapattis for tea and we sat and talked. He was going to come with me to Nakuru and stay at the Bible College for one night, then travel back home the next day. Joseph popped in with a present from Mama Knight and all her love. I was packing that day. I was so excited to be on the move again. Once I knew I was finished, I couldn't wait to be on my way. Kenneth came and we had sausages and chips as a going away treat. This was to be our last meal together. "Father, bless this young lad so much, please. He has been more than a son to me. He has looked after me, laid his life on the line for me and protected me at every turn."

Joseph and his wife arrived; then Beldine, Julie and Eric and grandma and grandpa. We talked and shared. The whole family had loved me so much, Father. Goodbyes were so difficult and everyone wanted me to come back. The chips and sausage did not go far so we had jam and bread. Everyone said his or her piece. How they thanked me for coming and talked about the work with Joseph. Joseph prayed; then it was my turn. It was so difficult, but the Holy Spirit helped me and I said it was Joseph's father who wanted help, and the family his church. After I had finished speaking, I went round and prayed over everyone. We parted till dawn. "I cannot sleep tonight Father, for the excitement. I am going home." I prayed back every detail, for Joseph and his family, Gabriel and his family, and every pastor I have met; for the church of Jesus Christ to rise in Kenya and proclaim Jesus as Lord.

We were all ready to move off. "Bless this place Father. Bless everyone who comes in and goes out. Their basket shall be full."

Kenneth and I set off down the track for the last time. We reached the road for the bus. We had to travel to Kisumu to get the bus to Nakuru. Joseph came to us in Kisumu to say goodbye and waited with us until the bus came. "This is it Lord! Bless this man who just meets with You, loves You and surrenders to You."

We travelled down just about in silence. We arrived at Nakuru and got off. Then it was mid day, the four hour journey. I was not sure what to do but, because it was only mid day, we both decided that if we travelled on the matutu down to Grace Bible College, we could be home before Bridget had set off and save her the journey. So we got the matutu. Right enough we arrived at the road end at half past two. We set off walking heading for the school. At the road end we met Chris and another one of the new boys; hugs and kisses all round. They were so pleased to see me and greeted Kenneth with so much love too.

We set off up the road with the two boys carrying my bag. Someone had seen us coming so now we met Bridget and seven of the other lads - o the chatter. Bridget went and brought something for Kenneth to eat. He said his basket was empty so she returned with maize and beans and heated it up for us. The lads took Kenneth away to show him around. "O Father! It was so nice to be back." We talked and talked.

The boys were so lovely with Kenneth. He is well Lord and is accepted so well. The boys went to their sleep and they gave him supper. Bridget and I talked and shared all the happenings of the missions, all about Joseph and the whole family, about the hospital, and the intercession, which seemed such a long time ago. The doctor had given me a paper declaring all the treatments I had had, but only the symptoms, nothing had touched my body. We talked until we both just needed to go to bed.

In the morning, I was up with the larks, washed, dressed and went out to the library for my quiet time. "O my Lord! Thank You for such peace." I had nothing to say, I was just so thankful to be alone with my Lord.

At eight o'clock we gathered together, in the college, for our devotions, praising our Lord. The reading was Isaiah 58. Kenneth wanted plants to take back to put in Gabriel's garden. Bridget and I continued to share with the boys after lunch.

The time came for Kenneth to go for his bus. We all set him to his bus and we said our goodbyes. I thanked him for everything and gave him my Bible and then he was going off. I might never see him again, but there will be great rejoicing in heaven when we meet up again. We wept, both of us: the young and the old. He had been my shadow for three months. He had done his utmost in everything he did to take in my every whim even to the chips and the sausage.

One of the boys set me back to our little house. Bridget shared lots of things for the college while I had been away so we had to pray about them all. We went into prayer and continued until very late then went to bed. I mulled over everything, "Three months, Father." It was for every pastor in Sare-Awendo. The Father was really blessing His church, His bride; that's what I felt, when we held our service in the mother church; birthing in the bride and taking down every stronghold of sickness in Kenya; the spirit of the Mau-Mau. So lifting the curse of the blood from England and Kenya. "Father, when You go to work, You go to work. For me, Lord, all the wonder of the people I have met."

The next day, Bridget and I worked together to clean the house. We had our coffee and the boys came to see us and we talked till lunchtime. Bridget rested so I decided to take myself off for a walk. I walked and walked, talking to my Lord all the time. Every place had its own beauty. It was a hard land, very barren, dusty and dirty and yet one could get to like it. I kept going over and over everything and all the people I had met. I returned and Bridget made tea and the boys came round - such sweet fellowship.

We had a lie-in the next day, which was Sunday. We had borrowed eggs for breakfast and then went to church with the boys. We were going to James Park Church and we were asked to sing. We sang and sang. We then found a ladies' meeting which turned into a praise time and we just praised and sang. "Thank You, Lord."

Afterwards, Chris took us to his home where he was looking after a young brother whose mother had died when he was four months old. Chris was one of the eight boys at the college and was taking his exams for the ministry and so wanted to be ordained. Chris asked for prayer. I prayed covering most of what he had shared, then I prayed for the boy who had suffered with his eyes. I asked for healing, we hugged each other and it was time to go.

Now I was back at the Bible college, and basically not out on the mission any more, I believed Father was telling me to continue to pray for the whole of the land of the Sare-Awendo district, all the places I had been and all the pastors I had met. I prayed for the James Park's Ministry, for the church in Nakuru. Then the teaching of the boys: John Chont (teacher), Ronald, (the principal), "Change them all Lord, and build Your church. Touch everyone in this boys' college with the anointing of the Holy Spirit. Empower them as You empowered Your disciples. Precious Jesus, bring them into life-changing experiences and let them learn by being doers of the Word, just as You have taught me, Holy Spirit, and by the blessing You have given me. Let Bridget, although she teaches English, be the sounding board in the slightest thing as the boys just grow and hunger after You, so that each individual bit that she can see or realise, she will be able to share and talk with them and give them growth, Lord."

If you remember, Bridget had asked me to catalogue the books in the library the last time I stayed, while waiting for my letter from Joseph. I decided to continue where I had left off putting the books in order, with the headings and locations of the books and what they were about, so that the lads would not need to go through all the shelves to find what they were looking for. They would only need to go through the books about the subject they were studying. Wonderful really; I who could not spell or read on leaving school, Father would put me in charge of a job such as this one, but so exciting, because when subjects or titles leapt out at me I could read them, pray through them and learn from them there with my Jesus. What a mighty God we serve. I also knew He was blessing me in rest after our mission.

I picked up a book of the absolute surrender. As I read it, my God was speaking so much applying to the prophesies Father gave Christine for me even to the Scripture, so I got down on my knees and absolutely surrendered. I had done it before, but could I do it again? Yes, for we are changing and changing so our levels of perception change all the time. "Our intimacy is so beautiful, so take away, Lord, anything that is of the world: I desire only You and Your will."

So because of the books, another growth and learning. Father was teaching me. I spoke out and confessed when the things I read applied to what I was doing, or to me. This book, which I am writing, testifies to what I have read and applied to myself. That night, Father showed me 1 Peter and 2 Peter; how Peter was changed. I studied and meditated on my beloved Jesus, His lifestyle, how He preached and how He would do things while He was here on earth; the Word Christine gave me, only my Lord could bring to pass, nothing I did. "Finish what You have begun Father. So change me Lord, as You changed Peter."

I picked up Colin Urquart's book "When the Spirit comes." I had read it many times, many of Colin Urquart's books but Father wanted to show me something new. I read and read. My fellowship was so with my Father and Jesus and the Holy Spirit. The Holy Spirit is my teacher, "Now, come up higher, walk with Me, be with Me, love Me, receive more of Me." Again, confirming Christine's scriptures. My whole being was being renewed. "Come to Me."

I was doing my work in the library, but struggling. I left it and set off walking again praying back and calling out all He was revealing. "Tell me Lord. Show me."

After a couple of hours, I sat down by the wayside but I had my peace back. "Praise You Lord. I don't know what You have done, but I am free, so much freer."

I set off to come back home again. As He sent me ten pounds in a letter, I used it for the fare back to Nairobi. Even there again, the very detail; I had given everything to Joseph and so to come back, was travelling with nothing, yet here was the money to get me back to Nairobi. "Thank You Father for Your provision."

Bridget had to go to Nakuru, so she headed off and took the money to change it. I cleaned up and did my washing then I could come back in to my Lord. After yesterday's speaking, in a while, I was on my knees with my shoes off weeping in brokenness, confessing many things: the joy in His presence, and He was teaching me to receive the oneness with Him. "Be holy as I am holy. The oneness - as Father and Jesus are one, Jesus and I can be one."

Again, I finished and tried to do my chores. Bridget returned, we shared and had our coffee together. I went back to the library, to my book work. I set to, then picked up a book at the prompting of the Holy Spirit. The book was called, "This is the Will of God" by John H. G. Lake. It was all about being in the Holy Spirit. "As I am holy": I truly am astonished, my expectation in reaching the book and the pointedness of where my Lord was leading. I knew as I read this book that my Lord was really going to read with me and I repented and by faith myself received salvation and received Christian prophecies and absolute surrender in carrying out things in detail. Father was showing me that day 1990 there in Africa, I must die to self, I knew that, I knew that I no longer lived but that Christ lived in me. "I received it in faith Lord, that You and I were one; that through the fullness of the Holy Spirit, my fellowship was now with You and with You alone Father; with You Jesus through the Holy Spirit. I will only do what Father tells me, I must obey the awesomeness. The fear of God is the beginning of wisdom. I must obey; I must not grieve the Holy Spirit. Dear Lord help me! I desire to obey."

I shared with Bridget all Father had said and done, and Christine's letter, the Scriptures, how Father was affirming and affirming and showing me. I continued my work and bookkeeping. Around lunchtime I was disturbed so I stopped and just waited in prayer, praying in the Spirit. I lost an hour; then I was free. John came that day and brought me a letter from home, Josephine writing. I was so upset and weepy; it would not be long before I can go home. "Forgive me Father; just to read and read."

It was Sunday and we were to go to John Park's for lunch, so a lazy day. We got ready and had a long way to walk. Bridget first rang the Erero family to ask if we could come and stay the next Saturday. Malek answered the phone, everything was ok; we could stay until Tuesday night for my flight back. "Thank You Father!" We carried on to Park's for lunch. We had a wonderful time. Bridget got on to the electric piano and we sang and sang. Our Lord inhabited the praises of his people. Mr and Mrs. Park gave me a present of a brooch made from the feathers of the flamingos which were on Lake Victoria, for that was to be our next mission. Kenneth had been telling me we had to be so careful where we walked as you could step on to a crocodile and not know he was there till you stepped on him, the camouflage was so good - but it was not to be. Mr. Park decided to drive us home to Grace College as it was late. "O Father, such wonderful people, and this family of God just gets bigger and bigger." People we may never see again but what rejoicing when we all get to Heaven.

The next day, I must work hard; my time here is passing quickly and I am not finished in the library. I had to push on. Even this was important because Father had given me so much to read and everything He has wanted me to see was right there in the library.

Bridget brought a letter from Joseph and one from Kenneth. Joseph's letter was telling me that the man whose wife was dying met him at the door when he got home and was completely healed. "What a mighty God!" he said. The boys wanted us to have supper with them tonight as a goodbye, so we went to the fellowship - and the fun and the laughter and the tears. This is what God intended it to be like: such love. My last days at Grace College I worked very hard to finish all the write-ups and putting the books all in the right order. It was very late and dark outside but I had finished. "What a privilege Father and what I have learnt by being here."

I went over for supper and packed up that night as it was an early start next morning to catch the matutu for the last time. My heart was fit to burst. The boys came to set us on the matutu and after many goodbyes, hugs and kisses we were off. I was going through all things as we travelled one last time, making sure I had placed all things in Father's hands. We arrived at Nairobi. We walked to Kenya airport to confirm my booking. The office was closed, so we headed to the home of the Ereros, Madrakos. Everyone was pleased to see us. Bridget was concerned about my ticket, so her boyfriend drove us to another office. Praise our Lord! It was open and all is well. My ticket was there but had no name on it; I guess it was in case I was staying on, so all was well. The name was put on the ticket and we went to visit an animal park, where sick animals were brought, tended, put right and then released back into the wilderness. It was incredible really, but I saw nothing, not one wild animal while on my journeys. They took me to the snake park and we saw all the snakes of the districts I had just come back from. "Father, I was so thankful I never saw any of these while I was there, or that I did not see the park before I went." I am such a coward; if I saw an adder on the hill at home, I would run from it. We travelled back to Madrakos and Mr. Erero had come home. I thanked him quietly and I think he was generally quite pleased to see me. We talked and talked. The whole family wanted to know where I had been and what had happened, so I related my story, with intercession and all: I don't think they understood a lot of the intercession, but this is my life, so I cannot miss it off.

Two days to go and I was counting the hours, the minutes. "Father, give me something to do. Help! The days seem as long as the mission." Anne, next door, asked me in and so I witnessed to her - my whole trip. She and her family listened with baited breath, prompting me with questions. How wonderful! It took all day. By the time I had finished it was suppertime. "Thank You, thank You Lord." I went back in for supper. After supper, I started again with the whole family prompting me with questions - good questions too, Lord. They really wanted to know all about my trip and what I had been doing. It was time for rest. "One day left, o Father."

The family were all up early going off to work, so I stayed in my room, going through the prayer line for this family and the neighbour's family. I continued until lunchtime, remembering the hospital, the doctors, nurses and the thoughts of salvation for all of them; Gabriel and his coming home to his wife and family. Feeling I had remembered everyone I came out. Bridget was there with Malek so I helped her to clean through and then sat with Malek. We shared and took the afternoon easy. Bridget started to prepare the evening meal and, one by one, everyone came back in, telling each other about the day. I had my bath early and one by one everyone got ready for the evening meal. Mr Erero asked if we could bless the meal. "Wow Father! What a turn around." The first time ever, I think, but how beautiful, so we said prayers before we ate. The meal lasted a long time, not much time for chatting afterwards; but o, the day was over and tomorrow, tomorrow I could return.

I could not sleep because I would be going to the airport tomorrow morning. I decided to pray through the night. I went through but fell asleep. Next morning quite early Bridget and Harris would take me to the airport, but when I came out with my bags and everything, nobody had gone so it was goodbyes all around: one by one, the boys and the sister. I got a beautiful photograph of the family; then Mr. Erero. I thanked him so much for welcoming me into his home, thanking him for his good wishes toward me. We shook hands, then he left. Wonderful really, that they cared so much and wanted to wish me goodbye. Then it was time for us all; goodbye Madrakos and away we went. "Bridget, bless her for being there for me Father. Like Kenneth she had been on the ball every time and, like Margaret, she just knew what to do. O Father, I am so pleased to be going home." We said our goodbyes and Bridget and Harris were gone.

The flight number was called and we went to our boarding gate. Before long we were allowed through and into the plane. I had written to Margaret to let her know my returning date, so I prayed to precious Jesus that all be well. I cannot remember the flight but there were no delays and no trouble. We touched down at Heathrow Airport, England. It was so exciting to be going away, but it was wonderful to come home. I came down the gangplank after getting my bags when I could hear my name being called. This was Jim Hurst waiting for me. Margaret was going away, so she had contacted Roly who contacted Jim. Jim had driven right down from Duns in Scotland to meet me. "Father, thank You so much for this man." I hugged him and we went out of the airport. After we passed the M25 junction, I took over and drove all the way home while Jim slept.

# CHAPTER 12

# Another trip to London and the marriage of Josephine

*I*t was five at night when we arrived home. Edward was not home, nor Josephine nor David, so we sat in the car until someone came. Jim, having had a good sleep, said he would just get on his way for he had another two hours to get home. O, it was so wonderful to be home.

Edward came first and was telling me all about everything until the others came. I don't think I was ever so late in going to bed, my own bed; I praised my Lord.

By Sunday I was rested up and it was wonderful to see everyone again and sharing with them. Peter brought Peggy; Tony, Eddy and Helen came too, and it was back into routine: people were coming through the week for ministry, and the hours of prayer on Sunday.

I think the next part of my pathway was when Marion came one day to visit me with a friend. Now this friend was like Peggy and it was always a divine appointment. Father had reason for us to be together; so we had coffee and shared and then waited to see what was on Father's heart. We went back and forth until well into the afternoon. When we finished, Marion said that she and her husband Tommy were going down to Bournemouth the next week and why didn't I go with them? I said I would pray about it for I never went anywhere unless Father wants me to go.

Well, I got the 'all clear' and the following week I travelled over to Crook to Marion and Tommy's, at something like two in the morning and then we all travelled together down to 'Daybreak' guesthouse belonging to Anne and Neil. We arrived in time for breakfast and I knew this would be the beginning of many trips. I was introduced to Anne and Neil and everything was fine. So, "Why was I here, Lord?"

It usually takes a day or two to find my bearings and then be interceding for God's purpose. We would be going to a meeting at a place called 'Sri Lanka', another guesthouse but much bigger, more like a hotel, perfect and preferably for Christian work, seminars and such. We were going with Anne to the seminar, which was on that week. There was one gentleman speaking in the morning and another in the evening. The gentleman in the morning was excellent. The teaching was, "What the Spirit is saying to the churches. Revelation." He was extremely good and, "What is the Spirit saying to the churches?" so this seemed to be my opening to be in intercession for the churches. It was relevant; he could have been speaking about our church today. It finished at lunchtime.

We were away after lunch, we sat and talked and shared, how Marion had met Anne and Neil and how Anne had gone up to Marion's to stay; good fellowship. Then I was asked about my walk with my Lord, so I was able to give testimony. We broke up for the afternoon. Marion went for a rest. I went down to the pier, along which you could walk for miles. It was wonderful, right next to the sea. I love the sea, with its clean beautiful smell, plus I can pray my heart out as I walk.

I came back in time for dinner, beautiful homemade meals. Anne was an excellent cook. Neil was a tall fellow and gifted in acting. It was a bit like 'Fawlty Towers.' In the dining room, he could imitate anybody and consequently put people at their ease; new people coming in or people hurting or troubled; they had such ministry together. They dovetailed in to one another as they worked together. The main gift I saw was the gift of hospitality and the love, which flowed from both of them as they dealt, or worked, with others.

After dinner we were all ready to go back at night to our conference. It was the other gentleman speaking that night and he sang too, a beautiful singer; so our meeting began. Those meetings were always well attended. Well, from the moment that guy stood up, something was wrong, Lord, so I was straight into prayer. I prayed all the way through, not the content of what was said, not the singing, but the man himself. I just kept on in prayer.

When the meeting was over we travelled home. We were not very talkative, so I very gently approached the subject of the man. To my joy, Marion had picked it up too. "O Father, here we go."

We gathered together with the other guests for our hot chocolate; the last drink of the day, and then we went to our bedroom to work together for the guy. Anne came with us; Neil and Peggy went to bed. Marion, Anne and I started working through. We worked through the night until we had a breakthrough.

We went to our meeting the next morning. The speaker was brilliant. I prayed back on my walk in the afternoon, then went back to the meeting at night. There was a change, but more work was still needed, so I proceeded to continue in prayer through the meeting. We came home and went into prayer together again, with more of what we had both gleaned at the meeting - splendid.

This continued for four nights. By the fifth night it went into praise and there was a tremendous breakthrough - the last night. The praise was electric and the Holy Spirit was in complete control. What a night! What a breakthrough! What was so awesome was that the people began to respond and the young man was totally set free - released, to relate to, and set trust in his Lord Jesus. "O Father! What a privilege." We did not have to say a thing; our Lord did it all. "Humble yourself before our Lord and He will do it."

I used to want to tell people but, to my surprise, no-one understood about intercession and the more rebuffs I got, the more heartache I got so I learned to say nothing. It was closer and closer in with Jesus, trusting Him emphatically, implicitly. The more humbled you become, you know it is nothing you can do, only our Lord, but "All thing are possible to him who believes" (Mark 9:23). "Trust and obey, for there's no other way to be happy in Jesus but to trust and obey" (from a hymn).

Our week was over and it was time to come home, but many more such weeks followed.

One time it was the SDHS conference - Society for Distribution of the Hebrew Scriptures. Now this was a group of people given over entirely to printing diglot Bible sets (Old and New Testaments) in Hebrew and one of many other languages, and taking them out free to Jewish people. The late Joseph Yoelson-Taffen, the founder, was the man chosen by our Lord to do the work; he obeyed and now has representatives all over the world where the Bibles are given free. It was at one of these meetings that I went down to Anne and Neil's. The reports were coming in from every corner of the globe. At that time, the General Secretary, Mr Eric Browning, was telling us of Holland joining the SDHS organisation in mission. One could go on and on. We were praying about it on returning home, and Peter, Peggy and I were led to go to a wonderful joint conference in Holland, and again we heard of the contacts all over the world. One, Hillel Habibi from France, was extremely interesting, telling us that there were thousands of Jewish people in France.

Now, what came out of this, my going down to Anne and Neil's, was Anne's desire for prayer and to be an intercessor - which I might add, she was. She wept a lot, but did not know why. So finding out about the intercession was wonderful for her.

After going down there for three or four years, they would come up to me every year and we would keep in touch with each other and keep on in the prayer line with books and videos. One of these times there was a book Anne had read called, 'Earthquake in the City' by Clifford Denton and Paul Slennett. Anne was a very intelligent lady, very clever and could read through a book in double quick time. She read this book and thought I should have it.

I found myself praying through this book line by line; so much information. When I had finished, as I say, reading and praying line by line, I wrote letters to Tony Blair, sent a book and wrote down what I thought Father was saying. I also wrote to our Queen, sent her a book and, again, the letter. Last but not least, I sent the book and my letter to the Very Revd. George Carey.

I phoned a sister in Christ Jesus who was very high up in the highest circles and asked if she could give me a phone number of someone in London who might listen. She did, and I phoned the man and said who I was, which would mean nothing really; but I was very concerned about this book and was anyone doing anything about it?

He said, "Yes," he was calling a prayer meeting of a hundred people to Westminster Chapel to pray and seek God's face, but he could not invite me, as it was all organised etc.

"O," I said, "That's alright, I don't want to come, I just want something done and because you have everything in hand, I'm quite satisfied. Thank you so much - bye, bye."

About a week or a fortnight later, an invitation came for me to go to the prayer meeting in London. I prayed about it and talked myself out of it really, that I did not need to be there. I could pray and back the meeting at home. This was all in the November. Josephine came home one night from work at Otterburn Mill; the sale was on and she said, "Mam, try this on and if it fits, David and I will go halves for you for Christmas."

When I opened it out, it was a beautiful cardigan jacket, but on the left hand side the Prince of Wales emblem was embroidered. I knew in a minute Father wanted me to go. As you can guess, it fitted and you could buy the jumper to match, which I picked out from another colour of the cardigan. So, I bought the jumper and also a skirt to match in the sales - I had my outfit.

I praised my Lord and then contacted a lady called Tania. She came and stayed with me on a regular basis every year. She was an opera singer from Bulgaria but lived in London. She was thrilled that I would go and stay with her, so it was all arranged.

I set off by bus again and Tania met me at the station in London and we walked, or got the bus, to where we wanted to be. London is one of the most wonderful places. Because I was earlier than I needed to be, Tania took me by bus to where I should be and showed me Westminster Cathedral, the Methodist building, Houses of Parliament and where the Archbishop of Canterbury lives. "So, Father, what an inheritance it is that You have given us, the British people - so wonderful."

After we had walked and walked, she showed me where to catch my bus back to her part of London and we got all the buses into perspective and then out again at the other end and we walked home.

Well, my day came; I was so honoured to be going and, dressed in my new outfit, I arrived and went in. All directions were upstairs, so we went. I came back down; the toilets and café were downstairs, wonderful cafeteria really and opposite was the chapel. I went in for prayer, putting the whole day in Father's hands and went back upstairs. We had to sign in and were given a pack; I read it but was more interested in the people coming. For myself, I took a seat on the back wall. A minister from Wales was on my left and a guy from Jersey on my right. People were coming in and it was filling up. There was a screen up and it was being taped, so big stuff. The meeting began and, to my horror, we spent the whole morning with statistics, sheet after sheet going up on screen. Father, I thought we had come to pray.

Then, "Praise God," Clifford Hill stood up and he began to speak about our Lord and what he believed Father was saying. I just burst. I was sobbing in the Spirit and was having such a job trying to keep quiet because I was usually asked to leave, as they considered that I was thus far a silly and emotional woman, disrupting the meeting. But to my joy, the Welsh Minister knew it was the Holy Spirit and not me. "Wow Father! this is a turn up for the books."

Mr. Hill continued and away I would go again with the tears and the weeping. I was confirming through the Holy Spirit everything this man was saying. "O my Lord!"

At half past twelve, they would break for lunch. "Good gracious Father, we had just started, who wants to eat when you are in the presence of Almighty God?" I was dumbfounded.

It was like a stampede to the cafeteria for the queue. "O Lord, what a sham! This is the crème de la crème of the men and women for You Father. O my Lord, forgive me for my judging, but do they know You, Lord? Do they know Who they are talking to and what about?"

I hung my head in shame. "Precious Jesus come in and pour out a mighty revival and reveal Yourself, please!"

I descended the stairs but went into the chapel. "Dear Lord, we need a rocket to wake us up."

The Word says, "You search the Scriptures ... but you are not willing to come to Me," John 5:39-40.

They are so wrapped up in their situations that they never see our Lord standing by weeping for His People. "Please forgive us Lord; forgive us; forgive me for judging, I have no right. Who am I? Nobody."

Our break time was over and I climbed the stairs with a heavy heart. The thrill of coming to the meeting with God's people! I was invited to this holy gathering to meet with my Lord. Top brass. "O! my Lord have mercy upon us. Have mercy upon us when we think that we can do anything, for, without You, we can do nothing. Unless the Lord builds the house the builders labour in vain (Psalm 127:1)."

We came back to our seats and the man from Holland shook my hands, "Well done sister, well done."

I thanked him, but I did nothing, it was Jesus. To my joy Mr Hill stood up again to carry on where he had left off. At intervals the same thing would happen; I would confirm with the weeping what he was saying. After a long time, Mr Hill suggested that people might re-dedicate themselves to our Lord, and consecrate afresh their lives and whenever anyone came forward and really meant what they said, I would weep. If they stepped forward and prayed but it was just words, or whatever, I was doing nothing. For wrong reasons, I was silent. This went on for a long time. They wanted me to talk but the minister from Wales said, "She does not need to talk, the Holy Spirit has spoken. All we have to do is listen." I was very relieved.

By this time it was about four in the afternoon and the meeting was brought to a close. Everyone was packing up as so many had been invited to the Houses of Parliament to share what had happened in the meeting, so I was packing up too. The minister asked if I was going to the Houses of Parliament.

"No." I said, "Only top brass were going there."

To which he said, "It was you our Lord had used throughout the day."

So I went to the Houses of Parliament. We were ushered into a room where we all sat round a huge, beautiful, polished oval table and along the top were the bigwigs of our meeting and positioned in the meeting were the ministers of the Houses of Parliament (but not Clifford Hill or the Welsh Minister).

The meeting began and all the statistics came out again; no mention of God's heart. I sat and sat; "Nobody's going to say anything, Lord."

After about an hour, the main speaker asked was there any other business? I shot out of my seat and related the word Mr Hill had given which was in line with our Lord. Twice the Scripture came 2 Chronicles 7:14, "If My people, who are called by My Name, humble themselves and pray and seek My face and turn from their wicked ways, then I will hear from heaven, forgive their sins and heal their land."

I went on about the millennium dome, which was the biggest waste of money. Nowhere in it or on it does it relate to Jesus our Lord. I continued: the abortion in the hospitals was against what should be taught; we bend over backwards not to offend, but Christianity is not proclaimed in our schools - very few assemblies where our Lord is lifted up. The laws have all been changed in the Houses of Parliament. At one time, the Bible was our handbook and this Book was now put aside. This country was prosperous because we had upheld Jesus as Lord.

The silence in the room was awful; no one backed me up, no one agreed, no one said a word. I sat down and a moment or two later they closed the meeting. I was avoided like I might have the plague. I came out and went into a doorway and wept and wept. After I got myself together again I said, "Lord, that was a prayer meeting to pray for our country, and what have we achieved, apart from Mr. Hill and the Welsh Minister? How many came to pray?"

I left my doorway and caught my bus back to Tania's, very disappointed; only Jesus Christ, our Lord, can help us. "Please have mercy, Lord."

When I returned home, I shared what had happened and Josephine said, "O Mam! You won't be on telly, will you?"

I said, "No, our meeting was not important enough to be on telly."

Now Jimmy's brother, Lister, had a stroke and was taken into hospital so I was travelling day by day to see him and pray for him. He was in intensive care for one day then he was making good. By Christmas he had been there maybe two months. The doctors and nurses were pleased with him, saying he would make a full recovery. "Praise the Lord!"

Christmas came and Josephine and Chris, her boyfriend, came with me to see him. When we stopped and parked, Chris asked if he could marry Josephine. I was so pleased; it was such a blessing after the long haul with Lister. I was overjoyed for Jo; he was such a good lad. I was so thrilled.

We went in to see Lister and everything was fine. He was receiving therapy every day now and he was pleased with himself. He was pleased to see Jo; he really thought the world of her.

When we came out, all the way home it was wedding plans. They would like it at Easter if possible, and were so excited making plans. Chris's mam and dad were invited down and we talked. Chris's mam suggested I should marry Jo and Chris, so it was agreed.

Now, I am not ordained but we went about getting the chapel licensed for weddings and I could take the service if we had a registrar sitting in the vestry listening to the service: so far, so good. I did have the ASB 1980 book, the Alternative Service Book, which I had bought when I was in the Church of England when they first came out. Because we had registered the building for marriage, the registrar said the next thing would be for me to be ordained; but I had no witness to do that. Yes, we are equal to men in our Lord's eyes and He used women a lot in the Bible and they were leaders - but it was not for me.

Now this is how my Lord led me: every person is unique in the eyes of God, no formalities or 'What He does for you He will do for me,' but everyone is different; we are a peculiar people. I have emphasised this right through the 'Pathway of Faith'. You cannot copy someone else; you seek your Lord for your way forward, and He will answer you as He has answered and led me. All He looks for is the contrite heart; if you are teachable, you are reachable, but if you are a clever clogs and a 'Mr. Know it all,' you are working out of you own strength and heading for a downfall. I know nothing until He tells me and I can know nothing until He tells me and I pray and ask Him what I am to do.

My wedding dress was up in the loft and I suggested to Jo that she might like to wear my dress. When I was married, I paid £30 for my dress at Bainbridge's in Newcastle. Now that was a lot of money in those days. It was very plain, but bridal satin with two panels of lace down the front, a full back with a train. I carried my prayer book with a spray of beautiful delicate flowers on silk that went through my prayer book. This was my bouquet.

Well, Jo liked that idea, so I got the box down from the loft and took it out to see how it was. The pins that held the box together were rusty because the dress was so full with the hoops and buckram and petticoats that the dress had pin pricks of rust all over. I took it to all the best dry cleaning establishments and every one turned me down. They said I would never get the stains out, so I prayed, "Father, what am I to do?"

He showed me to do a coldwater soak overnight in the bath, with a touch of Domestos in the water, so I did. This I did three nights in a row and put it through the washer the next day, then the same the next night and washed through the day and the next night and washed the next day and it was clean. When it was for me, I hardly dared touch it and when I pressed it the night before my wedding I was terrified I did something wrong, but here I was steeping it in Domestos and putting it through the washer to get it right for Jo.

At this point, Father showed me to use the wedding and everything to do with the wedding as intercession for the Bride of Christ, so I was praying through every detail. Josephine asked Kate who was Andrew's daughter, Bridget who was Chris's sister, and Nina who was Sean's little lass three years old, to be bridesmaids. Sean was the son of Walter, Jimmy's brother. Liz said she would make the bridesmaid's dresses for the wedding present so this was wonderful. The bridesmaid's dresses were turquoise and so was little Nina's. We took the bow off my wedding dress so Liz could match the material for Nina to match Josephine. The men went to get measured for their hired suits. Edward and Avril took me away and bought me an outfit. Avril again put herself out and Chris's Mam and I went to Avril's to have a baking day - we would do the catering ourselves.

Josephine wanted the wedding in the sports centre, which had a big hall, and we split it in half: the reception in one half, and the stage for the band and dance for the do at night. We hired someone to decorate it - it was beautiful.

Next, Jo and I went to Morpeth for invitation cards for the reception during the day and evening invitations and order of service. The cards were beautiful, the same colour as the wedding dress, but we just bought the cards.

I had a friend 82 years old who did beautiful special writing and he wrote the order of service and what we wanted inside the card. We photocopied this and clipped it inside the beautiful cards. "O Father! It was wonderful - everything coming together marvellously."

My dress had come clean so I was pressing it and still praying through for the Bride of Jesus Christ to come forth without spot or wrinkle. It was nearly finished, only the bow to sew back on. Josephine took the bridesmaids through to Liz for the first fitting and brought back the bow so I pressed it and sewed it back on the dress.

Next, the Scripture was to invite the people to the wedding feast: as this was mainly family, it seemed to be all right. Then it was the invitations to the night do; about three hundred, a lot of young ones from right up the valley. Everything was set. Sylvia came with Richard who videoed the wedding for me, and on the day Avril's son Philip videoed for Josephine.

I was very nervous. I had previously taken a wedding in the Tower Gardens where the couple had been to the registry office and been married but wanted God's blessing, so I went through the marriage vows with them again and we sang. That lady had a grown up family in their twenties, and their partners and parents were there and one or two guests. But these young ones had no respect for what was going on; they were standing swilling down pints and shorts and sniggering and laughing, probably at me, but I did not think it was good enough. The Lord said, "Honour your father and your mother that your days may be long in the land that the Lord your God gives you." (Exodus 20:12).

So once I had taken the couple through their marriage vows, I put down my book on the ground and I started to preach to those young people about honouring father and mother, about how a marriage service is very important to our Lord and instead of swilling drink down their necks, they might have the decency to back their parents on the vows they were making. Well, the message went home. They all put down their drinks and were very attentive to everything that was being said and done. So, I preached the gospel as well, because it was very important for the woman getting married to have our Lord's blessing. That was all she wanted: to do everything properly and to know she was right with our Lord. O, it was a beautiful day and the sun shone for her. Her parents and his mum came up to me after the service and shook hands with me and said, "You really believe, don't you?"

To which I answered, "Very much so."

They thanked me again and again. Roly and Liz sang with me and the couple were overjoyed. We knew that the precious Lord Jesus was with us.

Well, it was time for Chris's Mam and me to join Avril for our baking day. We baked a good part of the day; it was wonderful.

Next, flowers had to be arranged for the chapel and the tables. Everything went like clockwork. I asked Father for a beautiful day and the sun shone so beautifully. Kathy played the organ. I prayed, "O Father, help me."

I had to go and prepare the salads fresh on the wedding day and then stuff had to be transported to the sports centre; time was getting on. I met Betty Oliver in the village on one of the runs and she asked if she could help, to my joy. I asked if she could help Avril and Edward. She went to do that and I went home.

The bridesmaids were coming to our house to get ready and Edward was giving Josephine away. Andrew was taking the photographs. I got ready and had to leave first to be at the chapel for the ushers, Kathy and the registrar. It was like we hardly had time to draw breath.

Noel was using his Jaguar car to bring Josephine and the bridesmaids. He was very proud. The car was gleaming and had ribbons and flowers in the back window. Josephine did the same as me and carried a prayer book with the spray. The bridesmaids had bouquets.

All the lads arrived: first, Chris and his best man, then David and the best man's brother, who were ushers. Kathy played some beautiful songs and choruses before Josephine arrived. The guests all came in then Josephine arrived. "O

Father, help me. Her Dad would have been so proud: she was beautiful. Please strengthen me." I could have broken my heart.

We had practised but I was so nervous and I hesitated at one point and made a mistake but I don't think anyone realised, so I kept going. After the service was over we had the signing of the register during which Kathy sang solo, which was beautiful. Then it was back down the aisle. Josephine was radiant. She asked Noel to stop at the church as she wanted to put her spray on her Dad's grave.

When we got up to the hall for photographs, I asked for whole families to be taken together as there are so few times when everyone is there all at the same time. Avril had everything just so, on the buffet table. Cold meats: turkey, ham and beef, with every salad you could make; and everyone helped themselves. The sweets were excellent too, all home made. I am not sure, but I think Avril made all the sweets.

Then it was time for the speeches and I asked Andrew if he would be compère and introduce everyone. It was really good and all laughed at everything he said and the way he did things was great also.

After we finished in the afternoon, there was a space where people could come down to the house to see the presents, before the evening do. Avril organised the food yet again for the buffet at night; she was so good.

By the time everyone came back, the band was there. Josephine and Chris were in the foyer until everyone was there, to greet them. Everyone enjoyed themselves. Not all came who were invited so the food that was left was given away to anyone who could take it, and the Scripture my Lord gave me again, was about how some were too busy to come at our Lord's invitation so He sent them out into the highways and byways to invite anyone who would come (Matthew 22:1-14); we had done that too, after it was all over.

The bairns had been going to Paris for their honeymoon, but our Lord provided them with a beautiful cottage in Elsdon; it was all ready for them. Some of the young ones took the balloons down and put them over the doors, in the garden and everywhere. The night after the wedding I cried and cried. "You blessed us so much Father. You did it all. How I managed to get through the wedding!"

It had to be my Lord, being in front of my family who are all perfectionists in everything they do. " Thank You Father, thank You."

I married Gwen after that and Helen, but neither of them was anything like Josephine's. We catered for Helen's wedding and just had it in the chapel - a cold buffet. Helen did not want a big do, but she wore my dress again. Richard played for Helen and a lot of the fellowship came. Peggy brought forth a Scripture like a prophetic word for Helen and Sylvia arranged the flowers and made up a bouquet for Helen's mam and Helen's husband Richard's mam.

By the time Helen was married, Josephine had little Yasmin, who was about three. Roly and Liz were there so Jessica and Yasmin gave the bouquets to the mums.

# CHAPTER 13

# A trip to Mull.

Next, I think it was my trip to Mull. I had a phone call asking me if I would go to Mull. The couple concerned were at Ottercops, a farm whose owner had been told by David Pawson the Bible teacher that it was "holy ground". David spoke there at an all day seminar, and made an appeal for men to be raised up for Jesus. 100 men came forward. Afterwards we had a baptism in the river: total immersion. The couple who phoned me were among those baptised. God even used the weather: the sun shone on the farm whilst it rained all around. Well, there was trouble on the Isle of Mull, so I duly asked Father and had the 'All clear' so prepared to go.

I stopped off at Ella's on the way. I did not know what to take; I had no leading at all, so I ended up going as I was. I stayed with Ella a couple of days, one of which was Sunday, so we went to Ella's church. Her pastor was on the stage all through the worship and before he gave the Word he called me forward to ask what I was doing, as I was shining for Jesus. I shared that I was going on a mission to Mull so he asked all the ladies to come forward and pray with me. The words and prayers were that I was fire cutting through the highways and byways and I was so blessed with the Word.

They took a collection for me and after the service I was given one hundred pounds. I was dumbfounded - what a mighty God, and the fellowship of the people being so generous in giving so much. We hugged and blessed each other then went back to Ella's.

She was a wonderful woman of God and really liked to get into the Word. We would sit for hours, going back and forth through the Scriptures. We differed slightly on one or two points, or opinions, but we loved each other so much that we agreed to disagree and to seek our Lord for His will, not our opinions; it was His will that mattered.

Next, we arranged that I would leave my car at Ella's and she would take me to the train station to get my train to Oban; so this we did. I had a beautiful journey up; the scenery was breathtaking and with not driving I could enjoy the scenery and see all there was to see. We came into Oban right where you get the ferry to Mull, but I was to wait for my friends. I sat on a seat bringing all things to my head, when I spied them coming along the Quayside. We met and loved each other.

Before we got on the ferry, they needed to shop. They asked me what I had brought to wear as it was extremely cold on Mull that time of year. If you remember, I had brought nothing, as I didn't know what to bring, so I went shopping too. I crossed the road and went into MacKay's shop which had a half price sale on. I purchased two pairs of jogging pants with tops to match and a beautiful double lined jacket that matched both outfits and everything was knocked down to less than half price. So, "Praise You, Lord. Thank You for Your provision over and above what we can think or dream of".

We met up again, boarded the ferry, sailed to Mull and headed off to their home. They filled me in on the way home. There were three churches involved, would you believe?

There was backbiting, bitterness, bitchiness and no unity; "Father, how sad."

Well I went to work straight away, donned my new gear and walked all around the areas, praying and speaking out; binding and losing every evil spirit. The Bible says, "Unless we take the strong man we cannot enter the house" (Mark 3:27), so I was taking down the high places of the principalities and powers of darkness, speaking righteousness over Mull, or the part of it we were in.

It was up and out and into work, every day a different direction and as high as I could get to speak out over the area. When I felt I had broken through in the Spirit realm, it was to get together to pray and praise Jesus. The couple's daughter came home so she started driving me further afield. We were great sisters in the Lord and two can put ten thousand to flight (Deuteronomy 32:30), so we were going great guns.

This went on all week then we all had a wonderful night to pray together. The cottage was right on the seashore and the sitting room had a window the length of the back wall, with a view right out to sea and across to the land on the other side of the cove. It was magnificent and while in prayer, we could see the seals playing in the bay. How wonderful, and our prayer meeting was just great, with Scriptures coming right, left and centre.

Next, we had to bring all the parties together, everyone from the three churches. My host organised the coming together and I asked for a buffet meal to be prepared as well, and the communion cup. Well, everyone duly arrived and we prayed to set everything before our Lord. Then it was to hear everyone's differences. Incredibly, for everything raised, Father had given the Word to correct it, explain it or stop it. Things were sometimes a bit heated but Father would pour on the healing balm and there was no argument. At the end of the day, it was just like a storm in a teacup. So after bringing in our Lord's Word to correct, there was repentance all round and weeping before God. We then prayed together for the work of our Lord to preach the Gospel and bring the churches together as well as the ministers and their wives; it went like clockwork. We broke bread together and served each other in such unity and communion was so special. Then we sat down to supper together and shared testimonies and talked all night of our beloved Christ Jesus. What a night of prayer and true fellowship, as minister shared with minister.

I was told the next morning that one couple had not come, so the daughter and I went to visit, taking all our Scriptures and everything Father had done the night before. This couple was not pleased, but I could not go until everything was out in the open. We discussed, talking through with all the correction from our Lord's direction, stopping gossip, back biting, criticism, binding a spirit of control, so when we finished they were in no doubt about anything. When everything is out in the open, then satan has nowhere to hide. Everything was cleaned out to the roots, so 'Praise Jesus', I was finished and could go home.

We had a day together just as a family with fun and fellowship, then they took me back to the ferry for the right connection to get the train back down to Edinburgh and I stayed with Ella for a day and then drove home.

# CHAPTER 14

# Plans to alter the chapel; and a mercy return trip to Israel

We had been praying to change the chapel for quite some time and Father had given us the Scripture to "Extend the tent ropes" in Isaiah 54 verse 2, and in our readings.

One night, Bob, who was a friend of Helen's, came in and, during the worship, he joined in the singing. He had a beautiful voice so, as we stopped, I asked him if he would sing for us. He was overjoyed and sang 'Jerusalem'. "O Father," it just melted your heart.

He was a man in his eighties. The Word was given, then we finished, and while we were having our teas and coffees I went over to talk to him. He opened up to me and poured his heart out. He asked if I would pray for him. That was fine; so I did. When people were going home, I was sharing the vision to change the chapel and he said that when he had worked he was an architect and if I liked, he would draw my plans. "O, thank You, Father."

He came up during the day, so did Noel. The members put it to Noel what we wanted so he gave his advice and Bob set to, to draw the plans. He drew them with the bedrooms upstairs, which would require steel girders to support the upstairs. I wanted the size of the main hall to stay the same for meetings. He was going back and forward with Noel, who was very good with the old man and said it was like working with Dad. He was Dad's generation and did things like Dad. He finished and we put the plans in to the council, who turned them down.

We kept praying about them. I came to the chapel one day and Father said to build it like the bungalow with the rooms downstairs and open plan upstairs for the 'Upper Room' - "O how wonderful!"

I got a call for someone to come and stay. I had to ask someone else because I could not use the chapel as it was. These people were so desperate that this man got another architect to come and share what my Lord said about making upstairs downstairs, the upper room for the house of prayer. He drew up a new set of plans, took them to the council, where they were turned down again; however, this time the people who lived round about the chapel had signed a petition to stop the work from going ahead.

It was decided to hold a meeting in the village hall to stop and oppose the whole project. I was quite willing to go and talk - in fact I had not given testimony at home, I always went out; but Josephine brought her boss home to see me, to ask me to drop it and not to go ahead with it, as it was looking like a lynching mob rather than a sensible meeting.

The day arrived and the bairns all came to support me. The upper room of the village hall was full and two members of the council sat at the top table. David sat with me at the side and Edward and Josephine were in the back. Eddy and Roly came as part of the fellowship. The meeting was opened and everybody started shouting at once.

The meeting was then called to order and a request made for one to speak at a time. The couple who lived next to the chapel, started first and said they did not want drugs and drink in our village. A young lass, at the back, started to laugh and said that when a certain lad who lived in the village was drunk he was one of the worst people you could meet, so the lad sat down.

Next, some were shouting that people should look after their own families, in cases of drugs and drink: that was shouted down. Those who were shouting didn't understand that Jesus is the only One Who can truly help drug and drink addicts. Then someone said I had already broken the law by allowing people to stay at the chapel. Josephine piped up and said she thought that that was what church was all about: a place of refuge. That shut down that argument.

It then came to the couple who had stayed and how they were dangerous. Avril said she had found the lady fine and, when asked how she knew anything about it, she replied that the lady had worked for her and thought it was great to give someone back their self worth. So once more the argument was defused.

The next thing raised was, who would pay for it? I said, "Jesus."

After the mocking and laughter had died down, Eddy and Roly tried to come in but were both shouted down. The meeting was brought to an end after that and people began to move away. My whole being ached inside for the people.

Really, we all parted with sighs of relief that I was not hung, drawn and quartered. I never closed my eyes all night.

The next day, I had Bridget coming to see me as she was back home in England. When she came I shared what had happened and that I was still in under everything. Bless her, she said, "Well, that's alright, I will help you."

We set off and Bridget read the Word and we prayed. I knew I was slowly dying to self for the people of the village who had mocked and ridiculed me, and our Lord. Bridget was reading about the crucified Christ. She read and read of how they came to get Him in the Garden, how He was mocked and scourged and brought before Pilate, then sent away and brought back and slowly, bit by bit, hung on the cross and was dying inside.

We worked together until three in the afternoon when Jesus died. When Bridget was finished, she said we should have a cup of tea. I said, "I am so tired."

Bridget said, "Well, close your eyes while I make the tea."

I did close my eyes and within seconds, two thousand years flashed past and I awoke refreshed. Bridget came back into the room and said she saw me believing. If she had not seen me she would not have believed it could happen, but she said, "You hung and died there this afternoon for the people of this village. Father was forgiving them for what they had done last night."

We had our tea then went back to the Word to pray in the resurrection; after that we were finished and I was free. "O Father! Thank You, thank You."

A week later, Father had me knock on all the doors of the village to collect for Doctor Barnardo's Homes and the people were shocked when they opened their doors and I was standing on the steps. When I said I was collecting for the Children's Homes the relief on their faces was something to behold. I knew what Father was doing, both for them and for me. If my Lord had not been with me I could not have had the guts to go to the doors after what had happened.

It was about this time, that Ray came to see me and said that if he paid my fare and everything, would I go back to Israel and pray for a little boy who was very ill. I said "yes." But I would have to know it was my Lord's will that I go or I would go in my own strength and nothing would happen. I said I would pray about it and let him know. Well, I did pray and yes, Father gave me the all clear to go.

So it was arranged and Olive, Ray and I flew out to Israel. When we arrived, Ray had hired a car and so we first got our bags and travelled to the hospice right opposite Lake Galilee - it was wonderful. Olive and I were in one room and Ray, off to one side, in another. Our room was big, had a shower, lovely tiled floors and was so clean. After we settled in, I left Olive to rest and went off to explore. The dining room was in another building and upstairs was a prayer room. This was my haven; like home, I could come and be with my Lord.

I came back down and Ray said he had contacted the family with the little boy. The boy was about seven or eight years old and had been sent home from hospital because they could do no more for him. Ray had arranged that we were to go down that night so I got my Bible and went back to the upper room to pray and ask Father what was wrong and what He wanted me to do. I prayed everything through until I had peace and then I had a quiet nap. Quite often, if there was going to be ministry done, Father would make me so tired I would need to sleep and it would be for ten or fifteen minutes but I would wake so refreshed I was ready for Father.

I went down, washed and changed, and we set off to meet up with the family in a church. It was a beautiful church and not just the family were there, but friends. There were so many and they were singing when we went in. I asked if there was somewhere where we could go to be private, so the minister and his wife, who were with the parents of the boy, carried him downstairs to a room away from all the people. Their daughter came too, as she was my interpreter to be able to communicate with her Mam and Ray.

I started by asking what had happened with the boy when he became ill. The mam would not co-operate; she stood motionless. Ray was going to step in and interfere with what my Lord was doing and I could not let him, so I very politely stopped him; but still mam would not budge. I asked Father what I should do and He said, "Get down and talk to the boy."

I knelt, took the boy in my arms and began to sob. The Holy Spirit was in charge. I sobbed and sobbed, holding the boy, and to my delight, the mam motioned and the daughter touched me on the shoulder. I lay him back on his pillow and stood up.

She began to talk very fast, weeping herself now. The daughter told me that her mother was confessing now. She had aborted three other babies and had tried with the boy, but had not succeeded and he was damaged from birth. I knew this was the case because Father had shared it with me. The cause was to do with abortion. I conveyed to the daughter that all mam had to do was repent before our Lord for each child, because children are a gift from God. Now this woman looked ill, her eyes were glazed, her colour was grey and she looked like a corpse or a zombie.

We sat down and she confessed to each child and I anointed her with oil and prayed the prayer of faith. Then she carried on and I did the next until she had confessed all three and the boy as well. Every time I anointed with oil to remove the sin, it was as if a layer came off and when we were finished, I asked her if she would receive salvation to which she said yes. So I prayed the prayer of salvation and asked her to speak it after me, first the daughter, then the mother. After that, I asked for the Baptism of the Holy Spirit. By now, her eyes were clear and clean like pools of fresh water, shining, and her cheeks were pink. The transformation was astounding.

Next, the father asked if he could also receive salvation and we went through the prayer of salvation and the Baptism of the Holy Spirit for him. Then, because everything was clean and clear with the mam and dad, Father told me to anoint the boy and pray for him. I got down again on my hands and knees and anointed the boy and prayed over him. The daughter began to cry and said he was saying he was healed. His whole body was burning and I said, "Let him go," but she was so afraid for her brother, she was holding him down.

Next, the minister and his wife asked if they could receive salvation and so I prayed and they prayed together; then I prayed for them to receive the Holy Spirit. When we had finished, Ray was sitting a little way off crying with sheer joy at all our Lord had done. The minister asked us back on the Sunday to take the service, at which Ray was overjoyed and accepted. As we came up from the room, after hugs and goodbyes to the family, I was counting back and realised that it was seven years since Roly and I were in Nazareth, praying from the balcony, so I shared my story with the minister. We came out on to the steps at the front door and he pointed straight up in front of us and he said, "Your monastery is right there. The church has just been built and now my wife and I are born again and baptised with the Holy Spirit."

So again, he said, "Our Lord has brought you back to see and be part of the miracles of your prayers, plus the miracle of our family." I wept with joy, seeing what our Lord had done.

We went back to our hospice at Galilee and Ray was bursting to tell Olive of what our Lord had done. I left them and went to the upper prayer room and on my face before the Lord. I praised and thanked Him. I was to discover many more prayers answered. Having the car was so wonderful and Ray took us to Capernaum the next day and (would you believe?) over the small excavated houses I told you about seven years ago, they had built a church. It was on stilts over the houses of Jesus' day, but you could still see them. We could not go in the church but the front, right across a wide span, was all glass so, while one is in the service, one is looking right across Lake Galilee; it would be stunning to worship our Lord in a building like that looking out over Galilee.

We then went to Elijah's church; Ray had made contact with friends who had talked about a service there, so here we were. We talked and shared with people from all walks of life; we spent the whole day there.

We then headed in a different direction to see a lady that Ray had met, and become great friends. We met and 'Praise Jesus,' she was an intercessor and did not know what was going on in her life. She would end up weeping and did not know why. O, it was wonderful to share with her and open her eyes to know she was not depressed, or anything worse; it was Father's heart. "O Father!" To share and open her eyes was like watching a rose unfold. She gleamed, her eyes shone like jewels sparkling in the light.

It was very late when we travelled back and again shared with Olive. Not many people understand intercession so we did not labour the point. We started to pray, and I could pray it all back. We went to bed, but about two o'clock in the morning, I woke and Father wanted me to go and pray in the upper room. I said, "Yes," and lay down again, but Father said, "Now!"

The pain in my hip, like Jacob, when he wrestled with God, was very bad. I got up very quietly, dressed and went upstairs to the upper room. "Right Father, I am here, what is it You want?"

Well, there had been some talk that Israel was very short of water; they needed rain. So I went to Elijah, when he prayed for rain. Elijah sent his servant seven times and each time there was nothing; then, the seventh time, he came back and said that a cloud had appeared, the size of a man's fist. Elijah kept on praying till the rains came. Well, I started with that Scripture and prayed and prayed 1 Samuel 12 v18. Samuel prayed for our Lord to send the rain. I was still in terrible pain, so continued in and out of Scripture all night and all day and at five o'clock, tea time, I suddenly remembered Olive; that she would not know where I was.

I got my things together and hurried down to our room to find Ray there and I shared what had happened; how I was in prayer, all night and day, for rain. Outside of our room the big outer doors opened on to a balcony with steps going either side and we had our breakfast every morning on the balcony. Because we were high up we ourselves had a beautiful view of Lake Galilee, between the trees. Ray was sitting on the balcony ledge when Olive and I came out. Suddenly it started to rain. It teemed, the thunder cracked and the lightning flashed. At that point, my pain left me and I was free. Also, then, Ray fell out of the balcony. I ran to the window and he was lying spread-eagled on the ground, laughing fit to burst. It teemed and teemed: "Praise You Father"

Next, it was Sunday and we were to go back to our church in Nazareth. We all got ready and went. We sang, and I did not know any of the songs, but I just sat in prayer watching everyone. The minister called on Ray to speak; he had an interpreter for him and I just had to pray. After a long time, Ray called me down and asked people to come for healing. I had no witness in my spirit that it was the Lord, but I went down and asked Father for forgiveness and prayed for the people anyway. Everyone was thanking us and hugging us.

After we left, I asked Ray why he had not made an appeal for salvation, and said that it was God's mercy and if anyone was healed it should have been salvation. So we repented of presumption and prayed our Lord's blessing anyway, for all who came forward and that He would touch them because the Word went forth and signs and wonders will follow.

Our time was over and we headed back to get our flight home. "What a wonderful time, precious Jesus" that He took me back to see answered prayer. Once again I was overwhelmed with my Lord and His love.

# CHAPTER 15

# A look around Otterburn Hall and the chapel is altered for my new home.

About a month or six weeks later, Ray phoned to say that the boy was in trouble. His mum had contacted Ray for prayer. I was praying and asking what had gone wrong and why was the boy sick again, when Ray phoned again, a week, or maybe a fortnight, later; he had received a letter from a lady who worked and lived here in Britain all her life. Her work had been in hospitals; she gave the patients physiotherapy, but, when she retired, she had gone home to Nazareth. Well, she had been going in to help make the boy comfortable, every day. After she had been, she asked Ray what we had done, because the lad had changed completely. She said he would talk to someone in the room and all he wanted was to go home to be with Jesus. He was telling his mum she must not worry, for this was his desire. The lady said that his desire was granted, and he slipped away, but she had never seen anything so peaceful or beautiful and the presence of his Jesus in the room was so wonderful that she wanted to come to this Jesus.

"What can I say, Father? You granted the little boy his wish, and the desire of the lady that she would receive salvation. O, You are so worthy. O worthy are You, Lord. Worthy to be worshipped and adored. Worthy, o worthy are You, Lord, to be thanked and praised and worshipped and adored."

I would like to share how at the end of September, the last day really, the call had come in to do a forty day fast for the Jews, starting on the first of October. I had accepted the call and prayed about it, and yes it was right. That night was the tragic death of Diana, Princess of Wales. The news the next day was terrible and the pictures of the cars and the impact it had on the British public. Everyone loved Diana. Flowers were being placed at the palace gates. The country truly was in mourning for Diana, and her two sons. How does one pray with such tragedy? All we can do is pray in the Spirit and the Holy Spirit will pray for us when we don't know how to pray. The Bible says, "The Spirit helps us in our weakness. We do not know what we ought to pray for, but the Spirit himself intercedes for us with groans that words cannot express", Romans 8:26.

We never need feel defeated and that we should not pray, because that's the very time to pray and our Lord will use us and turn the wrong the right way round. We should never feel hopeless as, "In all things God works for the good of those who love Him", Romans 8:28.

We should never say, "Never" and even if we feel disheartened, we should still pray and bring it before our Lord because our Lord will do it. "Not by might, nor by power, but by My Spirit," says our God (Zechariah 4:6). He can defeat any foe, which dares to raise itself up against the plans and purposes of our Lord Jesus.

My plans for the chapel had been turned down again, so the first morning, for our Lord's people, I came to the chapel and knelt before my Saviour and wept in repentance: "If I have done any wrong Father, forgive me, I do not want to have good ideas and tag You on at the end. I only want Your will and me tagged on at the end of it."

I was silent before my Lord and, no, I had not got it wrong; the glow of His presence, the warmth of His love and the tenderness of His nearness were with me. I rose from my knees and thanked Him. How I needed His presence; I love Him so. As I came out and locked the door the Scripture came, "Do not forego the small beginnings," or as Zechariah 4:10 puts it, "For who has despised the day of small things?"

I walked down the street and the board had gone up for the sale of the Tower. Now this is a most beautiful building with a walled in garden. I stood at the gate and said "Father, what You could do in there because of the walled in garden - it was like the city of Jerusalem, so I used it as my prayer for Israel. I walked round it. No one was there as it was empty and black and eerie; the trees all around were full of black crows squawking. The Scripture Father gave me was Ezekiel 36, the whole chapter, so I used it reading out loud declaring my Lord's will for His people. While battling for the chapel to be changed, and praying for the Jews, Father took me to 2 Corinthians 9:10, "Now He who supplies seed to the sower and bread for food will supply and multiply your seed for sowing and increase the harvest of your righteousness."

I had about £30,000 in the bank belonging to Maranatha for the work but Father would wake me up at night and tell me to send £5,000 to a particular place and then five and a half thousand pounds to somewhere else till I had £2,000 left in the bank.

My time of the forty-day fast was over and we were now into November. Ann was coming for her holiday so I went to the station to pick her up; there was so much going on. We talked and shared as usual - chat, chat all the way home.

Next morning I told Ann about the Tower, how I was in prayer for the Jews but because the Tower was empty and a walled up garden like Jerusalem I had used it for the intercessions for Israel. We had our prayer time then when we finished we walked along to the Tower.

Ann was very excited. The asking price was £400,000; it had been sold to the breweries for £40,000 and they had taken from it and taken from it. Also it had had manager after manager but no matter who had it, or what new ideas they came up with, it never made it as a hotel. So we came home and we were praying about the Tower. We had the Scripture about opening the gates for the King of Glory to come in (Psalm 24). We had our lunch and decided to go back and pray at all the gates; so this we did.

Well, while praying at the Tower gates, David was walking in the garden. This was the young lad who worked for Mr Harding; but it was a labour of love for he really loved the Tower, so we went to talk to him about the Tower. He said I should contact Mr Harding who was a historian and knew everything about the Tower, so we thanked him and came home.

I was praying all the time, "Father if this is You, open the doors, but if it isn't shut them firmly."

We got home and I phoned Mr Harding. At first he was asking why I wanted to know, but then he began to tell me. He went back as far as 1076 when the huge oak tree, just to the side of the Tower, was the place where it was first built of wood. Robert de Umfraville, who was a cousin of William the Conqueror, was given the Tower as the Manor House of the area. The site was always secure because it was built on a hill. The Halls acquired the Tower in the early 16th century and it remained in their possession until 1745 when "Mad Jack" Hall was a willing participant in the Jacobite Rebellion. Like the Earl of Derwentwater he was taken prisoner at the battle of Preston and was later tried for treason. He was found guilty and after five nerve wracking reprieves he was eventually hanged. In 1812 Sir Walter Scott, researching folklore, was a guest in the Tower. Mr Harding said staunch

Quakers, Pease & Co, were next to own the Tower, and that the crest was their crest - and it was not an eagle, but a dove with the olive branch, and the two lambs above were the Jew and the Gentile.

"O Father," I was so excited when he said the land around had reached far and wide taking in the mill, which was a corn mill. Then things were hazy but beginning to make sense; the land we had been praying for was all the Tower land. The Sanctuary was either a Chapel in the Tower or the Tower itself. We both were beside ourselves with excitement. Mr Harding said the Peases used it as a refuge for God's people.

"O Father," Ann's vision was for the Jews, my vision was for both and this was what the Tower had been. It was too wonderful for words. Now Gwen phoned and gave me a Scripture, Ezekiel 21:22 - "In his right hand is the divination for Jerusalem: to set up battering rams, to call for a slaughter, to lift the voice with shouting, to set battering rams against the gates, to heap up a siege mound, and to build a wall," (NKJV). The LORD gave the answer: Psalm 24:7,8 - "Lift up your heads, O you gates! And be lifted up, you everlasting doors! And the King of glory shall come in. Who is this King of glory? The LORD strong and mighty, The LORD mighty in battle." We prayed through the Scriptures.

Next I phoned the estate agents to ask if we could go through the Tower. The chap in charge said he would be unable to come but David the gardener would take us through. This was excellent. I contacted David and it was arranged. On the morning we were to go through Roly landed and I shared with him what we were going to do and asked if he would like to come. To my joy, he said, "Yes."

We prayed that Father would go before us and again, "Father, close the door if this is us and not You."

We met up with David inside the front entrance; my heart was pounding to know what Father was going to do. As we stood in the entrance hall I prayed again, "Take it Lord, Your will be done."

So we set off through the main hall; off to the left a lounge through to what the brewery had as the bar. We then went out and into the Conference room, out into a little back sitting room with the most beautiful wood surround over the fire place, and there in the centre was the coat of arms: the dove with the olive branch and the two lambs. Then back down a long passage with the ladies and gents toilets one side and down to the cellars on the other side.

Now centuries ago, when the war went on between the English and the Scots, even the stock was kept in the cellar. David said there was a secret tunnel which went right back and came out up the hill and this was their getaway. He had found it but was not allowed to continue in the tunnel, in case it caved in and he was trapped. When we came back up into the passage, he stopped and said a well was right there under where were standing, so they would have water in the Tower for the animals and themselves. It was very securely covered; David said the water was stagnant. To the left was a great big room and to the right the kitchen. Along another passage, off the kitchen, were the larder, the laundry and the store rooms.

You could see it, this beautiful mansion in all its glory. I could see it all. We came back through and there was a utility room with all the huge sinks for washing the great iron pans, the potato peeler, chest freezers, upright freezers and a walk-in cold room for the game etc. with the stone slabs to work on. Then into the dining room with exquisite wall to wall panelling, a magnificent big window and coloured glass. We came back out into the entrance hall. He then took us back through past the Conference room and up some stairs, along a small passage, up a couple of steps and opened the door into the library. O it was beautiful, like the dining room, wall to wall panelling and, like both the dining room and the little back sitting room, the beautiful fire place with the crest in the centre.

We went back along the passage and up into the main part of the building and the start of the bedrooms now. Ann, having a guest house, was jotting down the number of beds you could take. Then up on to the top floor. We came back down and along another passageway where the rooms were above the kitchen and we came down a back stairs to the kitchen door. Some of the big rooms had en-suite bathrooms, some rooms were family rooms.

All the way round, Father was showing me it was home, a home; no big set up. It would be my home, it would not be a hotel and it would not be a business. It was a home, and whoever He brought were His guests to His home. As we moved back through into what was the main tower it was as though I belonged. When we went off to the kitchen side I was moving out of where I belonged; I was still looking for what would have been the place of worship for the Quakers. I wandered back into the Conference room. This room was enormous, the whole of the chapel (Maranatha) would fit inside it. I walked right up to the window and this window had been a door, the steps were still there outside and, yes, this room had been the place of worship.

When I came back out, Roly had gone, and Ann and David were in the main hall. The size of the place! Ann said at least fifty beds. We shared all the way home. Josephine came round and I asked for the history books about the Tower which she said she would bring in the morning.

Ann was going to stay with her sister at Peebles but she phoned Neil and asked him to come up and have a look at the Tower. It was arranged. He would go to Ann's sister's and they would both call back here again before going back down south. Ann left to go to her sister's; I just waited.

Jo brought the book for me to read through but I did not glean anything we had not already got from Mr Harding. The days passed and Ann and Neil arrived back.

I asked the estate agent if we could look through again and the answer was yes but we would have to get David again so we made the arrangements and went after lunch. Again the joy of my Lord was so wonderful. We went right through then went home, not a word was spoken.

Ann and Neil were going back to Bournemouth that night; Josephine came in again and she broke the ice and we all laughed Still no real discussion but we talked and chatted. Jo went home and Ann and Neil set off.

I prayed it all back putting every detail into the hands of the Lord. I got little snippets of news that there were two buyers but that the cost to put it right would be as much as the asking price; nothing from the estate agents. John from Liverpool came up and I shared it all with him and we went along and we both felt it was like Jericho to walk right round it, so we set off praying all the time. After we did three times round John felt he was finished but I said I was not, I have to go the seven times so he said "well, I shall go with you". We continued to walk praying all manner of things, but the last time round it was all about Jesus the true bride, the Jew and the Gentile working side by side. When we finished we sat for a few minutes then went home. We had a prayer time together at home and then he went back to Liverpool.

After another week a letter came asking me to put in an offer and not to be afraid for they would not be tied to take the first offer. I took the letter and Peggy and Fred and I prayed together placing the letter before our Lord, like Hezekiah did. After we prayed we waited in silence. After a while I felt Father was telling me to offer the two thousand pounds I had left in the bank of Maranatha just the same as the fifteen hundred that we bought the chapel for, when it was valued at fifteen thousand. So I spoke and said to Peggy and Fred I had to offer the two thousand I had left in the bank after sowing the seed.

Peggy said, "Yes, the widows mite, the tuppence." She also said it would be given to me for a peppercorn.

I thanked them both and travelled home praying all the way that my Lord would write the letter. I set to and my Lord did write the letter. I shared in the letter how the tower belonged to our Lord and the meaning of the crest and the dove with the olive branch, the vision of the place of refuge and how it had been a place of refuge. I shared the Gospels in the letter then my offer of the widow's mite, the two thousand. I received a letter back saying they had received a much higher offer and they were sorry but it wasn't final, so I kept on praying.

I phoned Ann to tell her what I had done and the outcome. Now Ann and Neil wanted to sell "Daybreak" and move north, so I shared that the little cottage next to the chapel had come up for sale so Neil travelled back up to see the cottage. In the meantime I made arrangements with the man who owned it for them to meet so Neil could look through. Well he loved the cottage - his words were, "It is like a rough cut diamond."

He took photos to take back and slipped in to Hexham to get them developed, while the lad went back to discuss the asking price and other things with his father as he and his partner were going on holiday the next day for a fortnight. When Neil arrived back the lad phoned to say his partner had promised another couple to look through so his hands were tied.

Neil left to travel back down home. Now Ann and Neil never put their guest house, Daybreak, on the market. Some people were there who had gone and stayed for holidays, for years, and Ann shared how she could be moving north to work in Northumberland. The people were so upset when they went back home, they asked in their church if anyone was interested in buying a guest house as the one they had been going to for years was for sale. A couple came forward and said, "We are," so they went down to see Ann and Neil.

In the mean time, the father of the young couple selling the bungalow next to the chapel, phoned me to say that the people who were interested had dropped out and I could have the key for Ann and Neil. As a God-incidence, a relative of Ann and Neil had died in Carlisle and they had decided to pack up and head north and, if the worst came to the worst, they could put their furniture in the chapel and stay with me.

Neil prayed and Father said moving out date was the tenth of June. This was also a couple of days after the funeral of Ann's relative - when Father moves, Father moves!

Now they packed up and left. The next day I was given the key to the cottage so Ann and Neil could just move straight in. We were not able to wash everything down as we could not find the stopcock to turn the water on, and I was unable to get the couple to ask where it was until the funeral was over at Carlisle. Ann and Neil and Ann's dad travelled up to Peebles to Ann's sister's as she was going to have Ann's piano.

On the Saturday morning Ann phoned me to tell me they were on their way from Peebles and would be with me in two hours and I said, "I have got the key for the cottage you will be able to move straight in." They were ecstatic with excitement and joy. The man had said they could pay rent until all the documents and solicitors were sorted out. "What a mighty God we serve."

The Tower had been sold, but the plans had at last been passed for the Chapel. Now this was when Father told me to sell my house and give the money now to my children for their inheritance.

Roly came that weekend and in the conversation he said that his mam and dad were coming out of the farm and were looking for a place in Otterburn so I said, "I am selling my place."

Roly's mam came round to see it and the next thing was they wanted to buy and the price was right and we put it into the hands of our solicitors and in a very short time it was sold. Mr Johnson, Roly's Dad, said I had not to worry I could stay in the house till he was ready to move. So Hallelujah! I split the money three ways and gave the bairns their inheritance. There were no problems this time, so everyone was thrilled.

David put his money into buying his house for himself and his partner, Josephine put hers into buying the council house she was in and Edward put his into a building project that he was busy with. They each gave me back some, which was about a tenth of the amount. I was thrilled that they gave back to the Lord, which I put back into the changing of the Chapel. I prayed, "O Father! Words cannot express." I just stood speechless and thanked Him for what He was doing because the plans had gone through and we could begin the work of changing the Chapel.

Because the bedrooms were to be downstairs and the walls would be the supports for the upstairs it would cut the cost of steel girders so that was a good start. The windows were going to cost around £5,000 and more but I did not want to have the windows that were there because they have to open. Then our joiner came to me and said, "Rosie I can make the existing windows to open." "Praise Jesus."

Then there had to be Velux windows in the roof for the upper room, and because the Chapel was built in 1904 the Velux windows that had been chosen would not fit between the wood panels of the ceiling, so they went back and smaller Velux windows were chosen, thus saving again. Time after time my Lord would change things and it worked out cheaper.

The next thing that happened was that my sister in Jesus and myself were talking about the work and progress and she said she would like to give the central heating. We had it costed out: boiler, radiators and everything would come to around £5,000 and she gave the money for the central heating. She also said she had furniture she did not want, she would give that too, which was a dining table and six chairs and a trolley in beautiful wood that actually matched the rich wood of the ceiling. She also gave me two chairs; one was an armchair recliner, and the other a straight-backed chair.

The work was going well; then another couple gave me fourteen and a half thousand pounds, absolutely tremendous. I knew these wonderful people were giving to our Lord and His work but it was very humbling when I was the one to be privileged to live in this sanctuary of our Lord.

I had asked a beautiful young lad, Patrick Green, if he could put a dove with the olive branch in its mouth on the window of the inner door, which he did, with the Bible verse Genesis 8: 10-11 - "And he waited yet another seven days, and again he sent the dove out from the ark. Then the dove came to him in the evening, and behold, a freshly plucked olive leaf was in her mouth; and Noah knew that the waters had receded from the earth". He sandblasted it on to the glass and he did lots of artistic things like this in his workshop.

Next the kitchen: Avril scoured the newspapers and got an oak kitchen with beautiful oak doors. The lad was a lovely lad and kitchens were his business; then Josephine came round and said she would pay for the kitchen. Then it was the bathroom and en-suite. Avril took me to warehouses to choose tiles and she organised for the tiler to come and do the work; things were really getting on.

In the meantime, Mr Johnson needed to move so I had to move out. We moved everything to Avril's until the Chapel was finished and I stayed with the bairns. I was with Avril and Edward first, then Josephine and then Ann and Neil.

Father was doing things in the valley. Keith and Mary came first to stay and while we were praying Mary said our

Lord was showing her wars. I said, "Well, Otterburn training camp is just up the road."

"No," she said, "It is not that."

There were the border battles between the English and the Scots. "That's it," she said, "Border battles." So Keith and Mary repented for the part the Scots played in the battles and I prayed and repented for the English. We went back and forth well into the night. We were thrilled and the next day we knew our Lord had done something in the heavens.

Next Barry and Liz came to stay. Now Barry is related to Josephine's Chris and had been born and bred in Byrness village, the last village before you go over the border into Scotland. He left the district twenty-five years ago and had come back to stay, to show his wife where he was born and bred. During the day they were off touring, and the first day Barry had taken Liz to the Roman wall. When he came back he was telling me there is a place up on the Roman wall declaring every religion is welcome but Christianity. So after we shared and talked about their day Liz wanted to go to rest but Barry and I got into prayer. We began by bringing down the Roman wall plaque binding every other evil in our valley and lifting up the name of Jesus. Barry had pictures of the hangman's noose over Elsdon so we tackled that and a number of other things. We prayed and prayed, and worked into the night. Barry said he had never had a prayer meeting like it. What a joy.

The next thing was the cleaning of the water spirits. Peggy was being led about evil in the water, and the source to the water going into the houses is up above me, both reservoirs; so we had to blow the Shofar and declare our Lord's decrees - Numbers 10:8 "The sons of Aaron, the priests, shall blow the Shofars; and these shall be to you as an ordinance forever throughout your generations." I borrowed Avril's hunting horn. Peggy and I set off to the burns and rivulets coming into the reservoirs. Peggy had the Scriptures. We

pulled up as near as we could get to each place and walked to
the head then blew our Shofars and declared the Word of our
Lord over the rivers and burns and we put salt in each one
- II Kings 2:19-21 "Then the men of the city said to Elisha,
"Behold now, the situation of this city is pleasant, as my lord
sees; but the water is bad and the land is unfruitful." Elisha
said, "Bring me a new jar, and put salt in it." So they brought
it to him. He went out to the spring of water and threw salt
in it and said, "Thus says the LORD, 'I have purified these
waters; there shall not be from there death or unfruitfulness
any longer.'" " Then we drove downstream till we came to
where the river branched off and blew our Shofars again and
declared our Lord's Word and put a bag of salt in each river.

Now we were very close to the Roman wall and we had
both talked about the Mithraic temple which was where the
plaque was declaring, "No Christianity." Mithraism was
a religion the Roman soldiers worshipped like a sun god,
also the Persian god of light. He became known as the cre-
ator of life after killing the sacred bull from which the sky,
earth, animals and plants were born. According to the myth,
Mithras was born of rock and armed with a knife and a torch.
As a warrior deity he was particularly suited to soldiers and
imperial officials and many Mithraic monuments have been
discovered at military borders like the Roman wall. The
Mithraic liturgy was celebrated in caves, at the far end of
which was a picture of the god about to sacrifice the sacred
bull. Mithras was also associated with the planets and stars.
We parked and walked to the Mithraic temple. You can walk
into where the plaque is - well we did that. We prayed and,
as we were coming out, another couple were coming in and
I stepped off the path, on to the grass, to let them past and
down I went. The gentleman helped me up and I walked
back to the car but had severe pain in my leg.

We had one more stop to go to finish what we had started
but Peggy had to drive, because I could not put my foot

down on the pedals with any pressure. When we got to the bridge I could not go with Peggy so she just had to walk on to the centre of the bridge and put the salt over and read out the Scriptures. Peggy then drove me back to Josephine's and I phoned Neil and asked him if he would take Peggy home.

I walked on the leg for three days and Josephine kept telling me to go to the doctors. Because I could walk on it I thought it couldn't be broken; however, after three days it was swelling up so I consented to go. Josephine took me straight to the hospital because it would need an X-ray. Well it was broken in two places across the anklebone, and we have a little bone alongside the anklebone. He put a plaster on and said I would have to go back because of the swelling and because they would have to break it again and set it properly. I was praying, "Father, no way, let the swelling go down and both bones be in place to Your glory Lord."

Well I did go back and guess what, they took the plaster off because the swelling had gone down but both bones were perfect, he could not believe it with my walking on it as well. "Thank You, thank You, thank You Lord."

Because Ann and Neil were in the cottage all on the flat I went to stay with them and we had a great time. We watched a video, a wonderful romantic story; it really was lovely, I love romance. Well, time was moving on and the chapel now had the floor in but no stairs for a while.

On the last night of the old year we had no electric light but we had stairs. Peggy and Fred, Ann, Neil, Ann's mam and dad were up. I am sure I was at Josephine's. I had my plaster off now and we went into the Chapel for a midnight prayer meeting 2000.

After that, about the end of January, I was allowed to decorate and Ann and Neil worked with me. It was March by the time we finished everything and then it was carpets and furniture. We got them second hand then Avril took me to B&Q to match it (or the Co-op, I am not sure) but it was delivered in flat packs so Ann set to and put it together. I laboured and helped her to line things up then I could move my things from Avril's and Edward's. O the joy of having my own place again.

Next I wanted to dedicate it to my Lord's work so I asked Laurence if he would come back, and with Roly, Jew and Gentile standing together, dedicate Maranatha to my Lord for His work. It was agreed. I am not sure how many came but it was a wonderful night and we stood together to proclaim Maranatha for Jesus Christ my Lord.

A day or two later Neil was working outside and our Lord gave him the Scripture of dedication, I Kings 8:63b - it was the one He gave me, so Ann, Neil and I prayed the Scripture.

Now people that used to come to Daybreak started to come and stay, so really the vision has been going on in Maranatha. Since I moved in people were coming in as others left, some that I was not sure about, some who really wanted help and some who only wanted a holiday. If they did not want to know my Lord or move on with Him or need help in themselves, I was having to say no and stop those who were coming for the wrong reasons. So, after being very busy with people it began to change. People were coming to pray and two of such people were two ladies who came every Friday. We would be in prayer all day mostly for the Jews, but for things of the world situation as well. Maranatha House is a house of prayer for all nations (Isaiah 56:7 quoted by Yeshua in Mark 11:17).

Now these ladies were going to Rome and asked me to go with them. Well, I prayed about it and it was right for me to go. Again my purpose was to cover them, and pray and back them in what they were in - so it was, and we were out. I had my fare to go but that was all. We were out on the first part of the mission this day and we were crossing the road. The roads in Rome are so wide you have to have your wits about you to get across. Well the two ladies were in front of me and I was following them over and in watching the road I picked up a bundle of money. I got to the other side and we prayed about this wad of money; where would I take it to hand it in and so forth and so on. I had such peace to use the money for wherever we had to go or whatever we had to do. This money paid for everything; all our meals, all the fares to go to the places we had to be at, everything. It truly was amazing.

We had our prayer time together every day. We had an en-suite bedroom, lovely big room with three beds. We had no air-conditioning to begin with, but we asked for a fan. I could hardly sleep at night for the heat. When our work was finished and we travelled home I gave what was left of the money to the ladies. Again Father provided our every need; the ladies were thrilled and we continued to pray every Friday.

Next they asked me to go to London but this time I wasn't given the leeway to go. I went with them to buy things to go with and I was unable to go shopping. I stayed in the car in prayer all afternoon. Now, as I have said, I don't always know for what or for whom I am praying but it lasted all afternoon. The two ladies returned and we travelled home. I received a phone call to tell me about a little girl who had had an operation to insert a plate and tubes into her head. She had been rushed to hospital and when they operated, they cleaned the plate and the tubes and she was all right. I knew as soon as I received the call that this had been my intercession all that afternoon. I prayed back what was in my heart now that I knew who it was, and I was clear.

A couple came to stay; they were to take a meeting in a Hexham church about the freemasons. We all went to support and, as we were reading and praying back the thirty three degrees of freemasonry, people were being set free of all manner of things; so we were learning a tremendous area to break through on deliverance of freemasons' families to see people being set free: as the men and women take the oaths, they bring the curse over the family. "O Father!" I bought the manual and was able to use it with two families where the parents had been well up in the freemason lodges. Two men in our village were in the freemasons and I tried to show them what was involved. They would not believe me, declaring the good works the freemasons did. I gave them books to read but I was unable to show them the wrong they were in.

When I was at Edward and Avril's while walking my dogs one day, I realised that there is a triangle between the little church at the top of the hill, the lodge at Bellingham, and a point in Woodburn which had been an altar, the devil's altar. So I set off with my Bible and positioned myself in the centre of each line and began to read out the Scriptures over each part, in order to break up the power of the triangle. The Bible says to bind the strong man before you can plunder his house (Mark 3:27). On reading up after I had done this, opening the gates for the King of Glory to come in (Psalm 24) I discovered the altar had been stolen in an earlier century and was being taken abroad, and the ship was wrecked so that the altar was at the bottom of the sea. So praise the Lord for that, but I continued to declare Jesus Christ as Lord over the whole area, taking back the area for Jesus Christ to reign in this valley. So this was another part of the cleaning of the valley, first the blood, then the closing of the door to Christianity, then the cleaning of the water and now the cleaning of freemasons. "Father we are gaining ground, praise You, praise You Lord."

I said "the closing of the door" but we have prayed, Father, for that door to be opened to Christianity and closed to every other religion.

2001: the day the twin towers were bombed in America. I was numb almost like I was paralysed and just sat all day in prayer; watching on the news; the pain of families, people phoning loved ones saying, "Goodbye" as they jumped; other people running in panic to rescue loved ones or see if they could find loved ones. The agony in my spirit lasted for days - sackcloth and ashes. I was still numb, I just prayed in the Spirit. It was given out that not everyone was in the building that works there, so the massive figure that could have been a tremendous number of people killed, was not as high as predicted. But for the families of those who were in the building, the trauma still went on, trying to find loved ones in the rubble. My heart was weeping for a long time, for families and the pain. Fatherless children, wives weeping for husbands lost, the utter despair was still very real and coming to terms with the fact that life would never be the same again.

Eventually the pain started to subside bit by bit and very slowly things came back; numbness going, confusion going, shock beginning to ease slowly, and I was able to let people go. I had a prayer line for all these situations, taking each one and continuing to pray through till peace came. I would get through one set of circumstances and another set would arise. Praise Jesus. "O comfort ye, comfort ye My people" (Isaiah 40:1).

The circumstances led into prayer and intercession for the generational bondage we carry, and I found myself breaking generational bondage to the third and fourth generation back to the tenth generation, to free people from sin coming down the family line; things they carried and were so unaware of the sin they were under. As we prayed back and confessed and repented for our forebears, things are being lifted off their shoulders. "My yoke is easy, My burden is light," (Matthew 11:30) my Lord said, so sickness, and all manner of things, are being lifted off as we pray and confess.

Now after the twin towers in America we got word that David Wilkerson might be coming to Britain. His church is in Times Square in America and this is the man who wrote

"The Cross and the Switchblade." So we began to pray that he would come to Britain.

A man had come the year before, Angus Buchan from Durban, South Africa. We were involved with Andy and Jim as our leaders. We met at Scots Gap Methodist Church and people came from far and near to be involved, quite a number when everyone was present. We had a gentleman who came up from Top Barn Farm, David, and Karen his wife, a beautiful couple in the Lord. He brought a tape with Angus speaking on it and straightaway the witness in my spirit was for our Lord to bring this man. We were all excited, plans were going ahead, Andy would speak to bring us up to date and he would have all the leaflets we needed to advertise, big posters and hand bills. We prayed for where the venue would be, everyone pulling together. A treasurer was appointed so we could send in finance to pay for the venue. David and Karen would come back and we would have a time of worship and then break into groups for prayer.

After putting places forward the most central place was Kirkley Hall agricultural college. It was decided we could have Thursday to Saturday nights. Then it was to send out all the invitations. I also put hand bills in every pub from Byrness village, right down to Four Road Ends, back across to Knowesgate and back up home.

Our first night came and we were there early to pray over all the chairs as we put them out and then a prayer meeting with Angus and the team. Music was by Johno (Jim's son) with another lad, and Lizzy (Jim's daughter, Johno's sister) singing with another girl. There were quite a few doors, so different ones were assigned to welcome people in and give out bits and bobs. People started to come, I am not sure how many the place could hold but the centre from front to back was full.

The music was good, very good, then Angus spoke. He was very good on his obedience to what You, Father, told him to do against the odds, but he did it and Father blessed. He made the appeal and some came forward. Then we had to get names and addresses for follow-up. I did not go on the Saturday - I stayed behind and prayed.

He and all the team were at church on Sunday. We broke bread together and it was lovely, really good fellowship. Then we were setting them off on their journey to the next venue. Jessica and Jim supported them in their work in South Africa. Angus had an orphanage on the farm and he went out all the time preaching the gospel. He had a huge wagon in which he travelled all over.

Now this New Year we had the word that David Wilkerson was definitely coming but it was for leaders, pastors, ministers, etc., and the venues were all booked, so there was no opportunity to have him come to our area. "O Lord, we really should like to hear this man."

Peggy and I came every week together for prayer, and so here we were, in prayer, and in our prayer time the subject of David Wilkerson came up. "God's messenger to Britain. Please, please Father, have mercy on Britain."

While we prayed we both knew the witness to go to one of his venues and, in the 'Prophecy Today' magazine, the nearest was Perth. Peggy phoned immediately and because we were intercessors we could go, so Peggy booked there and then. Now I knew another prayer lass who had a house in Perth, so I said I would contact her to see if she were going, and could we go and stay with her in Perth. When I got home I phoned Sheila; she said she did not know if she were going but would let me know. A day or two later Sheila rang me and said, yes she was going, yes come and stay, and we might start to pray three days before. This had been my prayer, that we could get the prayer work in beforehand. So it was all arranged. Peggy and I would drive as far as Edinburgh where Sheila lived, and then she would take us up into the Highlands of Scotland.

# CHAPTER 16

# A conference in Edinburgh, Christmas at home, then preparations for Ethiopia

We were very excited about it all. I remember Peggy came back with me after our prayer day on the Monday and we set off together from here on the Tuesday. Sheila had sent me a map to get to her home in Edinburgh so off we went. Now my little dog could go with me to Sheila's, she loved him. Bengy was a Cairn terrier and he was now 17 years old but he loved people. He would come upstairs to all the prayer meetings and he loved the people who came to stay. When he was younger he would take me for a walk, but at this time I would take him. He had such a character and we would play Peek a Boo along the passage and he would love to have something I was having. All my neighbours used to come to pat him and have a word with him and he would lick their hands and love them back. The story of Greyfriars Bobby is so true, his loyalty and love in the book. When he was young I lost him, he was such a hunter and he picked up a scent and followed it right over the valley. I went back and forth calling for him, then I was told the gamekeeper had picked him up in the next county and had taken him to the police station in Hexham, so I travelled over to pick him up. Another day I lost him at the Hall; he was chasing the rabbits. He would not touch them but loved the chase. I could follow him all over the wood by his yelps of delight as he set off after another rabbit. He went all day and would not come to me and late on at night I went back to see if he had given up yet and to my joy he was lying up against the staff back wall absolutely done. I picked him up and carried him home, so thankful he was OK. I was not so keen to take him off the lead after that so I bought one of the leads that extend right out, or you can keep them to heel. Now Father showed me we were the same, He could not give us the freedom - He had to keep us on a tight rein to protect us too.

Well all the way Peggy was thrilled with the scenery. As we began to come into the heavy traffic outside Edinburgh Peggy was reading the map. We were doing fine and we came up a slip road. I was going to go one way and Peggy said, "We can't go that way."

I panicked and followed through with the traffic. We kept going and I said, "We are lost."

So I pulled in and found a phone box and phoned Sheila. She told us what to do, which we did, but still came back the wrong way, so I phoned again. She came out to meet us and we were so close. It was silly. Never mind, Sheila parked my car and we packed everything into hers and off we went again. I was so thankful.

I loved my car and could drive anywhere on the country roads but I didn't like being in busy, busy traffic in town. But "All is well, Father" and we are really on our way now to go to Perth. We travelled in some magnificent countryside. Sheila's house was built on the bank side of Loch Tay and the sitting room wall was all glass - you could sit and look right up Loch Tay with the rolling hills right up each side. You never saw anything so beautiful.

We were there quite early as Peggy and I had set off from home at six in the morning so we were up to Loch Tay for lunchtime. Because we had three days to pray I knew Father was saying for me to do an Easter fast, just water for three days, so that was fine - I drank herbal tea. We unpacked and Sheila made lunch for Peggy and herself. Peggy was so in awe of the beauty of Sheila's house and our Lord's creation.

We settled down after lunch to pray. Well Father started with us; first we were confessing wrongs and repenting of things, then we were ministering to each other, then we had to get history books out as our Lord started to reveal things. We discovered that Perth had been the capital of Scotland at one time with a thriving port, ships going in and out and very prosperous, so we went into history to see what happened, to repent of it, breaking down the wall - standing stones - taking the strong man. We worked till late, Sheila made the meal and we just talked and shared, then we retired.

Day two, after breakfast we walked the dogs then came back into prayer. Father took us back into repentance. More came up to deal with among ourselves, then into warfare for Scotland again. It was very intense all day. We broke again while Sheila made meals but we were straight back in there. We worked till dark then retired.

Day three arrived. Now today it was taking back the land for Jesus Christ our Lord, so we were praying for David Wilkerson, God's prophet. We were praying for ministers and pastors from all around. We covered the days he and his son were speaking. We took away every detail and brought it before our Lord. Now Sheila made the meal earlier as we had to travel about an hour to Perth for the first of the meetings.

There was the opening session. After such a wonderful time of worship David Wilkerson came forward. He was a man in his seventies but as much on fire for God at seventy as he was when he was young. O, my Lord, this man knew my Jesus: no false message, no beating about the bush. He stepped forward and declared, "Welcome to the church of Jesus Christ."

O my Lord! It was like sitting at Jesus' feet, everything he said was from Your heart. "Father, all I ever had believed he was saying."

He confirmed and confirmed everything. As he finished he made the appeal and - remember this conference was for leaders, ministers and pastors - the front was full. O I was on my face before the Lord. Answered prayer was overwhelming as he prayed for these leaders and pastors and ministers over and around the Scriptures and said more than we can think or dream of.

We travelled home absolutely bewildered; this was only the first night. I cried into the night all Father was doing for Scotland. I prayed it all back, overjoyed to see all the men go forward but more than that really, for he called all the wives to come, wives who had stood by their men but were hurting as much as the men, tired, weary and frustrated. O this man really was God's apostle to our land.

We were up with the larks ready to go to the first sessions of the day. David again, the "Touch of God" - this again was profound in detail. The "Touch of God" is the calling to come up and come out. To come up is to come to an intimacy with our Lord in prayer; we come to listen to Him, to let Him talk to us. David says, to let our Lord feed him - "O my Lord how wonderful."

I was a little afraid that I was wrong for I just wanted to be with my Lord. I would go out and do what I had to do but I couldn't wait to get back home and be with my Lord. I never stayed if I was finished; I just wanted to come home. If people came to stay, I would do all I could: cook and clean etc. but o the joy that flooded my soul when they had gone and it was just Jesus and me. "Again forgive me Lord. Forgive me I only want to be with you." It makes sense just to be with Jesus. Jesus could have been speaking just to me, so great was the blessing hearing this man preach. "Thank You, thank You Lord."

Now Gary, David's son, is equally as good as his father but he is speaking to young pastors and ministers and telling them not to follow formulas because it wouldn't work; the only thing that works is to follow Jesus. "Well done, Gary." He explained time after time how he copied some well known man even to dress like him but it did not work. The meetings were exceptional, the teaching right down the line - back to being a desperate 'die to self and live for Jesus'.

Then it was spiritual warfare again; Father was showing me the intercession, breaking the curses and setting families free. Binding this strong man and overcoming the enemy in prayer, in intercession, in spiritual warfare. "Give him an inch and he would take a mile. The minute the attack comes go straight back to our Lord. Turn it round - don't accept it - pray - take every thought captive before God - place every detail before God - leave nothing to chance."

"O Father," listening to this man David is like sitting at Jesus' feet; it is like coming back under the holiness of our Lord. Every word is like fresh manna yet it is confirming all Father has ever said. This man is God's man speaking with the true anointing of our Lord Jesus Christ, speaking what is in Father's heart, putting into words all the things confirming the depth of our Lord.

Every night we prayed back all he had said, and all that Gary had shown by example: all the mistakes, releasing the pain in the hearts of young pastors, because we had got it wrong, but repenting, confessing back and taking the consequences. "Being open, being real with our Lord and growing up: if we are standing still we are stagnating. If we are constant in seeking our Lord we are growing. We will never know it all till at last we see Him face to face. Over all these years my mistakes will stretch to John O'Groats and back, but Father does not condemn me. Pick yourself up, dust yourself down and start all over again. We must stay teachable, we must stay humble; each time we fall we become more humble, because we know in our strength we can do nothing, but with Him all things are possible. To him who believes, and the more broken you become, only he with pure heart and clean hands can come up the mountain. Don't model yourself on someone else only on Jesus. He and He alone is our example, come follow Him."

When the conference ended it was like I was full. I ordered all the tapes, which were seven. Peggy and I travelled home, it had been a feast.

I had a couple stay with me in the following days and because it was friends of Ann and Neil I invited Ann and Neil in every night. We ate together, enjoyed fellowship, and prayed. When they left they gave me thirty pounds, and I was asking Father for a recording machine so, when David's tapes of the conference came, I could copy them and send them out. Well I was in Morpeth and I was looking everywhere with no joy; if I found what I wanted it was very expensive. I was about to give up but I was prompted to go to Safeway's and there as I walked in the door was exactly what I wanted reduced to thirty-nine pounds. "Praise You Lord" - the full price was double but half price was what I had, "Thank You, thank You precious Jesus."

I brought it home absolutely excited at my purchase, and tapes at Woolworth's were also on offer, 10 tapes for £3.99 so I bought the tapes too. So when my tapes came from the conference I started to copy them. Now this is another mark of God's man. He would not take anything for anything he had done, and he declared we could copy the tapes. He was not here for what he could get, he was here for what he could give. "Get the Word out," so with the privilege of having been there I copied as many sets of tapes as I could and sent them to everyone I knew. Out of the hundreds of tapes sent out the feedback was very small but that was not my concern. My job was to tell, as in Isaiah 6:9 "Go and tell this people: keep on hearing, but do not understand; keep on seeing, but do not perceive." Mine was to get them as far and wide as I could - that was my job. It took me weeks to copy and post but the Word went forth from Maranatha, out into the farthest parts.

We don't understand what our Lord is really saying for we are but mortals and we see through a glass dimly (I Corinthians 13:12). We shall never know till we go home. All these years down the road but my journey is still a learning one. I know nothing; the closer I get the less I know, I go in obedience to my beloved Lord to do what I don't know; only He knows. The Bible says: "He will use the foolish to confound the wise" (I Corinthians 1:27). "If we say we are without sin, we deceive ourselves and the truth is not in us" (I John 1:8). We should be ever changing to be more like our Lord.

Now our Lord is "the same yesterday, today and forever" (Hebrews 13:8), but we change. We see a little more, we understand a little more, as when listening to David Wilkerson. Father confirmed and confirmed all he had ever shown me. It was put into words; the blessing was profound and just made me reach out to my Lord for more. Teach me Holy Spirit, teach me. "You shall be holy, for I the LORD your God am holy", Leviticus 19:2.

We were in the month of September when sharing and talking and we counted up when we last saw each other. I realised that particular October was the beginning of the seventh year since I started with the Tower, so I started to pray round it, because of the forty days fast for the Jews. I really felt I should do it again, praying for the Tower. Seven years is a very significant time for our Lord so a fortnight into the fast was when Father showed me that was the time to write my book, "Pathway of Faith." I was quite excited about it and made a start right away. I had so much to write: about all the places I have been and all the wonderful people I have met on my journey. Well, I was sitting at the kitchen table and my phone went and a gentleman said, "Hello Rosie, are you going to be in?"

I answered, "Yes."

He said "We are at Hexham so we'll see you in half an hour."

I got stuff out of the freezer to make us a meal, or them a meal, so all was well; and right enough, in half an hour Richard and Sylvia came in. What a lovely surprise. We had not seen each other for a good long time. We were sitting chatting and Richard always asks what I am doing. So I laughed and said, "I am writing my book."

I shared how it was the seventh year, which is the year of completion. I also laughed and said, "I don't know how it will come together because of my lack of ability."

Richard replied, "Rosie you write it, we will record it on to tape. I will take it and type it and put it on to the computer and all you have to do is take the floppy disc to the publisher."

Now we did this so Richard could take it away with him that night, and when I had finished as far as I had written both Sylvia and Richard said it has to be on tape too so people can listen to it as well as read it.

By the end of the fast I had been asked to go to Ethiopia with Elisabeth. Elisabeth is a specialist in medicine for lepers and worked a lot of years in Ethiopia but still goes back every year to check her pupils. I had the witness immediately but I waited for Father to confirm through two or three witnesses. To my joy on sharing with Peggy she also had the witness, so "Hey presto Ethiopia here I come."

I was writing like mad to get my book right up to date before I went so my mind would be free to listen to my Lord, for the work or purpose for going out to Ethiopia, and of course for my Lord's provision. I was not altogether sure, so "When in doubt do nowt."

I kept going back to Richard and Sylvia's to tape my book. After a while Peggy and I were continuing to pray about all manner of subjects. Durham church was uppermost on the list, but Peggy always linked Durham with Israel, and it came to our attention that there were 24,000 Jews in Ethiopia, and Scriptures came so, again, Father confirmed to me about going to Ethiopia.

While out walking with Bengy the sole of my shoe came off, I managed to get home walking with it flapping. Coming back into the house I said, "Well Father, I will need new shoes if I am going to Ethiopia."

I took my shoes off and stuck the sole back on with Uhu glue. The next week I went to Peggy's and when we were finished our praying, Peggy asked, "Rosie what size shoe do you take?"

I said I was a seven but I am nearer an eight now as my foot is broad. She went away, came back with a pair of beautiful shoes and, handing them to me, she said, "Try them on."

Well I put them on; they looked and felt comfortable. I said, "They are beautiful," and Peggy said "Well, I was an eight, but I take a size bigger now so if they fit and are all right you can have them."

Well, we laughed together as I told her what happened to my shoes in the week and how I had stuck them together again and what I had said to our Lord. Again confirmation I was going to Ethiopia. This was November, remember, and there was so much to do as Elisabeth said it would be January. So the next day I phoned Elisabeth to say I was coming, I told her about the shoes and then she said, "Well, the money for the air fare had come in too. Praise Jesus."

Now we had to pull all the stops out. I had to make arrangements with my doctor for all the vaccinations you had to have and a certificate to say you had had them, so it was two a week for six weeks. I had never been to the doctors since I was in Kenya, ten or eleven years ago. He thought I was going to another doctor, so he had to get my files back.

We laughed as I told him, "I am never sick". Then the injections began. He asked me every week if I was all right, and every week I was fine. He really did investigate everything to do with Ethiopia and updated my policy as well making sure I was covered for everything.

By now it was nearly Christmas so my cards were out, I had my presents for friends and family and I even had birthday cards written for February because I would be away two months. Next it was to ask about my little Bengy. I felt I was to ask Noel and Joan as I always went home to Rothbury and looked after their dogs whenever they wanted to go and see Paul, Noel's son. Bengy liked being there, he was used to the house and he loved the company of Noel and Joan's dogs so I prayed first that Father would go with me and things would be alright.

Well I need not have been concerned at all. "O ye of little faith."

Both Noel and Joan were so pleased to have little Bengy. Bengy had had two strokes and now was on heart pills but Joan and Noel said did I realise he may not still be here when I got back as I was to be gone two months? Well, I did realise and I prayed about it and was prepared, so that was all arranged.

I came home and checked through my list. Ann was knitting me a coat for my Christmas with Jesus knit into the yoke. I was thrilled - things were going well. Elisabeth phoned: we had to apply for visas to go, so she posted my form down to me to fill in and send. Two ladies came for prayer week and while we were together I shared I was going to Ethiopia for two months. Well we started to pray and halfway through one of theses ladies wrote out a cheque and when we had finished praying she said "our Lord has told me to give you this." Well, I was thrilled, a cheque for £50. I thanked her so much and we parted.

My letter came from Elisabeth; I had to fill in the form and pay £50. I was so surprised - here our Lord had gone before me and the money was there. I duly filled in and sent my letter with a cheque for my visa and I phoned my friend to tell her about the £50 cheque. She was thrilled that she heard our Lord but better still she had obeyed - "What a mighty God we serve." Next I took my cards to the little fellowship at Newcastle and shared with Jim and Jessica and the fellowship that I was going to Ethiopia for the two months. The date we now had was the sixteenth of January till the sixteenth of March. I asked if they would pray with me as this would be the last time I would see them not only before Christmas but before I go. It was beautiful; everyone prayed a prayer for me. I was so blessed. After we had our teas and coffees I was making ready to go and Jessica came forward and said the Lord had told her to give me the gift and the money was a hundred pounds ... Well, I sang all the way home, the excitement of God's provision and the love of God's people.

Christmas was beautiful. I always go to Jo's to see the bairns open their parcels and Jo invited me for Christmas dinner, so I went. I was waiting for the phone call to say the bairns were up and Jo phoned at eight o clock. When my bairns were little (before I was saved) the excitement of Christmas was so wonderful. The lead up: hiding the presents beforehand, and trying to get things Jimmy and I thought they would want. O what fun, I loved the carols and the joy of getting things ready, baking the Christmas cake and getting the puddings and Jimmy loved the rum sauces. Everything had to be so right and the bairns were on their best behaviour, for they believed that Santa's little men were listening up the chimney to see if they were being good. They were up at 5 or 6 in the morning with excitement.

When I received Jesus as my Saviour my joy was great, but it became even more beautiful as I learned all about the Jews and how Jesus' birthday was really the Feast of Tabernacles (September / October time). The Jewish people kept Hanukah, which often coincided with Christmas, and they exchanged presents too. The story of Hanukah was God's rescue of the Jewish people from extermination by the Syrians in 165 BC. Jews expect their Messiah to come on or around Feast of Tabernacles. For them, Christmas is not our beloved Saviour's birthday because they still await His coming. I felt disappointment at first, and concern, as we were told how our Lord's birthday coincided with a pagan festival, and the early church put the two together. So it was confusion, concern of were we wrong to celebrate Christmas. How could we celebrate Christmas, the most wonderful thing that happened after all the years, the joy and gifts at Christmas, all the love shed abroad at Christmas? I really was earnest in prayer about Christmas and consoled myself that for me the real meaning of Christmas was its being the Lord's birthday. When the gifts were given and wonderful Christmas dinner was over, above all was the joy of my Lord's birthday. I have to say that for me now, with my bairns up and away, I can enjoy the festive season but with a greater joy that Jesus is with me always, not only at Christmas or Hanukah.

Jo phoned to say that my grandchildren had woken up, so I went to their house for the opening of parcels. Well, it took about three hours of laughter, joy and fun, opening all the parcels and "Santa" had brought everything on the list. After this Jo was going to make breakfast so I asked if I could go and take Bengy for a long walk which fitted in well to be back for half one or two, for lunch. I left Jo's and called in to see David, Hazel and Zak. We just had a little time together as Hazel was having her mam for Christmas lunch so I moved on and came home and Bengy and I went out for a walk. We always went down to the mill and walked round the field and the mill, then home and, as we came round from the back of the mill, there were Edward and Avril to wish me happy Christmas. O it was wonderful!

They went off home and Bengy and I went home. Then I went back to Jo's and we had a wonderful day. The bairns knew I was going away again after New Year and I had everything in order for while I was away. The time flew by till it was time for me to take Bengy down to Noel and Joan's. Two days after I said my goodbyes and I left to go to Edinburgh as we were flying from there.

# CHAPTER 17

# My time in Ethiopia

*I* had been to Ann and Neil's fellowship up over the border and Margaret prayed for me too. It was so great to have the prayers of support. I received another letter from the Newcastle fellowship with another cheque for a hundred pounds; then another letter, from a praying lass, with two hundred pounds. I was so thrilled and prayed, as this was His money, for Him to show me what to use it for, as it was from people who had to work hard for what they had and I did not want to squander the money entrusted to me. I wanted to be a good steward of God's resources.

Elisabeth and I travelled to Edinburgh to sleep at Mary Clare's house, as we had to catch our plane very early in the morning. We set off from Elisabeth's, Gorbridge near Peebles, in a blizzard; it was snowing very heavily. We took the main roads as there would still be traffic, whereas the back roads and short cuts would work out more hazardous. We arrived safely at Mary Clare's house and unpacked the car. My car was to stay at Elisabeth's and we asked the lady next door if her grandson would start it once a week or so. We chatted for only a little while as we were to have such an early start. I had my bath before going to bed, so leaving

Elisabeth to have hers in the morning. I was straight off to sleep after thanking Father for everything of the day.

I woke at three o'clock, before the alarm went off, so again I could thank Him for this protection in the night and handing everything over to Him for the day in front of us: the flights, the baggage, the weather and every detail.

The alarm went off and Elisabeth went for her bath. Having had mine last night, I got ready. We had breakfast and packed our overnight things and secured our bags. A friend of the family was coming to take us to the airport. She arrived on time and packed the car with our luggage and we were off. No problem at the airport - our bags went through fine. We had them weighed together as I was travelling light so Elisabeth could take out extra stuff for the people she knew out there. The bags passed the weight allowed ok - praise Jesus.

After a while, not long, we boarded our plane. We both had heavy hand luggage but it was ok again.

The first part of the journey was from Edinburgh to Amsterdam: a two hour flight with an hour to wait in Amsterdam, before we took off again for Nairobi, which was seven and a half hours away. We had to wait, as they were bringing a refugee on board, in handcuffs, who was being sent back home to Nairobi. The man was very distressed, crying out and he kept trying to break free of the man holding him. Once the plane was in the air there was nothing he could do but cry. I was praying to our Lord to calm the lad and give him peace. The men with him were reassuring and being very good in the way that they were responding to the situation. They had their plan and how they hoped it would go, as they were working for him not against him. I prayed through as I had heard being discussed, placing as much as I could before God.

Next we had two men in front who really were afraid of flying. They were drinking very hard, so I took all that back to Jesus. Elisabeth had gone to sleep, so she was fine.

Then a young girl, in her early twenties, was sitting next to me and as we chatted and got on talking, she shared she was going out to Kenya as a missionary. Because I had been there we talked and talked and shared. The seven and a half hours passed very quickly; it seemed no time till we touched down in Nairobi. As we said our goodbyes I gave her one of Roly's CDs and we said we would pray for each other.

What a joy it was to see one so young setting off on the mission field, with the zeal of our Lord shining in her eyes. "O Father," what a privilege it was: like wanting to share so much, which we did, for our journey, but to tell of the pitfalls I have made; the lessons we must go through to know what Father is really saying and to know the difference between what we think He is saying. We only get a bit and before you know it we have presumed what He is saying and we run with it and when it goes wrong we think "well, what happened?" But when we sit with our Lord and wait, He explains and we realise "if only I had waited."

Elisabeth and I had to get straight to the boarding gate for our next flight to Ethiopia. We made it just in time. We boarded our plane and settled in for the last lap of our journey: another two hours to Ethiopia. It seemed such a short time till we touched down there. We got through the landing procedure and passed the customs to collect our luggage. It was not there. Elisabeth went to see what had happened but it was all right: our luggage was at Nairobi and would come with the first flight on the next day. I knew it would be OK because we ourselves had only just made our flight; no way could they have got our luggage off the flight from Amsterdam, so all was well. By this time it was midnight but praise the Lord we were able to change some money from our travellers cheques into Birr, the currency of

Ethiopia. We then went outside and our lift was there to take us on the last lap to the hospital. "Praise You, my Lord, safe and sound. O thank You, thank You."

Elisabeth introduced me to this lad who was one of the drivers of the hospital. They chatted and I just sat very quiet taking in this part of Africa. The city of Addis Ababa seemed vast with the skyscrapers and tall buildings, big, big hotels, different kinds of buildings, which at this time of night loomed up out of the darkness. Elisabeth would call out to tell me what each one was. It was very evident, even at this early stage of touch down, that Elisabeth loved being here. Her parents had been missionaries in Kenya. Her father had ministered out there and Elisabeth had been a doctor in the hospital in Addis itself for a number of years before she became involved with the leprosy hospital, outside the city, where we were going. She knew a lot of the history of Addis and had made many friends here, so to come back every year to do more tests and write up all about progress, she was in her element. Because it was so late, we were taken straight to our house, in number five.

We thanked our driver very much and we had a quick look round. There was a main sitting room cum dining room, small bedroom and a large bedroom, bathroom and kitchen, with hot and cold water, a bath, absolutely wonderful, and of course a proper toilet, not one where you had to squat. This was marvellous - I really didn't know what to expect; there were even electric lights. I had had none of these luxuries in Kenya.

I had never slept our entire journey and I was quite tired, so we said our good nights, gave each other a hug and went off to our bedrooms. I got ready for bed, but then I just wanted to talk to my Lord giving to Him everybody we had seen, and all the different incidents that had happened, then my bairns and Bengy, after which I went straight to sleep.

I woke about seven and all was quiet, so I lay still and began my day with my morning reading, and giving the day to my Lord, "Thy will be done," as I did not know my reason for being in this place. After a while I heard Elisabeth moving about, so I went out. We got into a routine straight away and continued for the whole time we were together. I would bath first as my breakfast was fruit, while Elisabeth had poached egg, done a very special way: an auntie, I think, had shown her what to do, so I left her to it while I got bathed and ready for the day. By that time we were able to sit down together, I to my fruit, and Elisabeth to her egg. The first lesson was the birr in currency: one or two birr bought a kilo of bananas or oranges. The fruit and vegetables were so cheap: a bagful of avocado pears cost two birr, potatoes one birr, carrots one birr and sometimes celery, so to live on fruit and vegetables was very, very cheap. But then I discovered the wages for a month were a pittance so "Praise You Lord" that the food was so cheap.

The staple diet was a stew made with pulses ground to a powder and mixed with a bread that bore a likeness to crumpets with the holes in. It was not thick like a crumpet but doughy and rubbery, the size of a huge dinner plate, and they ate it at every meal. The stew called wat was too hot and spicy; it burned your mouth off, and the bread dough called injera tasted sour as though it were off, but the Ethiopians loved it.

After breakfast I always washed and tidied up. Elisabeth was going out to meet everyone at RE, the hospital. I was to go with her, so off we went. Wandu was first - o what a lovely lad, and he spoke good English. "Praise You Lord." Wandu and Elisabeth chatted away, catching up with each other on all their news; then we went down to meet Howard at RE head office. We asked if we could send e-mails home, and Howard was so helpful: "Of course," he said. I had e-mail addresses for my boys but not for Jo, but I had Noel's as well, so we sent off that we had arrived safely. They also said that it was for the hospital so not to use it again.

Elisabeth took me round every department, introducing me to all the different ones of the staff. As we headed back to our house we met Gabra, who was head of the department that we were under. He let the house, was in charge of the staff, and he also let the rooms to all the people who came to train and do six or eight week courses. We were taken round to see the rooms and laundry, kitchens and dining and sitting areas. I was also shown a magnificent old stone building - huge. This was the old hospital and I was taken round the new red brick hospital up to the eye hospital, and where the Aids people were. We went over to the training rooms where the students learned all about Aids, malaria and leprosy, the three big diseases of Africa. Then we walked out of the compound right down to the far corner and I met Sister Sinkernich, a Catholic nun. She was an Ethiopian who had a mission for children and old beggars. She was beautiful. She had a tiny chapel in her corner and she said I could come and use the chapel for prayer at any time. This was wonderful - from my sanctuary at home, Father had given me my space with Him. "O my Lord." I was so thankful. "So Father, now show me my work."

Well, apart from cooking and cleaning and washing for Elisabeth, my work was prayer. As the days passed I was gleaning the information that Elisabeth told me. The compound had been a Mission but then the government had taken over, and now it was "big business"! The people paid to come to train. We also hit one thing after another. There was no office for Elisabeth to work in and so a table with all the computer equipment had to come into the house; day by day the atmosphere went from bad to very bad. The hostility was becoming quite something. So this was my job - the more I prayed the more I saw that I was bringing to my Lord, with Elisabeth and Wandu working in the house.

Praise Jesus for my sanctuary along at Sinkernich's. Father was showing me the Ethiopian Jews - 24,000 in Ethiopia - so I was to be like Daniel when he prayed for Jerusalem three times a day. He gave me the Scriptures to pray three times a day starting with Exodus chapter 32 verse 13, "Remember Abraham, Isaac, and Israel, Your servants, to whom You did swear by Your own self, and said to them, I shall multiply your seed as the stars of heaven, and all this Land of which I have spoken I shall give to your seed, and they will inherit it for ever."

Next, Leviticus 25:23, "The Land, moreover, will not be sold permanently, for the Land is Mine; for you are aliens and sojourners with Me." Then right over to Psalm 83, speaking out every word of the whole Psalm; then Psalm 147, every word. Proclaiming then it was Isaiah 43:5-7, then Isaiah 45:21-25 - "Powerful words, Lord." Next, over to Jeremiah 31:7-10, then 33:6-9. How exciting, the Scriptures were coming thick and fast. Ezekiel 36:22-28 was next. Now on to Zechariah 12:10 and 13:1-2. Now Romans 11:25-27, then I Peter 4:17 - now this Scripture was for us: wake up, Church.

I would read my Scriptures out three times a day and this would lead into other things at the same time - my Lord was showing me other things. As I walked to Sinkernich's little chapel, I had to go past the hospital where all along the front so many people were waiting to see the doctors, so many people with limbs missing. I have never seen so many, some blind, some with withered hands, no fingers, just stumps; with leprosy the fingers drop off. I would get past the hospital, then there is a wall right down to the chapel full of beggars, again so many with limbs missing. Some walked with flip-flops on where the knee should be and on the hands, their backs were so deformed. Depending on the day, full some days, other days maybe half a dozen or a dozen, and the same ones would beg. I had nothing I could give because I was doing this walk regularly.

After a while those who could speak English would talk to me; they would invite me to share what they had which was bread and water but I was able to share my faith in Jesus, and who I was with and why I was here. I would get to the chapel and go in but I was speechless; I had nothing to say to my Lord. I wept unto my Lord for the sickness and poverty, and the three hundred orphaned children that Sister had. I wept and wept. Then outside the compound in the Leper Village they just stayed, shunned, because of having to wait for medicine, just like when Jesus was on the earth. They were not allowed in town or anywhere else, so it was the Leper Village, made from tin: no sanitation, no water, no electricity, just squalor.

The weeping lasted for two weeks before I was through the pain in the heart, with the intercession. Then Sister asked me if I would write thank you letters for her to people who had sent cheques for her and her work. I was told that the clothes were sewn on to the children so they could not be pinched. Sister said that when the parents had died the children would attach themselves to others, and this was encouraged, so Sister would buy their clothes and food and pay for them to be taught, but they all lived in families which I thought was a very good idea.

By now prayers were being answered and Elisabeth was given an office in the training wing so I went round to take coffee, and Elisabeth introduced me to the Doctor in charge of the training. "Well, o Father, what a beautiful man!" He could speak perfect English. On the shelf of his office was "Praying Hands". As he talked he wanted to show me round, he was so proud of his area for students; he showed me the computer room and the lecture room. He told me not to bring coffee any more; Elisabeth and Wandu would receive coffee with them.

I learned so much about the human body: the medical thing. Elisabeth took pills for every thing every day but my Lord protected me - I never had anything. Elisabeth wanted me to try the different tests they did, to see all the diagrams they had done, file after file they had to go through again. Elisabeth was so brilliant, she explained and talked of nothing else but I could understand that my faith is in Jesus not medicine. Now don't get me wrong - I know that God has provided all these things too, but I felt that the witness was in the men and women and medicine, not bringing our Lord into it at all. So as this man was talking I was bringing the thankfulness that our Lord was in charge. When we were finished he turned to me and said "I believe everything you are saying." He had been brought up by missionaries in India.

Well, I was so thrilled. I believed that this was God's man on the compound because he knew Jesus. The tears were rolling down my face. "O Father, here we go." I walked the compound to take it back for Jesus, to ask Father for Jesus to take His rightful place here. My prayers now were for the workers to know that this place belongs to our Lord and that they worked for Him. Things began to change, the atmosphere began to be put down and a love began to flow. The guards on the compound all asked for a Bible. Elisabeth went into Addis to buy the Bibles and came back with two kinds: the full Bible in the Ethiopian language but she also brought the New Testament in Ethiopian and English.

Now this was wonderful because of two girls who were Elisabeth's children, whom she watched after treatment for leprosy from being young. Well, when they knew that she was back they came to see her and as we talked they wanted to speak English. So we started by their coming every week and reading the English out loud, then reading the Bible in their language and discussing what it means. So we were having English lesson come Bible study come discussion all at the same time. Now that Elisabeth was working in her office I could pray in the house and save me time walking to Sister's. Writing letters for Sister, teaching English, praying with people, cooking and cleaning, my days were wonderful.

Our neighbour two doors down in House A3 was a Korean girl, Yushine. She asked me to teach her English so I went at night after I had washed up. Again it was wonderful as she too owned a Bible in English and Korean so we would read and pray. She asked me if I would cook an English dinner for her and her friends, so I did. I cooked roast chicken, Yorkshire puddings, about three vegetables, roast potatoes and boiled potatoes mashed and creamed. They were thrilled and like the African Kenya there was nothing left. They did not eat the bones but licked them clean. The fun we had as we talked and shared about Jesus. In every nation and every creed, when you talk about our Lord we truly are family, rejoicing together; laughing, praying, lifting up the name of Jesus and He will draw them to Himself.

Next, Sinkernich asked if I would like to go on a trip with the bairns, seventy of the smaller ones. So yes, I wanted to go. The children are so well behaved; they stood in line for an hour waiting for the bus and Sinkernich and they never complained, never winged, never a peep out of them. I thought how different it would have been were it our children who have so much; they would have complained and cried and winged. Well, time had come so we all piled on to the bus. One of Sinkernich's girls was in charge and what a job she did. The bairns sang all the way there. Because I was English they sang all the carols they had learned in English over Christmas. I was so pleased and joined in with them.

We arrived at the Menagesha Suba State Forest, the oldest park in Africa. It had nurseries growing trees. Up in the forest itself, wild animals: 82 species of mammals and 186 species of birds. It was a beautiful day. Three guests with us had done a sponsored cycle ride. Listening to them, it had been some tour. They were beautiful, raising £18,000 to give to Sinkernich for the mission. What a joy, what a blessing; "away I go again, Father." The tears just rolled as one of the men was talking and sharing about his trip and how he wanted the bairns to have the money. Sister was thrilled. Then it was picnic time: one doughnut and a small bottle of pop. Each child got a balloon. "O Father, Father." On the way home each child was given two sweeties - not a bagful or a bar of chocolate - two sweeties. "O Father, please, please help these bairns."

Prayer really being answered for Elisabeth and Wandu - they got through fifty nine items of the data base that day.

Sister was so pleased with my letters to the churches for all their help. We went into the school and got so many of the children to write letters too. Sister asked if I would write a report on our trip so I did; she was overjoyed.

Saturday again and we were going to the market today. Now this is held at the international church. It is every charity, every organisation that has come into Ethiopia to help the people, and the amount of stuff was incredible: all stuff made to raise funds for the people to help the people. The garden vegetables then farm produce, eggs, butter, pâté, rugs, leather goods, cotton outfits, tie-die, candles, wood, stall after stall - all charities come in to help but putting the people to work and showing them how to do it. What a market, what a work! I did get bits and bobs to bring home for my bairns and to support the hard work.

That week Wandu took me to Beysuahu's church. I was praying all the way through - Holy Spirit was not allowed to move, very sad. I did tell Beysuahu that we needed to pray for his church.

After church we were invited for a meal at the house of the little lass who comes for English lessons. This was in the same area as the church, so Elisabeth came to meet us and we set off together. We arrived and were all introduced to Mam and Dad, brothers and sisters. We ate together in the main room and everyone else stayed in the kitchen which was a shame, but only the young lass could speak English. We read a passage of Scripture and prayed together. The meal was the way they cook but Winashet, one of Elisabeth's girls, had tried to make some how we would eat it. All these years down the road I was not as adventurous as I was in Kenya and so I had managed to get through things I knew I could eat. After our meal we talked and talked, or they talked in their languages. I just sat and watched again - it was like I had taken a step back in time and we were back to when our Lord was here on earth. The lepers were shunned because of the nature of their disease in accordance with the primitive ways things were done. We finished our meal with real coffee; the beans were ground in the stone with an instrument made of stone.

It was time to head home so it was all our goodbyes and thank yous. Everyone chatted together as we walked back through the area towards home. For me again I was silent with the beauty of this nation, and the poverty of this nation. "O Father: the Ethiopians are mentioned in the Bible forty-seven times - they had nothing material-wise, but the ones I have met, the ones Father has brought across my path, are rich in their love for You, Lord. They are bold in prayer and believe Your miracle working power." They have faith to pray - and Jesus said "if you have faith as small as a mustard seed ..."

Today Sister asked me if I would write letters with the children to the American children who wanted pen pals, so here we were. What a sense of humour our Lord has - me writing letters! I cannot spell back home; when I write letters I sit with the dictionary to make sure I don't spell wrongly.

The news has been on the telly and the talk on the compound is heavy falls of snow, but it had melted quickly and so flooding and all kinds of things were turning up on the streets of New York - snakes and everything coming up the manholes. So into prayer. So far it is three times a day, like Daniel, for the Jews in Ethiopia for our Lord to take them home. I was praising Him for the mighty move He had brought on this land. Father showed me today to press on to get the victory.

Four letters from home, two from Peggy and Ann, one from Sheila; such joy and encouragement. I got such a boost and drive to get in there. The prayer line is so important.

Beysuahu came this afternoon so it was in the Word and prayer with him. After tea back out to A3 to the little Korean girl leaning English. Work till late so no prayers first tonight - straight to bed.

I have made friends with a little monkey; he comes every day for his banana - and today he stayed with me all day. He lay on the window ledge while I worked all day.

One of the students came round today to show me a picture of her husband. She is so in love with him - it is beautiful. We just talked and shared.

Beysuahu came today. We were in the Scriptures, all about marriage, I Corinthians 6 and 7. Beysuahu's job is counselling at the church so it was good to talk and share with him, to help him with his understanding and how important it is; so teach right down the line the truth of the Word. He is so hungry Father wanting to know. "O Father, speak to him, bless him with Your presence, go with him in his work for You."

Another day: "What will You bring today, Father?" Well, Wandu and Elisabeth came in for lunch. We must have talked about many things when Wandu began to weep and get down on his knees. Elisabeth says demonic, but Father was showing me Scripture: Genesis 12:13 to the end where Abram tells a lie about Sarai his wife. Well, we calmed Wandu down and he then told us he had not dared to tell Elisabeth that he is married and has two boys. He has worked with Elisabeth for three years but he looked at me and said "You know our Lord" and he, Wandu, was afraid our Lord would tell me before he did, so he wanted to confess. Well, we were so thrilled about his wife and children, but I asked him to repent before our Lord, which he did, and then I prayed for him and he was healed immediately. He had suffered with terrible headaches for three years and had been taking medication, thinking it was blood pressure, but as soon as he confessed his sin the headaches were gone. He was elated! "What a joy, Lord, to rejoice with him." I told him he must get in touch with his wife and tell her he is free and everything is alright. What a day of rejoicing!

Winashet arrived for her lesson and we prayed together then straight to work. We had been going for half an hour when Mesaret, another of Elisabeth's girls, arrived. She also wanted to learn English, so we set off again and the girls took turns to read the word. We worked on till half six so when Wandu and Elisabeth came home I had nothing prepared for dinner. We ended up where we all had egg in a bun and fruit.

Wandu brought me three letters, one from Peggy, one from Joan and Noel, and one from Josephine with little letters inside from Matthew and Yasmin. O, it is wonderful to hear from home. Jo's was all family news; Joan and Noel's was all about Bengy and Peggy's was all about our Lord and what He was doing. "Thank You so much, Father."

After I washed up I went round to Yushine's for her lesson. Praise our Lord we went to the Bible to John 7 from verse 14. We read through, Yushine reading three or four verses then I would read and explain. We studied till ten then I came home.

Now we were preparing to go to Chencha where Wandu lives. He was very excited about going home so we had started praying for transport and what we had to take. Now before I left home Jessica gave me an address for sister Jemba. Jessica called her and said that I might not meet her but might be able to make contact. Well, to my joy Sister

Sinkernich knows her well, so she gave me a phone number to get in touch. Sister seemed pleased to make contact and said she would send a vehicle round to pick me up on Friday. So I was all ready and did extra prayer times in the morning to get my requests in three times for our Lord's people and everybody else, and so I was waiting for my truck which arrived on time.

We set off, the driver and a beautiful girl and myself. We arrived at our destination and the young lass then said she would show me Sister's work. We proceeded to walk for miles round the community. Sister Jemba goes into the slum areas - the worst areas - and sets off with the poor of the poor; but they build new houses so they set the men to work new roads, all by hand, no big machines to shift the rubbish. Everything is done by hand. They go from door to door and ask the people what they want so they have their own clinic and doctor and nurses - so more employment. I was talking to the doctor - what a wonderful guy with such a heart for the people.

We then went to a factory where the women worked. The grain was laid out on huge sheets to dry in the sun, then put into bowls and the women have to pack the lentils clean, taking off the black skin and leaving them orange, like we get them back home. Then there was a machine to grind them to powder. They had a shop to sell the pulses both cheap for themselves and as a going business to bring in more capital. Next to it was basket weaving and they made all kinds of things, again to sell. Then I was taken to where the raw cotton was brought in, spun into thread into huge cones and then some girls were weaving it into material. About six looms were going. O, I was so thrilled again: all women bettering themselves.

Next we went up the hill and into a warehouse and more men making furniture. Man, this was marvellous. From the weaving it was into a factory and they had patterns so they were cutting out clothes - about six sewing machines working flat out. I was taken to the shop again to see them finish everything from baby clothes to adult also. There was a section on embroidery.

From here I was taken to the nursery - all babies so mums could work, then play school for toddlers then infant school and on to the high school and college. Even handicapped children were taken care of so mum could work. I was praising our Lord all the way round. Then it was community hall for the elderly where they were fed and looked after and entertained and some of them even worked if they could and if they wanted to. There were as many old as children but every one was cared for and they were so happy. As I walked in with my young chaperone everybody shouted so I shouted "Hello" back.

We then headed back to head office and I would see Sister Jemba. I was taken to the head of the table as guest to sit with Jemba and I was asked to give thanks for our meal. The working party in head office would be about fifty people who planned everything, each one specialising in his or her specific talent, with Jemba bringing them all together to fulfil this tremendous work.

After our meal I went back to Jemba's office. She asked me if it would be possible to come back and pray round one area which needed prayer against witchcraft. Well I never got back but I still prayed for the area, coming against the principalities and powers of darkness.

Now Elisabeth wanted to take me to see Katharine who worked at another hospital but with all I had seen with Jemba I wanted to stay behind and go back through everything so as not to forget anything. Wandu went with Elisabeth so praise Jesus I was excused.

Monday we go to Chencha. Now this is where Wandu lives. He, like us all, is so excited to be going home. He talks about it all day. So we are packing to go: all the files and the laptops have to go. It is like when your bairns are little and even for a day you had to remember everything. Six o'clock start, so Father help us to be ready. Elisabeth is a very bad time keeper and leaves things till the last minute. Wandu and I are packed as ready as we can even with the equipment, then we wait. Well praise Jesus, at last we are ready just before our transport comes.

Again "we praise You, Father", as our transport is a lad going to Awasa to do some work in the hospital there, so we are half way there at Awasa. We get everything into the back of the truck. Elisabeth is taking medicines that they cannot get at Chencha and 3 boxes of Bibles for the churches there. Wandu talks of pastor Solomon who he says is a great man.

Well, we are off. Elisabeth knows this country like the back of her hand. This is her home; she was brought up here, she loves it here, so she is pointing out things and places to me; she knows it all. The journey takes us till lunch time with two stops for the driver to stretch his legs, and we get a drink at the office of Elisabeth's surgeon. I have made sandwiches so we are quite happy, everything going well. The people sell their produce on the side of the road, so from time to time we stop and she buys a bucket full of tomatoes, then a little bit further on and it is mangoes, then water melon. Because there is nothing where we are going these are our provisions for the week. Next, bananas. By the time we got to Awasa we were laden with fruit and veg.

We arrive and to our dismay we have to stay the night as there will be no transport to Chencha till tomorrow. Wandu is quite upset but praise Jesus he pulls himself out of it. We are taken out for our lunch by the resident doctor, Dr Daniel, and he pays for it and for our driver - but then it is what to have: Elisabeth says stick to eggs so we order omelette, but the Ethiopian lads go for the works. It is a massive plate just like one of our meat plates back home with all kinds. They both offer; we try a bit of this and bit of that - all raw! We accepted, but mine was the smallest bit I could take.

We then went off to find a hotel. Well, it was filthy. The loo did not flush but praise Jesus for the loo - we did not have to squat. Next there was a shower. The water was cold, but again, "thank You for the shower". It is so hot in Awasa that to have a cold shower is brilliant. Elisabeth and Wandu went off to the lake where there was a bird sanctuary and every bird under the sun is there, plus crocodiles. I did not go as it was quite a walk and in the heat of the day I knew I would be foolish to try. So I rested and in the quiet of my room I was able to be with my Lord and could pray back everything. "Dr Daniel is beautiful, Father, and he knows You and loves You". We hit it off like two peas in a pod. The talk was that he was coming with us as he was interested in Elisabeth's tests.

Elisabeth and Wandu arrived back at tea / dinner time with darboo bread, a flat unleavened bread. We had darboo and banana for tea and supper because where we were it is black dark by six o'clock in the evening, so it is easy to eat. We joined together to read from our Lord's Word and pray. By the time we finished it was quite late and time for bed. Again we had an early start in the morning so off we went and woke very early. I went for my shower and got ready for the day. We were all ready and packed up to go. Elisabeth went for Wandu and we had banana and darboo for breakfast. Dr Daniel arrived with his driver who also knew Jesus. My heart just sang. Such beautiful skin shining like ebony, and eyes so beautiful. "Father, Jesus truly was looking out of those eyes."

We packed everything into the truck and were off. Well, what a journey. "We talked about You, Lord, all the way, and the countryside we were travelling through was out of this world. Again we were passing lakes so the wild life was great and Your creation was breath-taking, Father; and the privilege to talk to these boys, mostly encouragements. Praise You Lord. Such beautiful lads just worshipping You Lord. O pour out Your blessing on these lads, Lord. How they loved You." We stopped for breakfast and once again these lads were eating raw meat. Dr Daniel was teasing me to eat it. I said very politely "No, thank you." Elisabeth and I had omelettes again and the lads were laughing at me but it was not mocking. It was such fun, I just laughed with them. The twinkle in their eyes was so wonderful. "O bless Father, bless such fellowship. It is so rare."

After we finished we got back into the truck to continue our journey. We arrived safe and sound and we were taken straight to the mission where Elisabeth and I would be staying. The last part of the journey was like a race track round hairpin bends, but up and up it went for miles and miles. We saw a family of baboons. I took photos but they moved so quickly I didn't know if I had got them or not. Whole families of the very old to the babies - what a sight. I could nearly have touched them if they had let me. They were so close to the road, or track I should say, and when we got to the top it was like a plateau of lush ground. A whole tribe of people lived here, with farm land and quite a lot of buildings. As I said, we went to the mission, which was on one of the higher points. Again, like Addis Ababa and the hospital, I was here to take back the land which was our Lord's. The moment we stepped down from the truck Father said "Take off your shoes from your feet, for this is holy ground" (Exodus 3:5). "O Father!"

Elizabeth and Dr Daniel were about to go on to the hospital, so I was left with all our baggage, fruit and vegetables. The lad who had the key was not there so I had to sit and wait. There were hugs and kisses and tears as I would not see Dr Daniel and the driver again until we meet in Heaven with our Lord; they would go straight back to Awasa after seeing the hospital. What a privilege! "What a privilege, Father, to grant me to meet with Your boys of this land." My heart was bursting as they drove away.

I sat down to survey my surroundings. Very derelict; the little chapel is all boarded up and has not seen prayer or praise for a very long time. "O, how Your heart is grieved, Father." The rest of the compound was not too bad. Gardens looked kept and tended in a fashion. There were lots of buildings. The mission house was a long building, again a proper building like a bungalow. I believe it had solar power to heat water and there was electricity and water. This was a little paradise in the middle of nowhere. Again, there was such beauty in the rise and fall of the land. The cattle and sheep looked well kept, not skin and bone. The pasture land for food looked green and lush, not barren and dry and a desert, like Addis.

Tea time - the lad arrived back at his house on the compound. He got the key and let me in. "O Father, worse than I thought." The dirt and the kitchen were thick with grease, so "my work is cut out for me here, Lord. Clean up the whole mission," but all there was to cook on was a wood-burning stove. Another one of the lads brought me wood and lit my stove. "O my Lord!" He then proceeded to fill the log box beside it. "So to work, Father." I filled every pan and a huge kettle. Remember, we still had to boil our drinking water. Soon the stove was going great guns. I started by cleaning every pan as the water boiled, and benches, walls, table, the stove and a gas cooker, then also the floor.

By now it was late and I had not been in the rest of the house. Four bedrooms, two bathrooms, one long marble floor right through with everything leading off the passage. Dark, damp, dirty, but "hallelujah Jesus," a loo. Again the flush did not work properly but you could juggle it and with patience it would work. I made up our beds and then cooked something for supper. Wandu would be going home as he just lived down over the back of the mission. I felt quite pleased with myself that I had got the kitchen clean and would start the rest of the house tomorrow.

Elisabeth arrived with so many people to meet me, including Wandu's pastor, Solomon. This man walked everywhere so I was uncertain where he himself lived, but he went everywhere. I was so pleased I had made a start so they were not coming into dirt and filth. Some could speak English, some could not. Pastor Solomon could not but we embraced in the Name of our beloved Lord and we were on the same terms: "He loves you" to "Precious Jesus." He talked to Elisabeth, who could speak the Ethiopian language very well. They all left and we ate and read "Your Word, Lord." We went to bed. It was again black dark by six. I did not wake until about seven. Elisabeth was up and dressed and making her breakfast. Because there were two bathrooms we had one each and left our things there. Very little was said. Elisabeth said we would only be here a week. She was ready to go to work by eight and was out and away. My guard came again and lit my stove, so I was able to have toast. Who would have thought toast could taste so good? What a blessing! Short-lived, as when I went into prayer I was to fast like Esther - so "OK, Father."

I covered the work at the hospital and the little mission and everything at Addis, and Jemba, warding off the evil that she felt was preventing one area from making the grade like the rest. I worked in the prayer line until about eleven o'clock and had my coffee break. I then started to tackle the rest of the house. As I was cleaning the house I used it and the different things I was seeing to pray for the hearts of the tribe up here in the mountains. Our Lord loves this people. There must be little changed, for the mission had not been used for years. I was asking Father to pull back the bolts to open the windows of Heaven (Malachi 3:10): "Open the mission, Father, so that Your people will come in and worship You in this place. It is holy ground, so bring Your people here, Lord, to meet with You, with hearts open to receive You, Father." As I cleaned I had all the windows open and my worship tapes on. People were calling out to me as they went past.

Elisabeth had bought a sack of sugar and huge bars of soap for mothers. This was her bribe to get as many as possible to come to the hospital for tests. She had writing books and pencils for the children and shirts for the men. My cleaning and things were going well, and I had been left the sack of sugar to bag up into about two or three pounds ready to give to the mums. Well, it was going so well that Wandu arrived back to get some more bags, so we put them up together and off he went. We just sang all the time we were working.

After I finished my cleaning I made supper for us and when Elisabeth and Wandu came back we had been invited to Wandu's parents' home for coffee, so we had supper. Pastor Solomon returned with them so he ate with us. We had soup and darboo then fruit and coffee and tea. We then washed, got ready to visit Wandu's family, and set off down through the compound then out and down over the back side of the mission, and duly arrived.

Waggai, Wandu's father, owned land and had cattle and sheep. He and his other sons had just finished harvesting the corn. Their house was made of breeze blocks, like most of the houses here, quite big with lots of rooms off the main room, just dirt floor; no electric, so candles or lamps. To our surprise Wandu's mum had made a meal. With our having eaten it was a struggle but we managed a bit. The family was huge so nothing would be wasted with all the little ones. Pastor Solomon would pray and read the Word first. Wandu had to interpret what he was saying. The Scriptures were Matthew 21:22, Psalm 121, John 10:27-30, Deuteronomy 33:27. He preached on the Word, then we would eat the meal. Mine was scrambled egg which would have been great had I not already had my supper. I ate a little then had to make my apologies as I was full, but as I say no one minded as plenty little ones to eat it up.

After supper photos were brought out and so everyone was eager to tell us who they all were. This family was better off than most Ethiopians, hard workers. The mother would carry as much as a pack horse on her back like most of the women. When we came into Chencha, one woman was coming towards us carrying a tree. You would not believe how hard the women have to work. To get past us in the truck she went sideways on. The tree was something like thirty foot long and here she was coming down the road.

Waggai spun and made the cloth on a loom. He took us through to show us how he used his loom. He also worked as guard on the mission compound. Now Waggai knew Jesus, like Wandu, a beautiful man of God. Well they began to sing in the Ethiopian language and like the African music but it was different because they were singing praises to our Lord. Waggai asked us to pray for two of his daughters. One had sugar diabetes and the other was schizophrenic. Elisabeth prayed but I felt Father was saying to break the curse from the family. I did so, and the unclean spirits came out of both of them, and the family sang all the harder giving thanks to our Lord. When Father tells us to do things we have full confidence that what He tells us to do will take place. For Jesus did nothing unless Father told Him (John 14:31). We then decided it was time to leave and again everyone was walking with us to the compound gates.

I slept well and woke at seven, and Elisabeth was up and doing her breakfast. Because of my fast I just had water. I worked till lunchtime again in the prayer line then continued my cleaning of the house. I worked well and in the afternoon I was finished. I was pleased and asked Father if we could clean the chapel next.

By teatime Waggai came to the door to introduce me to a young man called Hailem who also works on the compound. He was a beautiful humble man. We embraced in Jesus' Name and we just went off "talking about You, Lord." Here, right up in these mountains, God has His man. He took me to his office to show me his work. He was translating the Bible into his own language. He had done Genesis and Exodus in the Hebrew Scriptures and Matthew, the first of the Gospels. "O Father, what a wonderful lad, truly Your son. He just loves You, Jesus." We talked and talked.

I asked Hailem if we could clean the chapel and he would not let me get dirty. He went for the key and took down all the boards and muck and dust and cobwebs on the outside. He got two more men and the three of them worked like navvies cleaning stuff they could lift outside which they lifted out. I was allowed to wash all the chairs and stools and forms and things outside. They worked hard and we finished late afternoon. Hailem and I finished the job off in prayer. What a day! Hailem was jumping with joy. I was quite excited myself as to what Father could do. After Hailem went I lit my stove and prepared our evening meal.

The next day Hailem was back in the morning and we prayed together till lunch time. He left and I carried on with all I had been in. Come afternoon Hailem came back and we just talked and talked about Jesus. This was Thursday. Friday I prayed till lunch time then I went to Hailem's office and again we just went into prayer for his work. He shared other things with me, things that were troubling his heart, so praise Jesus, after I left I was able to bring all the things Hailem had been talking about to Jesus.

Saturday Hailem was away with his brothers in Jesus. He has four fellow pastors and they meet every week for prayer, and speak at different places. So I lifted them up and prayed for them and for every place they were in. Sunday I continued in prayer for Chencha, the area of the mission and the all the beautiful people I have met.

Monday we go back to Addis Ababa so it is cleaning through for the last time and packing up. Elisabeth got packed and said all her goodbyes, and of course Wandu would have to leave his family again, and we needed transport, so I was praying for transport. I went to say goodbye to Hailem and I was praying with him one last time when the truck came. Everybody came to help pack everything on to the truck. Elisabeth was taking everyone's photo. I was going round everyone for a last hug, a goodbye hug for we may never meet again till we meet in Heaven.

Our driver was a big man. He used to drive wagons but had joined the hospital work as it was well paid, but it was his own truck and could take other work as well. This man could drive: he did not want to stop for food but just wanted to keep going. He drove hard; Wandu wanted to sleep, but he hit the bumps in the bad roads with such a force that we, in the back seats, were thrown up in the air every time. So our heads were bouncing off the roof the whole way till we turned off on to a main road, which was three to four hours. Once we hit the main road it was much easier going but his foot must have been flat to the floor. We arrived home to Addis Ababa about eight at night but that was very good time.

I remember we did not get to Awasa till lunch time, from half past six, the first day, and we left Awasa at six and did not get to Chencha till lunch the second day; he did well. He had nowhere to stay so we made a meal and Wandu and the driver slept in the main room and we went off to our rooms. It was lovely to be back, so it was coming into His courts with thanksgiving all right but so much to go over and think about: everyone we had met - what an experience in itself. The two men were up and away very early the next morning. It was so early. I heard them talking, but I just turned over and went back to sleep till seven. I then got up for my bath. Elisabeth was up so it was back into routine as we only had two weeks left. Well, I am afraid I worked but my joy of going home was mounting. Everyone came back so my lessons carried on and when we went back to church we were welcomed. The man at the door said he had missed me so much.

On the Monday I washed everything - our coats and bags; I scrubbed everything, it was so dusty from our journey. Beysuahu came that day; he had got the job at the church. I was so pleased for him and we talked and shared till late, then he left. I was back teaching my students again, so I was out to my little Korean girl that night. The houses were full; all the students are back and this day I met the couple from next door who were from Sudan. He was a doctor and was studying tuberculosis and leprosy. Gabra came to take me to the craft shop to see if I could get some things to take home. The people from the hospital made everything as part of the hospital rehabilitation programme and to my joy it was just like what Jemba had done. Some were on looms making the cloth and others were making the clothes. Some ladies were doing embroidery and some crocheting. We went into the craft shop. It was like Aladdin's cave, full of beautiful coloured tablecloths, embroidered bed spreads, tunic dresses, you name it, it was full. I managed to get my few things and we came back. Next day I wanted to see Sinkernich so I set off; when I got along I had missed her by five minutes, so I called on her Secretary Mulukin Abate: "O Father, out of Egypt, the Ethiopian will come to God. This man is Your man. He radiates Your love and Jesus looks out of his eyes."

We had a great time sharing the Scriptures and then we went for coffee. I left and went back home. Beysuahu came in the afternoon with a friend. I made tea and darboo and banana and we talked and shared. Now the lady did all the talking. Beysuahu sat as if he was not part of the conversation; when he had come on his own we had just talked about Jesus and then got on with the Scriptures, but the lady went on about money and how she needed money for this and money for that; this was the sole topic of her conversation. Then after an hour and a half there was silence and I then said I was unable to help her, for I had no money, our beloved Lord had provided everything for me to come on this trip. Now she was silent; we then said, "Let us pray."

Again the lady did all the praying and because it was all in her language I was unable to join in, as I did not know what she was praying. So I prayed in my mind to my Lord for her and her problem with the money. I was weeping, knowing myself what it is like when you are desperate and need money, but my money was needed to feed and care for my children or a bill that had come in but "Father, You never failed me." Something came in from somewhere. Because I am white and from England I think this lady thought I would be able to give her everything she asked for; she was quite taken aback when I said I was unable to help her. "It must break Your heart Father when we think we should have what we want. You promise to supply all our needs but not our wants. You also say to feed the poor and the needy and care for the widows." But this woman had a husband and was well dressed, not like the poor, living in a leper village, who had nothing. I said "Father, You know if I had the money I would help the lady. I don't think I have turned anyone away at Maranatha. We have always done our best to help in any way I could."

The lady went silent, then said our Lord had given her a Scripture. I got my Bible and gave her one of the Bibles Elisabeth had with English and Amharic together. The Scripture was 1 Samuel 15 v 22-23. "O my Lord, what a word!" Samuel said, "Does the Lord have as much delight in burnt offerings and sacrifices as in obeying the voice of the Lord? Behold, to obey is better than sacrifice, and to heed than the fat of lambs, for rebellion is as the sin of divination, and insubordination as the evil of idolatry. Because you rejected the Word of the Lord, He also has rejected you from being King."

I was speechless before but I was struck dumb now and so was she. When God speaks, God speaks! She understood in her own heart her rebellion etc. against God.

Nothing more was said until we said our goodbyes and they both left. I went back to the Word and read it again and prayed for the lady. "Thank you Father, that you had the answer to her prayer and her begging for money, with no bad feeling or anything, because our Lord corrects us because He loves us. So praise You, Lord, that You spoke through Your Word."

I went to my little Korean girl that night. This would be my last visit as we would be preparing and packing for us to come home. She gave me a bookmark, and one of the boys had made me a rose out of an Ethiopian bank note. He had cut a plastic bottle in half and had stuck the rose in the upside down bottom and then put the top half over the rose for protection. It was very well done, very effective and artistic. Yushine was in tears and said she would miss me terribly but we talked and shared till she was laughing and then we hugged and I left. It was going to be very hard to say goodbye to all these beautiful people; we really had grown to love each other.

The work was finished, the files were now being packed and all the equipment boxes packed and labelled as to what was inside. Everything being ready to store till Elisabeth goes back, I guess, but I am not sure. Now I still had money that had been given to me. I wanted to come home and share how this money had blessed, and how it had been used and not wasted because of the work with the letters, the children and the pupils. In my heart I would have liked to give the English and Ethiopian Bibles to the school, so the bairns could read for themselves and they would be confident in writing back to their pen-pals. I was quite excited about this because they also would be reading the Word and our beloved Father would be healing the memories and traumas in their little lives. "Yes Father."

I asked Elisabeth if I could do this, as she would have to get the Bibles for me; so it was agreed. Elisabeth went into town and came back with a full box of Bibles for me. I had enough to buy a full box, "O thank You, Father." I could not wait to be able to take them along to Sinkernich. I finished my chores and Wandu said he would come too and carry the box. So off we went. Because it was afternoon only two or three of the beggars were there but one came forward to talk to me. It was the same one every time but he could speak English. So this may be why he always came to talk to me, he was spokesman for everyone. So we had a chat and I said I was going home. His face fell but I said I would not stop praying for him, just because I was going home. We hugged each other and Wandu and I carried on with our box.

Sinkernich was not in so we took them to Mulukin, my wonderful Egyptian Ethiopian. We talked and shared, then I said my goodbyes as I may not be back. As we hugged it was like I was holding someone precious to our Lord, like touching a precious child of our Lord whose ancestor, who knows, may be a line of the lost tribe; I don't know. It was holding someone our Lord loved very deeply; as we departed Mulukin wept and so did I. I never dreamt it would be this hard - it never had been before.

I was silent all the way home and Wandu was too. Sinkernich arrived the next morning to thank me for the Bibles. She could see also the potential of the children being able to read our Lord's Word. We laughed and it was just so wonderful, what a privilege - I felt I had known them all my life, and the bond was really like blood brothers in our Lord. The last few days passed. Beysuahu came back, and the girls too. Mesaret arrived and bless her heart she had prepared a full meal for all of us - it was like a party. We heated everything she had made on our little stove. We sat down together; we laughed and shared as we ate our meal. It was quite late when we finished so we washed up and it was more goodbyes.

We now had only two days left for Elisabeth to pack. Everything in the house that she had brought over the years was all wrapped and packed into boxes. On our last morning the truck came to take everything back to stores, then he came back and took all the boxes that had to go back to Sinkernich's storeroom for Elisabeth coming back. Then, last, the driver came to take us to the airport, so we loaded up his truck with our luggage. Wandu came with us to the airport and this was our last goodbye. We held on to each other and sobbed and then we went through the gate and he was gone. "What memories! You don't forget people who love You Lord."

Elisabeth and I boarded our plane for the start of our journey back home. I was praying again to cover our flight and baggage, and the weather both en route and when we arrived so I would be able to get down home, take off and up, up and away. I could look down for my last look at Ethiopia.

We arrived on time in Nairobi and we had so many hours to wait here till we got our flight to Amsterdam. Elisabeth lay down for a sleep but I could not sleep. Once more it was thinking and praying and smiling, recapping all the people of that land, their lives, their families, the places. "O my Lord, what a two months" - a bit like Kenya, really, taking back the land, the missions, and the people, serving Elisabeth with all manner of ways. Encouraging and loving all I met; teaching - well I'm not sure. "We just prayed and read Your Word, Father, and had a good time together."

Before I knew it they were calling our flight over the intercom so we gathered our luggage and set off. Again everything was fine and we had to wait in the lounge before boarding. It was here that we met Douglas - what a lovely man - and his son. He was American and he had been to an annual convention. He was sharing things that had happened; while we were in Chencha I hadn't known why I was fasting till Douglas was now sharing about his conference. So I was thrilled as he talked and shared, and away went the tears again, praising our Lord for all the wonderful things God had done. We sat and talked and shared till it was time to board our flight. This was our seven and a half hour flight.

Elisabeth slept all the time as she did on the flight out, but I had no little lass beside me coming home; everything was very calm and I cat napped. We landed at Amsterdam and made our way to reclining seats. We found them and made ourselves comfy for a couple of hours, till it was time for our Edinburgh flight - I did sleep then. We then ate and made our way to our boarding lounge. When we arrived, our flight had been delayed so we just had to wait a little longer. Soon it came over the intercom that our flight to Edinburgh was now ready to board, sorry for the delay etc. etc. We got our seats and soon we were on our last lap home.

# CHAPTER 18

# Home again and counting blessings

*I*could not believe it, we seem to have been away for ever and a day. My thoughts were going always how everyone would be, if the weather would be all right for me to travel home. My mind was going fifty to the dozen. We arrived and went for our luggage, then through everything you have to go through at air ports and out, and there was Dotty waiting for us. "O bless her."

We went straight out to the car and headed for Mary Clare's house. We packed the luggage straight into Elisabeth's car and then went in. Dotty had to leave as she had another job on. Mary Clare wanted to make us lunch but I just wanted on the road for home. Elisabeth said she would take me down to Peebles where my car was and come back to Mary Clare's, so we set off. I was so pleased; we met Granny from next door and her oldest grandson. I gave her a present for herself and one for Douglas who had been turning the car over all the time I was away - "Lord, bless him." She started straight off! I thanked Granny and her grandson, and Elisabeth for bringing me down, and I was in and away.

"O Father - home!" The fields were so green after the bare barren earth of Ethiopia. The lambs were in the fields too and the sun shone all the way home. O I got home and came inside with my luggage and shut the door and went up into the sanctuary. "O Father it is so wonderful to be back home" - my tears just flowed. "We have so much Father, I feel such gratitude."

I was so thankful to be home, I sat and talked to my Lord. I just wanted to stay with Him, I was so grateful for such comfort in my home. The bairns would all still be at work so after a while I decided I would go and get Bengy, so I set off for Rothbury. Noel and Joan were pleased to see me. One of my purchases was a crocheted tablecloth for Joan for a thank you for looking after Bengy. I stayed for dinner telling my story of my trip, then I headed home. I went along to Jo's and got a welcome home from Matthew and Yasmin and gave them their little prezzies and told them all about the people who had made them. Then I called round to Hazel, David and Zak's again with such a love from Zak, and I gave them my bits and bobs for them. By the time I came away from there I phoned Edward and Avril to say "Hello, I am back" and I would see them tomorrow.

"O what joy, precious Jesus, that I can come home to You. What dedication Father, these missionaries I met from Nigeria. Ann spent her whole life going where You told her to go; she was checking out RE Hospitals at Addis to see if this were her next post. They have to stay so many years, whereas for me, the time I have to stay is months or even weeks and then I can come home. Thank You, thank You, Father. I remember, way back in the beginning, when I came home from Japan, I wanted to be a missionary to go to all the different places just to work with You, Lord, and I guess really this is what I have done, but with a job that had to be done in each place. O my beloved, my Redeemer, my brother, my friend, my husband, You have been all these things and more, and this is not the end, this is just the beginning."

Reader, if you don't know Jesus as "my beloved, my Redeemer, my brother, my friend" and would like to ensure that "this is just the beginning" of a new personal relationship between Him and you today, please be encouraged to pray to Him along these lines:

Tell Him that you are sorry for leaving Him out of your life (that is what sin is) and for any and all of the resulting wrong things that you have done during your life. Ask Him to forgive you by the power of His blood shed for you on the cross. Thank your Heavenly Father that He took away all your sin on the cross of Jesus.

Ask Him to come now into your heart and be your Saviour.

Ask Father God to lead you into all truth (His Truth) and to guide you in all your ways (Proverbs 3:5, 6).

Tell your Father in Heaven that you surrender your life to Him today to be His disciple in order, in obedience to His Word, to deny yourself, take up your cross daily and follow Jesus (Luke 9:23).

Be baptised in water, and ask Him to fill you with His Holy Spirit (Acts 2:38, Acts 19:1-6) so that you may know how to talk with Him regularly (pray without ceasing, I Thessalonians 5:17), read His Word the Bible daily (Ephesians 6:17, Hebrews 4:12), and seek fellowship with other Believers (Hebrews 10:24, 25).

A useful way to start your daily prayers is to pray back to the Lord, in your words, Luke 9:23 (perhaps continue to verse 26) and Ephesians 6:10-18.

Lightning Source UK Ltd.
Milton Keynes UK
UKOW041910191012

200894UK00001B/17/P